Winning Through

Executive Career Transitioning

Guiding you through your Transition to Success in the C-Suite

Winning Through

Executive Career Transitioning

Guiding you through your Transition to Success in the C-Suite

by
John Petty and Sandra Calvert

First Edition: January 2021

Published by Sandra Calvert and John Petty via Sanvon Investments P/L

The publisher and authors are not responsible for third parties (their websites or content) that are not owned by the publisher.

Australian library cataloguing in publication date: a catalogue record for this title is available from the Australian Library.

- ISBN   978-0-646-83081-0
- eISBN 978-0-6450607-0-6.

Our dedication of this book is to our loved ones
Siobhan, Tim, Coralie and Andrew
who encouraged us to help and GUIDE YOU.... our reader,
as the next successful executive.

Special acknowledgement to our Mentees for diarising
their days in preparation for the move and then in
their new roles in the C-Suite.

Contents

FOREWORD

Written by Kevin Chandler, Founding CEO of Chandler Macleod Group, Australia's largest human capital services firm, and author of AbilityMap, a leading Career and Personality Profiling Assessment tool.

Written by Kevin Chandler, Founding CEO of Chandler Macleod Group, Australia's largest human capital services firm, and author of AbilityMap, a leading Career and Personality Profiling Assessment tool.

The World of Work, Recruitment and Employment has dynamically changed. Writing the Foreword to this book by John Petty and Sandra Calvert has given me the opportunity to put the World of Work, Recruitment and Employment into a new perspective, as recent events have changed the employment landscape forever. These changes must be fully appreciated by employment candidates otherwise they will remain unemployed and unemployable for a long time.

My new perspective led me to develop the latest employee diagnostic tool, AbilityMap, that I happily share with you along with a few key insights of ATS [Applicant Tracking Systems]. These two tools combined will give the key advantage of how to push your success to WIN the job.

My AbilityMap is designed for the Recruiter, the C-Suite executive, and the Board, when assessing the appropriateness of their candidates, being management to C-Suite roles. This mapping tool allows Board Members and C-Suite executives to identify critical required competencies for performance and match the competencies of the role with the skills and aptitudes of various candidates to gain the best candidate for the role.

Sharing secret insights of how the ATS works and the intelligence of the keywords that underpin searches will see your chances of successfully Winning the job increase. These are special insights that Recruiters don't want you to know, but are necessary to win through.

I trust that you will also find this book enjoyable and enlightening.

PREFACE

You have been in your current job for five to seven years: you have mastered it and are well recognised for your current contribution to your organisation, but you face the inevitable. You are no longer viewed as a fresh new visionary, with outsider knowledge and the latest techniques.

You have but a small window remaining to leave your current organisation, to advance your career, or remain and move up. The clock is ticking. The risk trade-off is to not make a career move, knowing that you will be deemed as losing value each day you remain. Time to reassess! Time to look for a new challenge or horizon either within or outside your present position and employment.

Observing the strong team that you built that surround you, you see the need for vitality, the injection of energy and new approaches to be introduced to your position by your successor. You have succeeded in your role, yet realise your value could be invested either in a new position within your organisation by way of promotion, or moving on to a new organisation.

If you decide to move on, how do you review what you need to know about the new organisation and map it ready to win the job of your dreams and then hit the ground running?

We help you to assess what you thought you knew in terms of your skills and talents and business reputation and your value to the organisation and what should happen to the organisation and your position, if you were not there anymore?

So you decide to think about moving on and hopefully up.

TO WIN YOUR NEW POSITION

Jobs are advertised [and sometimes not advertised] in different places and in different ways to promote the organisation and the available position.

Recruitment has changed dramatically over the past five to ten years, from the older newspaper inserts to digital platforms.

Technology and new recruitment models and avenues have seen candidates apply for the position that you want to win, with only the few who invest time and research, winning the job. That is where this book will become your greatest piece of executive advancement property that you can invest in.

For every senior position, you will be compared to over 200 applicants and more so in a recession or economic downturn. You can but hope, that you are in the final ten applicants to be interviewed, and then the final two or three to be considered for selection.

Is hope what you really want to rely on?

Wouldn't a purposeful and confident approach that sees you out in front be the preferable option?

You need to find that edge over the competition, cease competing and STAND OUT FROM THE CROWD. You want to bowl your interviewers over with a Knockout Presentation to have them wanting you, not you begging them.

You want to win and perform to get the job offer. So that was the easy part, winning the job with your award winning presentation that is a summary of your plan for the organisation. You accept the role and then next step is to make your mark in the First 100 Days in the new Job.

How can you present your plan for a new organisation that you have not yet stepped into? How can you win the role and then deliver it to your business without seeming presumptuous?

As personal business coaches, executive mentors and recruitment specialists, we see many candidates who do not realise or grasp the concept, that the decision to move on from one position to another, is a serious endeavour. It catapults the candidate in a very intense and pressure packed 200 DAY PROGRAM: you need to successfully extract from your current position, to win the role in the new position or organisation, to then commence in the new position with real credit and authority, skills, intention and capabilities; WINNING THROUGH the first 100 days in the job.

Fortunately for those we have mentored over many years, sharing our guidance to ensure preparedness for the next role, is one that we now share with you, our reader.

This book is your roadmap of how to successfully and professionally transition, with respect and ethics, to another position or organisation and then prove your worth in the First 100 Days in the new organisation.

Commencing in your new job at Day One, your 'value clock' starts ticking. You have up to Sixty Days [60 Days] to have analysed and commenced implantation of changes in your new role. You have only Ninety Days [90 Days] from commencement until your new chief, the boss, will have evaluated whether you are worthy to continue, or they may take the approach to dismiss you during your probationary period, leaving you on the unemployed shelf. The First 100 Days in the Job is your golden opportunity to make a positive impact, to shine, but it comes at the end of your planned **200 Days** of your Career Transitioning Progression. Your 'Value Clock' is ticking down fast.

Follow this 'HOW TO' book, to successfully manage the decision to MOVE ON and UP in your career.

Kevin Kelly[23], CEO of Heidrick & Struggles suggests that 40% of newly appointed leaders will fail, be pushed out, fall out or quit within the first 18 months in a new role.

His TOP 5 REASONS for FAILURE as the nearly appointed leader being:
1. Tried to do too much – too smart or aggressive for their own good or the new organisation.
2. Did too little – guided but did not assert authority – not a true leader.
3. Operated in a vacuum: did not communicate or involve others - the team.
4. Tried the 'my way or the highway' approach and not successfully.
5. Politically or culturally tone deaf – did not get it and missed the messages.

With those levels of failure rates [40%] of new appointees, it is a serious issue to match the position and the candidates for a successful appointment.

We trust that this book will be a great help to prepare both the candidate for the position and the appointed interviewer in the selection of the appropriate and successful candidate.

This book is designed to help you with

WINNING THROUGH

Your "EXECUTIVE CAREER TRANSITIONING".

Written for the following audiences:
- Any Executive belonging to or aspiring to be in the C-Suite in either of commercial or private businesses but relevant for public sector or government roles
- Not for Profit and Community Service Executives
- University and other Executive Training Organisations
- Government and political decision makers
- Business Advisors and coaches
- Any C-Suite Executive seeking their next role as Director or Chair.

Although our preliminary focus is on the recruitment, selection and progression of senior executives, this book expresses how to select or be a senior executive in any type of business or commercial or Not For Profit organisation.

Revisit your career Journey through Checklists and Reassessments to determine where you are and what should and could be your stretch aspirations and ambitions for your future career.

Full of tips and hints of how to be successful in employment transition:
- Learn how to be successful in transforming your role.
- How to shorten the journey by taking the right employment options.
- Learn how to prepare and present yourself in your all-important Covering Letter and CV/Resume to get to the 'To Be Interviewed pile'.
- Practice and perfect your Interview style to SMASH your interview.
- Develop the INTERVIEW ACTION GRABBERS which are ONE PAGE summaries of proposed MUST DO's in the new role and your fabulous Career/Candidate Portfolio.

- Learn how to negotiate your new position and its compensation and performance package.
- Learn the COMMON MISTAKES that candidates make in trying to transition their careers and how to avoid them.

The authorship of this book: "Winning Through: Executive Career Transitioning" started as a Mentor–Mentee relationship some eight years ago: this relationship has progressed whereby the Mentor and Mentee are now both professional mentors and coaches, harnessing their professional techniques and lessons that have been developed and presented here for all to adopt.

John Petty has successfully interviewed and recruited hundreds of C-Suite executives and recently with Kevin Chandler [founder of Chandler McLeod], has formed the highest calibre search and recruitment firm, Chandler Petty CFO Search & Advisory.

The combined talents of our 'CFO of the Future' series facilitator and co-author, Sandra Calvert and John Petty's successful past twenty-five years as a professional Chair and founder of the CFO of the Future series, and author of the CCH best seller, The Australian Business Toolkit, former IFAC Australian representative and former national CPA Vice-President, have provided you key insights to see your career reach YOUR FLAG ON THE HILL.

GOOD LUCK on your career progression journey.

SECTIONS

01 PREPARE

1.1 Positioning
1.2 CV / Resume
1.3 Connect
1.4 Research

02 PRESENT

2.1 Pitch
2.2 Preparation
2.3 Interview
2.4 Negotiation
2.5 Accept

03 PERFORM

3.1 Reception
3.2 The First 30 Days
3.3 The First 100 Days

04 PERFECT

C-Suite and Executive Specific Role Tips and First 100 Day

Appendix

Index

Bibliography

Worksheets

INTRODUCTION

There are many career progression and recruitment books written and out there about the First 100 Days in the Job.

We wanted this book to be about the FULL journey from your decision to move on from your current position for whatever reason, to finally being a success in the new role/position/organisation of your choice, and all the steps and challenges in between

Apart from your family home, your career path is your most important investment and asset. Invest wisely as you WIN THROUGH the next 200 Days ... it will take that long ... yet be so rewarding.

From your decision to leave your current position, you will [please tick what you think you have prepared right now, before you continue in this book]:

- refresh your CV
- update your skills
- review the available positions and market conditions
- arrange your referees
- put out some feelers
- apply in earnest
- gain a few interviews
- make it to the final round
- hopefully win the race
- negotiate the package you want and deserve
- give notice and serve out a notice period
- start your job
- to then stamp your mark in the new position and organisation.

...that was exhausting and that is the 200 Day journey in front of you .. at best.

This is what our book and advice is all about, the old sayings, "Be Prepared" and "Don't be caught with your pants down".

The actions you take during the FIRST 100 Days in a new job will largely determine whether you succeed or fail. How you applied for, win the job, negotiated the job conditions and position [title and roles] and your changeover is so important and forms the Full 200 Days in the process.

This make or break period of transition is one that you can Win Through Successfully.

Your **first 100 days** in the C-Suite **begins** 100 days **before applying for the job,** to then endure many challenges along the journey, through to the First 100 days in the job. 200 days is designed for the CxO and new BxD; that is the C-Suite executive, no matter the title and the Director of the Board.

As you reflect on this next career move as a 200 Day journey, you need to be fully committed for that period ahead of you.

In the new job as a C-Suite member or a Director, it is all about:
- Attitude
- Communication style and protocol
- Priorities
- Contribution.

And what you do and say must be
- Planned
- Deliberate and
- Thoughtful.

Your journey requires three very important milestones that we have separated into the three sections, followed by a special tailored 100 days strategic guidance in the job, that has been compiled for eighteen [18] of the most common Executive roles in the marketplace.

We also have Tips n Techniques for you throughout the book. Look for this symbol to help you blast your career to new heights.
Each time you see this symbol you will know you have a new Tip or Technique that you must master and can then implement to accelerate your career progression.

Firstly we want to discuss why we mention and founded the concept of 200 Days.

Your 200 DAY Career Transition
The IMPORTANCE of 200 DAYS

What is 200 Days and why did we choose that number?

200 DAYS = 4800 hours;
288,000 minutes

but more realistically;

= 6 months, two weeks, 3 days and 8 hours

200 Days is a nice round number to go from where you are now to being a success in your new job – on your career journey – an exciting trip.

Note the Film '200 Days – A Trip Around The World Travel Film' – we will prepare you for your trip and your journey to new horizons in your employment and career.

The 200 day Moving Average [commonly expressed as 200 DMA] is a good technical indicator among stock market traders but is more popular among investors to analyse the underlying trend of stocks. It is an arithmetic average of the last 200 days closing price. The 200 day moving average is perceived to be the dividing line between a stock that is technically healthy and one that is not.

This book attaches a different importance to 200 days: being the 200 Days from preparation to performance in your new executive role.

Yes ... it is a 200 Day journey:

100 Days [prior to move in preparation]

+

100 Days [after moving into the new position]
= 200 Days

Now that you understand the concept of 200 Days, let's introduce the sections to assist your executive career transitioning journey.

WINNING a new job to then perform it SUCCESSFULLY requires your consideration of which APPROACH and STYLE you will use.

It is no use promising and then not delivering. Spotlights are on you as critics are lined up watching your performance. It needs to be better than good, it needs to be Brilliant!

We have structured this book in Four (4) sections:
1. **Prepare:** to harness the first 100 days before you apply for your next role with a winning strategy and well supported portfolio.
2. **Present:** an effective interview approach and style to win the new role whilst exiting your former role with grace and dignity.
3. **Perform:** to deliver in the new role, executing strategically within the first 100 days and then thereafter.
4. **Perfect:** your specific profile as the newest executive team member. We discuss what you must focus on and do correctly to be a success in these specific executive positions and include an overview of Board roles. You will learn what the key factors and differentiators in the various roles are. We added a few Managerial roles where a C-Suite executive is otherwise not represented.

The focus of this book is your journey as a Senior Management person and how over a ten (10) year period you can progress your career BUT it is adaptable FOR ALL CAREER JOURNEYS: regardless of your age, sector, discipline, domicile etc.

So regardless of whether your career journey involves;
- More of the same in a similar role but different organisation
- Moving to your Bosses position
- Need to step sideways for new skills and professional recognition to then move up again
- Developing Professional accreditation at external institutions
- Personally developing your career skills or CV through business coaching or mentoring.

We are about developing your career journey to achieve your lifestyle ambitions and aspirations.

Our focus is on where will you be and how you will get there in 10 years.

We have modelled this book on and over the journey: to be READY, SET, GO. You can continue to return to this book over and over again as you pick up on where you are in your journey throughout your career. This is particularly useful, especially as experts suggest that you will probably endure at least ten (10) recruitments, if not more, during your career journey.

Section 4: is particularly relevant for your personal development and advancement. We focus on what has been termed the C-Suite or Executive Suite where the senior executives reside and progress: we have initially introduced the IBM Global C-Suite [20] research and methodology as a framework but have then expanded our coverage to as many Executive positions as we have determined. The IBM Global C-Suite framework is depicted in Section four (4) covering the following 6 Executive roles as depicted below, plus a bonus few extra roles that are also common.

In this Section we have included pages of advice and practical steps for each of the most common specialist executive roles that exist within the C-Suite and other related disciplines and/or positions.

Appendices and Worksheets

To assist you we have compiled an Appendix packed full of examples and explanations of tools to assist you with **MEASURES THAT MATTER** within your organisation and your career, during the first 100 days prior to the job and first 100 days in the new job.

After you have referred to the Appendix, please turn to the Worksheets Section on page 289 to complete the exercises. We recognise you may wish to use an Interactive Worksheet. Please click here, or using your browser go to coachability.net.au/WinningThrough using your unique code **WinThrough$*** to register for your personal use worksheets.

The Customer-activated Enterprise

Insights from the Global C-Suite Study, IBM Institute for Business Value, 2013.

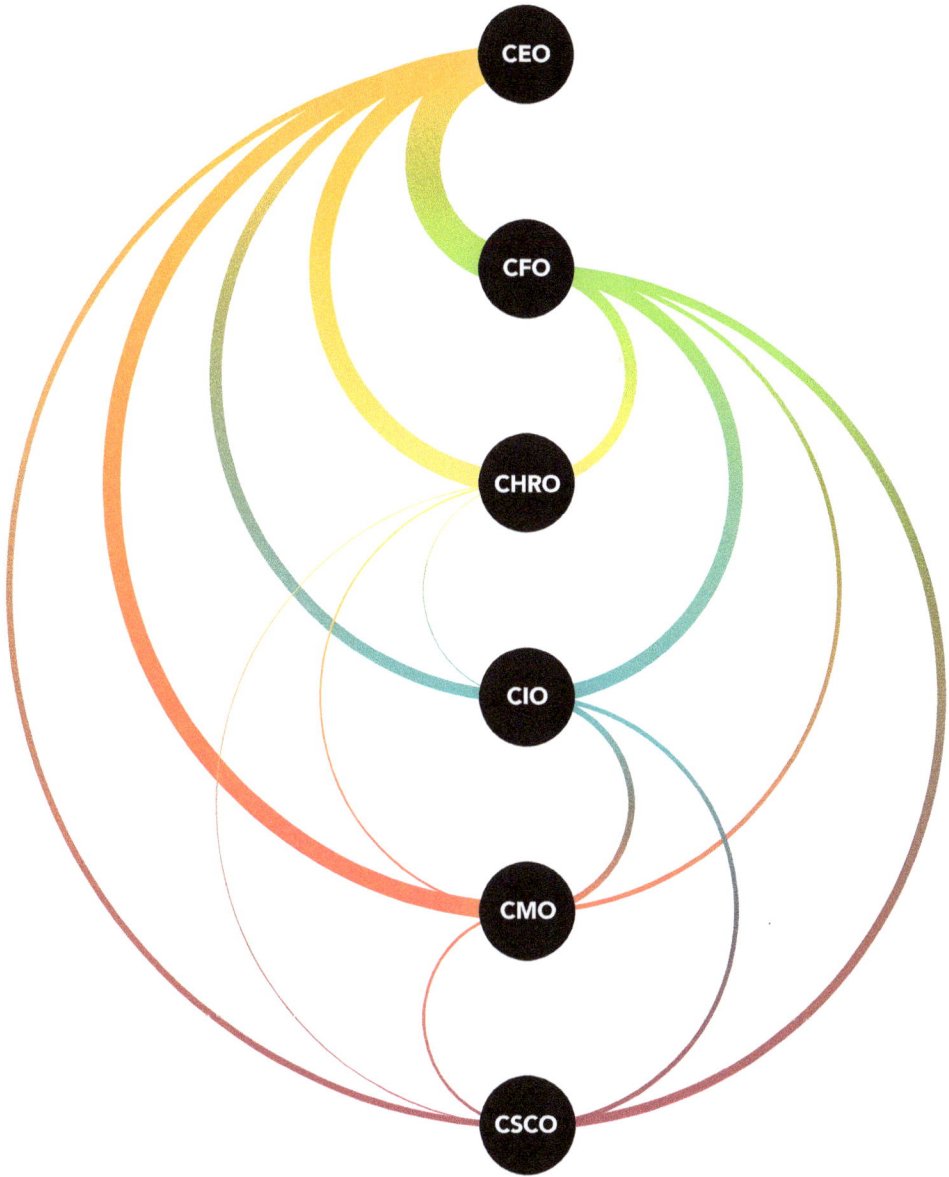

The specialist Executive Roles that we have covered include the following:

CEO	[Chief Executive Officer]
CFO	[Chief Financial Officer]
COO	[Chief Operating Officer]
CHRO	[Chief Human Relations Manager]
CIO	[Chief Information Officer]
CTO	[Chief Technology Officer]
CMO	[Chief Marketing Officer]
CSO	[Chief Sales Officer]
CRO	[Chief Revenue Officer]
CDGO	[Chief Development Growth Officer]
CGO	[Chief Growth Officer]
CPO	[Chief Procurement Officer]
CSM	[Chief Supply Manager]
CLO	[Chief Logistics Officer]
CSO	[Corporate Sustainability Officer]
BxD	[Director of the Board]
CHAIR	[Chairperson of the Board]

Our Section 4 'Specialist Centre' as well as focusing on the various roles in the C-Suite, will also cross reference or be helpful to the various industry or employment situations as covered below:

- Commercial, public owned or private businesses
- Public sector or government roles
- Not for Profit and Community Service Provision
- University and other Executive Training Organisations
- Political decision makers or advisors
- Business Advisors and coaches
- Directors recruiting C-Suite Executives

To start your journey, we ask you to complete the following two exercises of your Personal Career Skills Review and your Was – Is – Will Be.

PERSONAL CAREER SKILLS REVIEW

This book is structured around your personal career journey, from where you are now, to where you want to be in 10 years' time, with a focus on your skills, expertise, brand, roles, positioning and what makes you attractive and wanted as an Executive team member.

To assist you in this journey and to help with its development, we have developed a Personal Career Skills Review Model to help you to plan and equip you for this 10 year journey.

Please complete the following Personal Career Skills Review to help your strategic positioning and then prepare for your Career Journey.

Personal Career Skills Review

Current Personal and Career Skills:

Current Role and Position using these skills:

Current Skills not presently being used:

Where do you want to be in 10 years and how will you get there:
What is your ultimate Flag on the Hill Role? eg. CEO

Which positions/roles do you need to undertake to reach your Flag on the Hill?
eg. CEO via CFO

Skills Required to Reach your Flag:

Skill Deficiencies to Overcome:

Skill Development Program to reach next milestone and thereafter:

1.

2.

Figure 1: Personal Career Skills Review

Complete your Personal Career Skills Review worksheet on p289

WAS   IS   WILL BE

Your employment journey is not just important, it is critical to determining your lifestyle, and therefore the time you invest in yourself in this project will return results. Any advice or assistance offered to you should be well regarded and much respected.

Your journey is best depicted by the well accepted model of

WAS >< IS >< WILL BE

WAS: Your past achievements that are well described in your CV. You and your referees will cover these very well. They should reflect your past successes and what got you to where you are now.

IS: Currently, where you are now in your organisation and career journey. It reflects your record of success and the respect and regard you now have. Your CV is similar to Was, describing and applauding this position.

BUT you want to MOVE UP and ON in your career. As you study your past roadmap that led you to where you are now, you can appreciate the hard work and path you took to get where you are that is leading you into a direction of where you will be.

WILL BE: Future vision of the Flag On the Hill you aspire to reach and the accolades you aspire to achieve. This section is OUTCOMES focused.

Please turn to Appendix A1 to complete your Was and Is, however leave Will Be until you complete reading this book as you may decide to place your flag on a different hill.

Our WAS >< IS >< WILL BE: model once completed, should be reviewed earnestly upon each role that you take, and even better to be reviewed with your business coach or mentor.

Prepare

SECTION 1 - Prepare

1. New Days .. New Ways .. New Job Search Techniques

The Job Hunting market and process is behaving differently these days than it used to in the past.

The recruitment market and its supporting systems have changed forever .. and very dramatically.

Employer's expectations and wants are now *different*;

And employees are more selective and *disconcerting*;

So as a job seeker and job employer, you need to think and act differently.

The Average Job – Hunt Time

Another critical fact in the recruitment process is that the average job-hunt time and hence the time you will be out of a paid position and employment has increased very significantly and in some case doubled want it was five years ago.

Whereas it may have previously taken five to six weeks to find a new position: this period has increased very, very significantly to up to 12 weeks or even longer.

We are aware of a job hunter who took 4 and ½ years to get that new job – you say surely not – well YES it did. Obviously his old style of job hunting skills and techniques of the 1990's were not working or suitable in the 2020's but this is becoming such a true and serious issue: again showing the workplace is very different and your approach to getting a job must be different.

How long it takes to find and win a job depends on your job hunting skills – you need 2020 job hunting skills.

Average Job Time in the Job

Another development in the job market is that the average time spent in each job has diminishes greatly. Our Job Market / Employment Longevity Situation has changed significantly – candidates spend significantly less time in each job before moving on; i.e. in these New Days you will work in one position and/or for one employer for a much shorter period requiring more frequent job changes and job interview situations.

Where you have previously accepted and worked in a position for 5 or 7 years: this is now more likely to be less than 3 years before you change that role or employer.

Moreover, many employees are being forced to work or accept part time, or contract employment as a 'Fill in' position until that 'right' position arises.

So our market perspective for future employment is as follows:

- More part-time 'consultancies' or contract work or temporary hiring's
- More shorter period full time roles or expectations.

New Employment Modes

What is driving this new job hunting situation is the employers' reluctance to engage in full-time employment/commitments and the wish to adopt a more budget-friendly temporary or part-time role which can be terminated more readily. The author saw this new model of employment in 2000 when they wrote their book "Independent Contractors – Independent Lifestyle".

In the forward to this book Kevin Chandler of Chandler Recruiting and ex Chair of Chandler McLeod discussed this new way of work through "The Internet of Things" [IoT] –this is a whole new way of work and the resulting engagement between employees and employers.

There is a new and very effective description of the market in which jobs have now been described and developed: our jobs have now been redefined and recreated in a New Age / New Day best described as "The Internet of Things" or IoT as coined by Kevin Ashton[3]; surely a new market based on the internet; an ability to reach billions of customers in their homes and offices instantaneously is a new way of business and hence employment.

This IoT has created a new focus on the most appropriate Business Model for any organisation and much more focus will be placed on the candidates understanding of the Business Model and IoT in their role and contribution in any future employment in an organisation.

Increased Job Churn / More Roles

Another consideration in our New Ways / New Days is that candidates will wish to leave their jobs and apply for and re-apply for many more jobs than they did in the past; up to 20 job changes in their career.

This means keeping up with the latest job skills / recruitment techniques will be critical for all candidates.

Lastly how candidates will apply for and get jobs will be very different – MORE ONLINE and other contemporary models and avenues: whereas it was Newspapers and job ads in classified papers it is now ONLINE RECRUITING as below.

The new title is "JOB BOARDS" – with use of search engines: new terms like:

- LinkedIn
- Career Builder
- Livecareer.com
- Readyjob.org
- Facebook
- Twitter
- Indeed
- Glassdoor
- Instagram
- Pinterest
- WhatsApp.

2. Mindmap Landscape

A great way or tool to gauge or map your personal career path is using a personal MINDMAP or LANDSCAPE MAP; which we discuss and develop below:

The idea of a Mindmap Landscape or Mudmap is not new: it is a diagram used to visually organise and display information and relationships: it takes a central idea or theme and builds a map of the relationships that impact or flow out of that central idea. It is a great way to build out strategies to a central theme or issue.

You can use the Mindmap Landscape approach to depict your current position and skills and where they can take you in your career progression in the future.

Using the basic Mindmap Landscape format below depict your current career positioning and where you believe your career could progress in the future:

Name:

My skills:

I am appreciated for:

I like doing:

I am an expert in:

What is IMPORTANT to me?

Current & Past Roles Attributes:

I dislike or am NOT GOOD at:

My dream job:

My second [plan b] option:

Figure 2: Mindmap Landscape

Complete your Mindmap Landscape worksheet on p290

3. One Page Career MudMap

Alternatively you could complete the following One Page Career Mudmap which sets out your personal SWOT On A Page and the ACTIONS and DIRECTIONS that you could develop to progress your career possibilities.

SWOT: Actions - Directions - Possibilities

SWOT:	Actions / Directions / Possibilities
Strengths:	
Weaknesses:	
Opportunities:	
Threats:	

By completing this Personal 'SWOT on a Page' you can then develop the Actions & Directions that you could take to progress your career directions /possiblities.

Figure 3: One Page Career MudMap

Complete your Career MudMap worksheet on p291

4. Selection of Your Next Career Role

"Why are you applying for this role?" Yes..this is a left field but all too often asked question that the interviewer is really asking… why are you here?... Is it to add value to our organisation or to accelerate your career…perhaps you could not find another job so we are last choice as you waste our time and de-stabilise our organisation.

In what direction will you and your career head?

Where or what is your Flag on the Hill for your future career?

Will it be aspirational or based on reality and your current capabilities?

Is it to a medium size organisation, a large organisation or a public listed or a Not for Profit or Community Group: or a Public Sector role? Are they Multi-National, National or Local?

They all look appealing but how will selecting the next position lead you toward your career Flag on the Hill.

Do you have the requisite skills for that job or this career move at this time?

Have you earnt your stripes and accreditation/reputation or are you over-estimating your abilities and reputation/value?

Have you gained any / enough industry and personal brand recognition that will set you apart?

Are you experienced in the operations and people management skills required for a senior executive positions?

These are just some of the self-evaluation questions you need to pose as you think about moving on and preferably up with your career. How big a leap do you try in your next career move: is it to a new industry, state or country? Is it to a completely new role or from a 'for profit' into a 'not for profit' position?

We see far too many impatient executives who jump directly into the end position, only to find they drown quickly due to the lack of experience and/or the skillset required.

Yet had they pursued their next position to suit the career path toward their end goal, taking the interim step, the interim role they required to gain the experience and the skillset, would have meant the difference between success or failure.

How does one recover from failure in a career move? It follows you on paper and digitally, you must explain to your next future employer as to why your tenure was so short, exposing your impatience and lack of research and understanding which can be detrimental to their business should they hire you. If the 40% failure rate as mentioned in our introduction by Heidrick & Struggles is correct, then there are lots of executives out there seeking a second chance in a successful recruitment endeavour.

As a candidate moving on, once you have decided your future intentional direction and tempered your aspirations, you need to read on to learn how to win in the coaching, application, interview and selection process to gain that position that you aspire to attain.

Our experience is that you need to be mindful that it is a long distance event. It is a marathon, not a sprint, hence our Focus on **The 200 Day Transition in Your Career Progression.**

We will now take you through the full EXIT of your existing position, the RECRUITMENT process, which hopefully results in a SELECTION and then a JOB OFFER: and then as you PERFORM in this new job in the ultimate FIRST 100 Days in the Job.

5. Search and Selection Process Flowchart

How do we prepare you for your next role?

Roles are few too many for us to independently advise on. Rather than pigeon hole each role, we provide you with tools recruiters use for you to tailor to your next role as your hunger and growth as an executive increases. By understanding the process recruitment organisation's take, you can better prepare and appreciate how to successfully prepare and play in the job recruitment process that you must go through to successful transition from one position to another.

Why listen to us? A combination of recruitment, training and hiring experience providing insight to gain a competitive advantage over those who have failed to invest the time and resources into their own career growth. We want to succeed and in-turn, see your organisation achieve considerable growth as a result of recruiting the right person.

The following is a very useful flowchart of a search and selection process that a prominent Search organisation adopts.

This Flow Chart emphasises the matching of the clients/employers culture / behaviours / style with the candidates style/emotional intelligence, and particularly competencies to get a successful match and longer term employment situation.

The four (4) phases for the employer and employee of:

1. Preparation   – for moving on
2. Sourcing   – your options as a candidate
3. Recruitment   – considering candidates
4. Selection   – selecting the winning one.

Integrity & Validity of process

1. Preparation	identifying commercial objectives of the role
	matching personality style to culture
	identifying key stakeholders (internal & external)
	mapping behavioural competencies necessary for high performance
	customising structured interview documents and reference checks to identify specific skills and behaviours
2. Sourcing	detailed analysis of competitors to identify high performers
	primary research on market targets for potential candidates
	engagement of online and social media research databases
	formal search using existing networks in relevant geographic centres
	constant communication with client to inform progress
3. Recruitment	manage candidates with absolute care and discretion
	full review of candidate history
	exploration of abilities and potential in extensive competency based behavioural interview
	review candidates for rational, systems and emotional intelligence
	initial contact following qualification, cultivate interest in the organisation and the role
4. Selection	client interviews
	confirm shortlist, develop detailed reports on candidate suitability, interview responses, remuneration expectation
	preferred candidates reference checking. Referees may include clients' superiors, peers and subordinates
	negotiation of offer and employment conditions
	facilitation of smooth transition into the role. Regular ongoing contact with candidate and client

Figure 4: Search and Selection Process Flowchart

6. Researching the Industry, Organisation and Position

As a candidate applying for a new job, before putting your name up for that new position or in a new organisation, you need to research a number of critical aspects in respect of the organisation and/or the position.

Would you want to get all excited and go through all this effort and disruption only to find that either the business was approaching bankruptcy or liquidation or about to be taken over and asset stripped, or there was a massive board rift or there was an anointed successor and this was only a market test. Or you may win the race only to face an inevitable board rift and you may win the recruitment game only to face the inevitable sack following a board room revolt. Or your salary expectation is totally at odds with what will be or is being offered.

We so often see a 'selected insider' who is guaranteed the job and the business is either going through the motions or testing the market for a comparison and assessment of their preferred internal choice. Research will better inform you of the legitimacy of the job ad and reality of a job position and the market opposition.

Genuine Job Listing or Set-Up Recruitment Ad

Before committing considerable time and effort to submitting your job application [and getting all excited about the prospects], you must understand and clearly establish that this is a genuine job listing and not a pre-determined exercise to justify an internal incumbent: happens too often, unfortunately.

To be FOREWARNED is FOREARMED

Or maybe you learn that there has been two or three incumbents in the position over the past two years and the executive team is in toxic revolt and disarray.

As with all critical business decisions, it should be based on sound business research and intelligence.

You need to seriously assess the following due diligence checklist in respect of your future employer and the position being advertised.

If you are not supplied the information at first, request it upon offer of the position. If you are denied the information, this should be a good indicator of what is at risk. The table is split between information you can source internally (i) and externally (e):

Due diligence checklist

i	Financial solvency and future prospects / existence / security
i	Profitability/Sources of Revenue and Business Growth
i	Legal position, legal claims, reputation – good or bad
i	Strategic direction and unique positioning / capability
i e	Market position and reputation: Corporate Social Responsibility [CSR], ethics, brand positioning, market perception / qualities of products / services
i	Prepare your version of the organisations' SWOT analysis and your views of their way forward
i	Get copies of Annual Reports or Annual Returns and consider any contingent liabilities and valuable assets [tangible and intangible and whether owned or at risk]
i	If possible, see a copy of its strategic plan or prepare your version of a Strategic Plan on a Page for the business as you perceive it would or could be
i	Review the existing board structure and composition – [any known names or reputations – good or bad]
i	Consider banking relationships and current financial support and/or exposure of this new employer
i	Request current running balance account and declaration that all regulatory lodgements have occurred and are true to the existence of the declaration. Taxes unpaid or not lodged will be missing.
i	Finally, understand what may have happened to the positions previous incumbent: promoted and staying, removed, dismissed and moved on? Any skeletons in the closet?
i	Any critical subordinate staff resignations that will impact the performance of any selected successful candidate?

i	Ask what the business model (BM) is. Then assess if the current services and products offered are within the business model? Are the customers within the scope of the BM?
i	Current up to last two years board reports
i	Current management style and depth of reporting
e	Search the government website for banned or disqualified directors, persons and the organisation (ASIC, IRS, etc)
e	Review major customer and supplier relationships, currently held, at risk, won or lost recently
e	Conduct an Equifax SwiftCheck report
e	View any available industry reports or comparative surveys
e	Impact of present and emerging technologies or new business models which could be game changers
e	Competitive pressures and potential Blue Ocean Strategies / Dangers & Threats
e	Current market research / BOD research / CEO research

Figure 5: Due diligence checklist

If the recruitment is being handled by a recruitment agency, you are entitled to seek all the above information that you require before putting your name forward as your reputation is on the line as a genuine applicant.

handled by a recruitment agency

Getting Ready .. Be Prepared!

You may not even have a specific position or role to apply for but intend to be in the recruitment market in the next six months or so. If this is the case, then the following steps in preparedness are just as important and you have time to professionally get yourself ready for the application / recruitment / interview phases as listed in the following sections.

What can you do as you work out where and when to formally apply for a specific position:

- Update your CV / Resume.
- Develop actions/tasks/training courses and address any perceived gaps in your CV or professional portfolio – this may take time, training and investment on your part.
- Ensure your professional development and training hours are up to date and adequate.
- Consider and brief your potential referees, as to your progress, intentions, directions, support or guidance needed or requested.
- Consider and promote any career or position succession for your existing position to free you up to move on in a prepared and professional way.
- Increase your industry and organisational research and participate in industry discussion groups and networking events.
- Selectively have discussions with noted recruiters and search specialists to understand the current market trends, hot spots and nuances.
- Ensure your CSR [Corporate Social Responsibility] activities are up to date and fitting of your positions and aspirations – as a senior executive you must be able to portray a presence and contribution to your industry and the community – using your skills and position to advance your CSR and go one step further than financial donations, donate your time, your labour and plan for a new employee CSR program.
- Commence a formal mentoring program with you as the mentor and taking on a new mentoree.

Before we begin with your CV, we need to introduce ATS as it will be needed for your CV and Cover Letter.

Keywords in your CV / Resume – AbilityMap & Use of ATP's

The recruitment process [as described already] is now so refined that tools and techniques automatically help with the selection process – as described elsewhere.

Simply put – to efficiently process the vast number of candidates for a position, a or several key word selection editing techniques must be used.

You may not know what they are but you must know how to play the game and game your position.

Refer to the AbilityMap Competency developed by our colleague Kevin Chandler, the co-founder of the internationally acclaimed Chandler McLeod Recruitment, for the detailed description.

So what are these 'key words' and how do you know what and how to use them in your CV and application? Are they different for each job or role or level in the organisation or are they so generic that once you know them, you are assured of the role – read on.

As a recruiter of CFO's and with a specialty of selecting and appointing CFO's, we know the key questions and key responses that must be in any application for a CFO position. These are discussed in Section 4 of this book.

The recruitment industry use a well established but little understood app called an ATS that expedites the recruitment selection process through an automated digital technology.

An **Applicant Tracking System (ATS)** can also be implemented or accessed online at an enterprise or even at a small business level, depending on the needs of the company.

An ATS is very similar to customer relationship management (CRM) systems, but it is designed for recruitment tracking purposes specifically.

In many cases, ATS' filter applications automatically based on given criteria such as job application keywords, skills, former employers, years of experience and prior schools attended. This ATS method has caused many applicants to adapt CV/Resume Optimisation techniques similar to those used in search engine optimisation when creating and formatting their CV/Résumé.

Almost all recruitment agencies and most major corporations with an in-house recruitment function use some form of ATS to handle job postings, applicants, resumes and interviews.

ATS are built to better assist the management of resumes and applicant information. Data is either collected from internal applications via the ATS front-end located on the company website or it is extracted from applicants on job boards.

Recent enhancements to ATS include the use of artificial intelligence (AI) tools and natural language processing (NLP) to facilitate intelligent guided semantic search capabilities offered through cloud based platforms that allow companies to score and sort resumes with better alignment to the particular job requirements and descriptions, and also the corporate culture.

With the advent of ATS, resume optimisation techniques and online tools such as CVLift are now used by applicants to increase their chances of landing an interview call: you must be familiar with this ATS concept and utilise this tool to your advantage.

Benefits of ATS for the employer

Functionality of an ATS is not limited to data mining and collection, ATS applications in the recruitment industry include the ability to automate the recruitment process via a defined workflow.

Another benefit of an ATS is analysing and coordinating recruitment efforts to manage the conceptual structure known as human capital. A corporate career site or company specific job board module may be offered, allowing companies to provide opportunities to internal candidates prior to external recruitment efforts.

Candidates may be identified via pre-existing data or through information garnered through other means. This data is typically stored for search and retrieval processes. Some systems have expanded offerings that include off-site encrypted resume and data storage, which are often legally required by equal opportunity employment laws.

The combined resources available to recruiters mean that there is a new world out there that puts pressure on candidates to keep up to date and have a good mentor in the recruitment space.

You need a friend or mentor who can keep you abreast with the latest recruitment techniques and technology, otherwise your fabulous CV may just continue to be overlooked and unfortunately, you may be as well for that great job that you are eminently qualified for and you deserve.

How the ATS Selects

The ATS commences the review of your CV in the following order:

1. Job Title
2. Industry
3. Achievements.

Focus your attention to highlight these in your CV and then ensure that you have captured key words from the job description advertised.

CV Action Keywords

As a candidate, you now better appreciate how your CV / Resume will be assessed and automatically scanned in the selection process – you have to say the right words. We now follow on from knowing about ATS to knowing the 8-10 ACTION KEYWORDS that make your CV come to life and ensure selection.

We mention keywords in resumes a lot, for the reason of their importance for the ATS to select you. To expand upon this, the keywords are nouns that explain what actions you have performed. They are job specific and industry specific to the role advertised. An example of **Keywords** are:

- Degree, Certificate, Post-Graduate, PhD
- University
- A job title such as CEO
- Professional association
- Job related terms eg. business model, financial architecture, strategic modelling, corporate governance
- Software if a CIO such as Oracle or NetSuite.

Having researched your chosen job advertisement, you may recall words that repeated within ads for the job title and generic content of which you were applying, often these are keywords.

As you draft your CV and cover letter, be sure to peruse and highlight the keywords for your own check. If you have used too many keywords you may be overloaded so try to be concise when using these.

KEYWORDS also fall into two categories, Hard Skills and Soft Skills.

HARD SKILLS are technical job related skills specific to the job. An example of a CFO's hard skills:

- Budgeting and forecasting
- Statutory accounting
- Treasury management and funding
- Performance Management
- Business mergers, acquisitions and turnaround.

SOFT SKILLS cover aspects such as:

- Leading and strategic thinking
- Mentoring and coaching
- Training and development
- Community involvement.

Note that the ATS will not pick up untruths, but it will cross reference to pick up gaps and inconsistencies.

Tweaking Your CV

Here's something not enough job seekers appreciate about resumes (even though it *seems* obvious):

When an HR rep, recruiter, or hiring manager picks up your resume, they don't know anything about you. They have to scan over a single sheet of paper and, often in a matter of seconds, build a picture of who you are, what you've done, and where you're going. And then they have to decide: "Yes" or "No".

Their decision depends on a picture in their mind that's painted from just a few sentences and a handful of bullets and soundbites.

Do you know what this means?

Even the tiniest tweaks to the way you tell your story can make a HUGE difference to the picture they perceive in their mind of you.

Now, with that in mind...

Let me tell you about a fascinating experiment I carried out last week.

There's a resume app that is very useful: called Top Resume.

Basically, you upload a copy of your resume and this tool scans through it (using the same algorithms that Applicant Tracking Systems use) and gives you a fairly accurate look at the picture hiring managers' paint in their heads as they scan through your resume and consider you for a role.

Top Resume app - is a good way to view what your resume says about you, so that you know what kind of tweaks you need to make.

Anyway, I uploaded a hypothetical resume to see how hiring managers see it.

Just to keep things simple, this resume represents a young person who is looking to get into finance after graduating from college. My goal was for the resume to focus on this person's finance education and experience, while highlighting the fact that this person also speaks fluent Mandarin Chinese.

But, as it turns out, this wasn't the picture this resume was painting.

Top Resume analysed this resume. Although it picked up their finance background and correctly summarised their experience – it didn't even notice their Chinese language abilities, and instead (somehow) thought that they had some "exposure" to engineering. This wasn't the first impression I wanted, so I made some tweaks to this resume and uploaded it to Top Resume a second time. This time, the algorithms did indeed pick up on their skills and experience as a Chinese speaker (and correctly matched this person to jobs).

This experiment just goes to show that sometimes, **a few tweaks to your resume can make a huge difference** in the picture HR reps, recruiters, and hiring managers paint of you in their minds.

It pays to use a tool, an app similar to Top Resume to find out what your resume says about you and tweak it appropriately until it makes the right kind of impression.

Let's now start with that Job Winning CV followed by a stunning INTERVIEW PORTFOLIO.

8. Job Winning CV [Resume]

Some call it a CV [curriculum vitae]: others a RESUME. It is all about YOU and your career: skills, capabilities, offering, positioning, past achievements, references and selling YOU for the job.

WE MUST ASK: Is your CV up to date? Is it a stand out for this position and going to get you to an interview against over one hundred other keen aspirants?

On average we would expect over two hundred qualified candidates which can come in a rush and then dribble in over a three or four week recruitment period.

Timing of CV Submission

Consider the timing of your job application; when do you lodge your expression of interest? When do you show your hand and throw your name into the ring? Here is our wise counsel:

- In the **first** week, the CV is ready, a very keen candidate hits the 'Submit' button as they see the job advertisement and hit the recruitment sites or newspapers – they are ready, keen and probably need a job – commonly they apply for quite a few positions but keep missing out on interview or selection. Recruitment/Selection agents know to AVOID WEEK 1 APPLICANTS unless for some reason they are exceptional: but exceptional applicants have an existing role or jobs.

- In the **second** week, the more appraised and selective applicant will craft their CV and presentation/application and they will be a worthy candidate. They may already hold down a good job and will be considering their move vertically and more strategically: a worthy consideration.

- In the **third** week, the happily employed and 'just thinking' about putting their hat in the ring contender will emerge. They will be a strong contender and you as the potential employer will have to prize them out and over to your business.

At the **very last** moment or past deadline as they are very busy, probably not fully prepared to sell themselves and is a sort of knee jerk reaction – but a great qualified employable candidate applies. You must wait for this candidates' CV as they are less impulsive and more considered. Or is this the disorganised person who didn't really care? What are you creating for recruiters – mayhem to get through cv's as they all arrive on the final hour?

REMEMBER: It does take time to research an organisation and the position being advertised and offered and then assemble that Job Winning CV and full Application Pack and to research to ensure as a candidate that you and your application match the position and organisations' culture. Especially if you are busy or working on a Special Project or regularly travel overseas representing the organisation.

Regardless of when lodged, all candidate's CVs and presentation pack and covering letter will need to be assessed and ranked: GO - NO GO – or MAYBE.

So what does your CV need to look like to get you to the interview round? Remember you have to beat between 100 and 200 other contenders and it is likely that only ten (10) will get through the first round selection process: all based on your CV, Covering Letter and professional and industry experience.

You had your CV updated at middle management level in a format of approximately 2 pages, as this was the fad used by recruitment agencies to decrease the time they were spending on reviewing applicants for roles that did not require in depth analysis.

Is this the role you are still seeking? Or are you now looking for a senior executive position that will navigate the business growth using the CEO's vision, requiring analytical skills, experience and advanced toolsets and personnel demeanour? Perhaps you are seeking the role of an Executive Director of HR, COO, CMO, CIO or Finance or even as the CEO. Regardless, your CV must tell the story of why you would provide value to the business and stand out from the crowd.

So seriously consider the position and the type and style of CV that will suit this position. We discuss this in detail below with the various styles of CV's. As you do update your CV, think of how you harness your experience to tell that story that embraces your age against another with much less experience.

The 6-Second Resume [CV] Test
Much has been written about the 6 - SECOND RESUME [CV] Test.

Many credible studies show that the **average recruiter scans a CV/Resume for six seconds** before deciding if the applicant is a good fit for the role. It is that abrupt.

So you have **6 seconds to make your mark!** Let's aim for less.

It is important to construct your CV such that the reader can skim and identify your **most important selling points and commendation** for the position being considered.

Unfortunately, we have to confess that when we are considering over 200 CV's for a position, the 6 Second Resume Test/Review does have some logic and appeal. As an employer, you have a strong criteria and idea of what you are looking for and can very quickly and readily assess if each CV hits the mark: that it meets the essential criteria for further discussions and interviews; - style, qualities, accrediting skills, and a view of that special match of technical and strategic skills whilst fitting the organisational culture brief.

So with that 6-Second thought in mind, let's design your CV and Job Application accordingly.

Your Preferred CV Model - what does it look like?
For impact, the top third of your CV is a snapshot – your details, career profile, proven demonstrated ability, goals, qualifications, relevant skills and telling your career story.

We preach that your CV is your biggest piece of real estate, it determines your next role that provides your lifestyle and aspirations, to boost you into the top 10 to be asked back for an interview: so INVEST IN YOU.

Here we go!

The Preferred CV Length and Format

You have 6 seconds or less to make an impact and then you wonder how long a CV should be and if anyone actually reads it. At Management to Senior Executive level it is read more indepth the higher the role is.

Our extensive experience and research proves that a customised, personalised and professional CV of the 6 to 8 pages in length and format is critical for your selection to proceed to the next round of interviews.

Unfortunately, we see too many capable and employable candidates fail at the initial hurdle only because they have failed to invest in and customise their CV for the particular position and/or organisation.

MESSAGE: spend time and invest your resources to perfect your Resume/CV for the **particular position, role and organisation:** that is a well organised format, as outlined and easy to read – avoid long paragraphs. Focus on broadcasting YOUR KEY ACHIEVEMENTS and WHAT YOU OFFER.

You must avoid believing that your latest CV [no matter how good it is] is usable and suitable for every position you apply for: this is a FATAL MISTAKE.

Customisation is the secret to success. Customisation aligns your skills and experience to that of the reader, the recruiter.

You can buy internet based $250 to $500 CV templates which basically are a waste of money and time and unfortunately a waste of an opportunity: and once you have failed to have a 'call-up' after ten tries it gets a little demoralising and discouraging. Make your first go a winner: customised, purposeful for the position at hand.

Here is our advice on your CV: it comes from years of experience helping and coaching in CV preparation and also on the selection panel looking at tens of thousands of candidates through the eyes of Kevin Chandler former founder of Chandler McLeod, Chandler Petty CFO Recruitment and our surveys from hundreds of C-Suite executives :

CV Layout

You

Highlight your Name as the header: Jonathon Sunday [Your Name] followed by your Skill Title, e.g. MBA, Doctorate, Professional Recognition. Also add this to the footer of the document to ensure all pages remind the reader of who you are and of your qualification. Next we add your personal details that are standard for any management to executive and board role.

Personal Information

Residential Address, Mobile/cell phone including country code, Email, Nationality, Residency, Referees. An optional extra is to add whether you have a current passport and drivers license without including the identification numbers (further information will be requested upon your hire).

Referees

Always leave 'referees as available upon request'. We discuss referees in depth in section 2.

Academic Titles

Please help the reader by reducing your lifetime of titles. There is no need to place an undergraduate title that was compulsory for you to have achieved your phd or higher graduate degree. Eg, If you are a CA you do not need a B.Comm stated against your title. The B.Comm detail will be listed in your education section, as you highlight the greatest of your academia, being your CA.

To note there are now a number of differing MBAs, so we suggest you may like to add the additional letter to show the type of MBA studied if relevant. Eg MBA.SM MBA Strategic Management, MBA.M MBA specialising in Marketing. EMBA Executive MBA, IMBA International MBA.

Academia tip: If you are a CEO, display MBA followed by CA or CPA if you are accredited. If you are a CFO, display CA or CPA followed by MBA.

Number of Pages

The minimum number of pages for a senior executive will range from 5 to 6 pages for the average 35 year old upward. 2 or 3 page CV's are not meaningful and don't sell you for the position.

LABEL EACH PAGE with your name on the footer and the page number.

CV Content

Commence with a short paragraph of 3-5 lines to captivate the reader [interviewer] as you set the scene to elevate your value above your competitors using dynamic words but avoid buzz words. This is also referred to as your personal impact statement and may include your value proposition statement.

9. Personal Impact Statement

Your **Impact Statement** is a brief high level summary of your experience whilst highlighting your unique skills. The use of this statement can also be replicated in your covering letter that is discussed further on.

The headline will set the tone of HOW BRILLIANT YOU ARE: you understand the need to make an impact and you realise the importance of being value adding. This is your elevator pitch.

Your IMPACT STATEMENT states how you make or can make a difference using the classification below:

- Strategic – able to transform businesses or business processes
- Innovative and creative – bring new concepts or approaches
- The 'Go To' person – you will listen and can act
- A Champion of Success
- Managing and facilitating change
- Delegating for your higher level management as necessary.

Your IMPACT STATEMENT will be used in the recruitment process to demonstrate that:

- you are decisive and a leader
- you can be believed and relied upon
- you are a team player or team builder
- your ethics and values are of the highest calibre.

Which **writing style** to use? 3rd Person? 1st Person?

This is a topic well debated.

Do you want the reader to feel as if you own your profile and are talking directly to them or that it is written by a paid consultant or organisation who is not you?

We recommend writing as if you are speaking to the reader yourself. You want to captivate the reader so need to include the following elements:

Organisations you have worked for and should mirror your CV role titles. Add the organisation's logo and describe in 1-2 lines the organisation's business.

Skillsets listed including those listed on LinkedIn discussed later, should only be relevant to your latest role, along with any other major high achieving skills. Ensure you do not list basic broad words such as marketing if you are a CMO, rather choose the type of marketing, and say Commercial CMO or CXO if role is IT based.

The concept of an "IMPACT STATEMENT" will set you apart and stimulate conversation from the interviewer about you as the candidate, who has already assessed and developed their position of how they can and will impact on the business, if you get the appointment.

Let's examine a Personal Impact Statement example that emphasises keywords as shown here in bold that align the statement to that of the role offered:

Impact Statement of a COO:

*"**Experienced** Operational **leader** for APAC's fastest growing **logistics** sector, servicing **online multi-national** retail clients in textiles, furniture and electronics. Proven **cultural accelerator** creating advanced team DIFOTIS to win the International Logistics Best in Service **Award** 2020."*

Analysis:
The keywords in bold will direct the ATS to propel your CV to the top of the pile. It touches on the experience, the skills, the industry and size.

Impact Statement of a CFO:

*"**Mid-tier** to **Large FMG** CFO **veteran** for Australia and EU listed businesses on the **LSE** and **ASX**. **Strategic partner** driving **fast-growth e-commerce** and **blockchain** market leaders. **Increased EPS 6%** and **EBIT 20%** through **cost driven strategic finance modelling**. Team architect for multi-disciplined **FMG** cadetship to **CA, CILT** and **SCLAA qualification**."*

Analysis:
The CFO example highlights strengths, including experience, length of experience and skill level as a dynamic performer utilising lead technology. It then emphasises the ability to achieve results for shareholders and the organisation and how. It finishes with the value added within the business as to establishment and design of multiple cadet programs that result in support to the final post graduate level of membership. This example is packed full of keywords and ATS trackability.

Impact Statement of a CCO:

*"**CIM qualified VP Marketing** with experience growing market share and penetrating new markets for world-class luxury goods brands. Fluent in **French**, I have held country leadership roles in **Belgium** and **Singapore** and possess strong **Digital Marketing** skills. London-based, I am now seeking a Chief Commercial Officer role with an **entrepreneurial, fast-paced** luxury brand with **international growth**."*

Analysis:
Chris Mumford [22], managing director of the London office of Aethos Consulting Group, provided this example of an executive-level personal statement. This personal statement packs a punch. Mumford explains: "It's clear that the applicant is an expert in digital marketing, the inclusion of the French language capability and markets worked in conveys that the applicant has international experience, [and] an ATS will instantly match this person with roles in London." Also, note that the statement is keyword-dense as well.

> **Impact Statement of a CEO:**
> *"**CIMA, MBA** and **CA qualified veteran** with **international** recognition **awarded** in **RI's top 10 Global CEO's** as published by **Forbes**, as a power house **performance driven leader** of **high growth fintech**, harnessing **e-commerce** and **blockchain**. Established paid annual team community days to NFP charities."*
>
> *Analysis:*
> Using unique identifiers to push their recognised abilities as a highly qualified CEO will see this CV elevated to the top of the pile. The experience in the industries is mentioned with ability to utilise latest technology. Finishing off the statement is the Corporate Social Responsibility to establish paid days for employees to provide physical help to charities on an ongoing basis.

Tips: Impact Statement: When highlighting increases or decreases, always use ratios, not numbers. Ratios provide the metric of result that stands out in your statement whereas values do not.

10. Value Proposition Statement

This is a powerful newer concept that tells the end user, being the employer and organisation of the benefit and added value that you will provide. It is a very positive and useful promotional and personal positioning tool.

This is no more than one short sentence, ideally fitting the statement onto one page for the end user's ease of reading.

The Value Proposition Statement (VPS) [different to the IMPACT STATEMENT] can be inserted into your Personal Impact Statement or star on it's own under your name on the header. Using the similar concept of a business VPS, it is aimed at telling the customer what added value you will provide and what makes you different.

Put simply, our version of a personal VPS is to ask three simple questions *from the customer's perspective* in order to create the VPS:

Q1. What makes you different from other business partners?

Q2. Why should you want to engage with us as your business partner?

Q3. What will we solve for you?

An example of a VPS for a finance broker is:

Q. What makes you different from other business partners?
A. *A business finance solutions specialist*

Q. Why should you want to engage with us as your business partner?
A. *I deliver tailored results*

Q. What will we solve for you?
A. *To source better finance opportunities*

We take these 3 answers to populate the VPS: *A business Finance Solutions Specialist that delivers tailored results to source better finance opportunities.*

A further example of a VPS for a CFO:

Q. What makes you different from other business partners?
A. *A strategic finance business partner*

Q. Why should you want to engage with us as your business partner?
A. *I deliver meaningful reporting for dynamic informative decision making*

Q. What will we solve for you?
A. *Performance driven growth results*

We take these 3 answers to populate the VPS: *A strategic finance business partner delivering meaningful reporting for dynamic informative decision making to drive performance growth results.*

Skills List
Provide a brief on your skills emphasising the key areas of your experience on each line, for example:
- Strategic planning and competitive positioning
- Team development
- Change Management
- Anchoring structural change
- Business development and acquisitions: industry alliances
- Development of new business models or strategic partnerships
- Revised Board and management reporting and executive dashboards
- Executive compensation programs.

Each Role
The main content will commence with your current or more recent roles. The first line should state the title of your position [in bold] and the City and if relevant country in which you worked. On the right hand side, type the year you commenced.

Directly underneath input the name of the company and their current logo and website url. If the trading name or brand names are well known, also add these logos. [Make it a visible experience]

Write a brief on the organisation [two to three lines maximum] including the turnover, its products or service lines, and how you fit in: describe your contribution through your position.

Key Responsibilities
Outline your key responsibilities, including who you report to, or have hierarchal responsibility too, the number of subordinates that report to you and the portfolios you are responsible for - e.g. Property portfolio and trading portfolio: all functional service teams and finance, HR and people, OHS, Boards, Sub-committees, etc.

Ensure that any gaps or periods of unemployment are clearly explained - e.g. Full-time MBA study or seconded industry representation role overseas.

Key Achievements

Highlight at least three key achievements that were outstanding; above and beyond your primary role in each position or organisation that you list, for example:

- Acquired liquidated company to turnaround year 1 into a 40% Profit After Tax
- Introduced the contractor of the year award to show appreciation and encourage improved results that add value to our business
- A suggestion to change the business model of market channels to increase online sales whilst retraction of retail to introductory stores to provide a unique experience, resulting in a 55% increase in turnover in year 1 of a net gross margin of $65 million.

CV Key Achievements Tip: When deciding your tip, ask yourself:

Who is the end reader of this?

Does my CV lure the reader to want to know more, ensuring not to divulge too much, so that you can save the detail of how you achieved this amazing achievement for the interview, without being too light?

Referring to the above points, the first example leaves the reader wanting to know how you turned it around.

The second leaves the reader asking what was the award given and how was it advertised and taken up.

This also leaves the interviewer wanting to know what the experience was.

You now have something to discuss and expand upon in the interview.

Reason for Leaving

At the end of each of the 3 key achievements summarise on one line your reason for leaving. Eg: Promotion; Seek different sector experience; International opportunity. The employer will be judging why you left your role, and last role in particular, to assert the expected duration you may remain in the role you are applying for.

CV Roles Tip 1: Display roles as most current on your first page ending with oldest at the rear.

CV Roles Tip 2: For Roles that may be 10 years and older, we suggest you shorten these. For roles 20 years and older, simplify with title, company, url and period worked. No need to add keys and responsibilities.

Corporate Social Responsibility

At this point, you need to prove that your CSR for business is representative of your own stance you take voluntarily. We highly support and recommend joining your local Lions Club or local Sports Club to utilise and gift your skills to others. It may be as simple as cooking a snag at the Bunnings BBQ or providing marketing guidance or treasury support or management.

Interests

Finally, you need to add your own personal interests. The interests you display should be representative of the business your job application is targeting so that your personal interests compliment, align and can be utilised by the organisation and yourself on promotional days, such as: Golf, tennis, cricket, rowing, your favourite rugby or football team, musical instruments or styles where relative to the business, debating, etc.

Our example template is of an executive job winning CV layout:

Mary Bloggs, MBA CA

A strategic finance business partner delivering meaningful reporting for dynamic informative decision making to drive performance growth results.

Address:	88 Pierre Avenue, Westmeed, VIC, 3009
	[if applying for overseas role, include your Country]
Telephone:	+61 444 000 000
E-mail:	marybloggs@gmail.com
Nationality:	German
Residency:	Australian Resident and German Citizen [add this line in if you are not a natural citizen of the country location that you are applying for the role]
Referees:	Available on request.

Mid-tier to Large FMG CFO veteran for Australia and EU listed businesses on the LSE and ASX. Strategic partner driving fast-growth e-commerce and blockchain market leaders. Increased EPS 6% and EBIT 20% through cost driven strategic finance modelling. Team architect for multi-disciplined FMG cadetship to CA, CILT and SCLAA qualification.

CAREER PROFILE

- Finance professional with a consistent record of achievement across a number of sectors.

- Significant experience of working within a variety of business models and ownership structures.

- Experienced leader of teams with diverse ranges of size, skills, experience and expertise.

- Demonstrated ability as a strategic business partner; to learn new business quickly and liaise effectively with internal and external stakeholders.

- Proven change agent with a track record of successfully establishing business from liquidation or administration into a profitable position, as well as systems and process implementation.

- Possess strong strategic, commercial, operational and technical accounting expertise.

Figure 6: Executive Job Winning CV Layout

Group CFO
Abacus Pty Ltd (Melbourne, Australia)
www.abacus.com.zz

Trading As

ABACUS PTY LTD

2017 - current

Background
Abacus is an internal leader of medical apps for hospitals including surgical requirements. Servicing 15 major languages, the apps generate a consolidated turnover of USD 1.3 billion annually. Within the group, each app is a registered trading business, complimentary to one another providing a group consolidated GM of USD 800 million. Achieving a 20% reduction in costs in year one, the focus has been to strategically increase revenues 40% over two years, expand product lines identified by improved reporting and better service the subscription on demand helpdesk service.

Responsible for
- Being a key member of the Finance and Executive Leadership Team. This includes reporting to the CEO and directly to the Board.

- Driving strategy, planning, execution and compliance within the group. This involves working closely with the CEO and all COO to improve targets for each app.

- Leading all finance, risk and strategy reporting within the Abacus group including:
  - Management, financial and statutory accounting
  - Strategy planning, rolling quarterly forecasting and performance reporting
  - Consolidated and segmented reporting
  - Finance systems and all finance transactional activities
  - Cash flow hedging and reporting
  - Procurement, facilities and commercial contract management
  - Management and leadership of a strategic CFO team
  - Research and Development applications, management and board approved budgets in technical advancements
  - Liaison with auditors, banks, financiers, and internal and external bodies
  - Leading all mergers and acquisitions across the group.

CV / Resume 1.2

Key Achievements

- Successfully designed and developed a blue ocean strategy for surgical order app improvement for equipment required; per doctor [left hand or right hand], per surgery type, per patient's recognized other risks [eg. heart attack, stroke, high blood pressure]
- Development of strategic plan to Abacus Group Board of Directors, with execution contributing to a 40% increased turnover with a combined two year cost reduction of 35%.
- Successful ERP system implementation, training and co-ordination across the Abacus group, including in foreign languages being sold to.

Reason for Leaving: to return to the financial services market

CFO

Dynamic Financial Services Limited (London, UK)
www.dynamicfs.net.uk

DYNAMIC FINANCIAL SERVICES LIMITED

2012-2017

Background

The largest Financial Services provider of Stock broking and Financial Planning services with a total book value of GBP 3 Trillion. Regulatory adherence and legislative knowledge at government group bodies is represented by all senior executives. The CFO's task is to contribute, monitor and lead the firm with best governance and reporting both internally and externally.

Responsible for

- Board reporting
- Management reporting and forecasting
- Business model reporting and analytics
- Financial modelling and forecasting
- Legislative group body representation
- Business Workpaper Improvement
- Tax minimisation strategies
- Statutory reporting
- Business process development and implementation
- Improving financial controls, compliance and a regulatory and reporting framework.

Key Achievements
- Influencing parliament to include hedge fund reporting results as a financial statement, which we were leading across Europe.
- New sector and industry classification of clients that provided more meaningful management kpi's, resulting in a 15% new business increase whilst retaining existing clients, resulting in a GBP 450m revenue increase.
- Measures introduced to drive performance returned shareholders a 4% increase on prior year's Dividend.

Reason for Leaving: Career advancement required moving to Australia

Finance Manager	**2010 - 2012**
Sedost Limited (London, Britain)	
www.sedost.uk	
Financial Controller	**2007 - 2010**
Deutsche TWG GmbH (Berlin, Germany)	**2006 - 2010**
www.dtwg.de	
Chartered Accountant Taxation	**2002 - 2007**
Wolfsprunk Bank GmbH (Hamburg, Germany)	

PROFESSIONAL DEVELOPMENT

2018 CFO of the Future Series

EDUCATION

2019 MBA
Decker University
2002 Institute of Deutsche Accountants
Graduate Diploma – Chartered Accountant member# ABC777
1999 Degree Commerce
Universitat Dusseldorf

INTERESTS

Golf
Tennis
Travel
Technology Advancements in Quantum Computing

CORPORATE SOCIAL RESPONSIBILITY

Lions Club Melbdale	2017 - current
Victorian Soccer Junior League Federation	Treasurer 2018 - 2020
Deutsche debating club	President 2006 - 2008

GAPS IN YOUR CV/Work Timeline

Remember, if you have gaps in your CV, ALWAYS EXPLAIN THEM HONESTLY – if you have a number of short stints – call them contracts, then demonstrate and articulate the quality of your work and achievements and how it has created diversity and various useful experiences.

Explain short term contracts to achieve a specific task/s or interim positions and what proven outcome was achieved.

Pandemic and Natural Disaster Gaps

We know how hard some situations outside the control of you and your organisation may be. OH MY they unfortunately hit and hit hard when they do.

A once in a lifetime pandemic where the government enforces a long-term or in excess of a month lockdown on a business can be devastating.

An example is the tourism industry. Where during this you find the organisation could no longer financially support the years of no revenue and uncertainty, a retrenchment can be noted on your CV as the reason for leaving without fear.

11. CV on a Page and Dashboard Metrics

The HR/Recruitment market is constantly changing and the emerging trends in CV presentation are the use of:

1. CV Dashboard On A Page
2. CV Dashboard Metrics for Directors.

As we discuss the reasoning behind these they vary in their assertion of how and when to use them. A CV on a Page assumes that is all you need. It is slightly detailed and no other information is provided to expand upon the detail. A recruiter would view this as aesthetically appealing but serves little purpose.

This concept was posted by Yahoo CEO Marissa Mayer: it is well positioned on Google as "Yahoo CEO Marissa Mayer One-Page CV [16] Figure 7 on page 40, will Inspire Résumé Envy and Emulation" and promoted by Enhancv.com.

It promotes and applauds that it has a graph and other presentation tools. The article provides the best use of a CV like this " So, if your résumé is laden with egregious errors, or you're just not sure what to add or not add, take a look at this and prepare to be inspired." The article goes on to advise they capture her 20+ year career on a page. We let you be the judge.

Examine the document and then we will ask you to consider if this is right for you.

MARISSA MAYER
Business Woman & Proud Geek

✉ mmayer@yahoo-inc.com ☍ https://marissamayer.tumblr.com
📍 Sunnyvale, CA

EXPERIENCE

President & CEO
Yahoo!
📅 07/2012 - Ongoing 📍 Sunnyvale, CA
* Led the $4 billion acquisition of the company by Verizon
* Acquired Tumblr for $1.1 billion and moved the company's blog there
* Got to $1.6 billion in GAAP revenue in mobile, video, and social
* Tripled the company's mobile base to over 600 million active users

Vice President of Location & Local Services
Google
📅 10/2010 - 07/2012 📍 Palo Alto, CA
* Positioned Google Maps as the world leader in maps and navigation

Vice President of Search Products & UX
Google
📅 2005 - 2010 📍 Palo Alto, CA

Product Manager & Technical UI Lead
Google
📅 2001 - 2005 📍 Palo Alto, CA
* Optimized usability on Google's homepage to the smallest detail

Product Engineer
Google
📅 1999 - 2001 📍 Palo Alto, CA
* Joined the company as employee #20 and female employee #1

EDUCATION

M.S. in Computer Science
Stanford University
📅 1997 - 1999

B.S. in Symbolic Systems
Stanford University
📅 1993 - 1997

MOST PROUD OF

Courage I had
to take a sinking ship and make it float

Persistance & Loyalty
I showed through hard times at Yahoo following its acquisition

Google's growth
from 100k daily searches to 3 billion+

Inspiring women in tech
by being the youngest CEO on Fortune's list of the 50 most powerful women

MY TIME

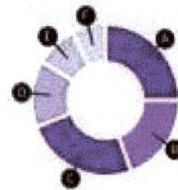

A Spending time with my children
B Publicly resolving Yahoo! investor issues
C Showing Yahoo! employees their work has meaning
D Building a biz-dev strategy for Yahoo's future after the Verizon acquisition
E Serving on the boards of New York and San Francisco ballet companies
F Creating spreadsheets for my amazing cupcake recipes

Made with admiration by ○ Enhancv

Figure 7: CV on a Page

If you are going to use the One Page CV approach, we ask you to consider the following:

Are you able to confidently write a One Page CV?

1.2 CV / Resume

What will the potential employer think of your approach and boldness?

Is it appropriate for your type of potential employer organisation?

Does it show disrespect?
Is it overselling you against the role?

Does it show innovation and modern thinking? Do you stand out positively and portray all of your attributes that you wanted and need to? For those with a limited career and not much to write, you may find yourself writing a one page CV.

We now step through the tips and considerations for a
One Page CV.

How to Write a One Page Resume

In general, most employers want a concise resume without a lot of extraneous information. They only spend seconds reviewing it [said to be the **6 second CV Review**], so the more compact it is, and the easier it will be for the hiring manager or recruiter to review.

In addition, many employers use software to screen job application materials, called **ATS** [Applicant Tracking Systems] – see following section, so making sure your resume is focused on the job you're applying for will help you get chosen for an interview.

In many cases, particularly for senior management roles, a longer resume might be in order. For example, graphic designers or visual artists might benefit from creating an illustrated resume, and academics, researchers, or long-time executives may need more than one page to capture the breadth of their experience.

Irrespective of the type of resume you choose, keep it concise and restrict to exclude waffle, small talk that drags on.

How Long Employers Want A Resume to Be

A Resume Survey conducted by US Saddleback [31] College found companies preferred the following types of resumes:

- One-Page Resume - 47.7%
- Two-Page Resume - 11.4%
- Depends on the level of the position - 34.1%
- No preference - 6.8%

The survey tells us that it really comes down to the level and type of the position. If you were recruiting casual summer staff, a one page resume has its merits, but for yourselves reading this at the senior to executive level, you must choose your resume type carefully.

If you do choose to fit your career on a page in written format, keep it short, simple and in listed form. We suggest you spend the time to seriously invest in a CV that TALKS TO THE READER and doesn't restrict your ability to highlight your amazing achievements.

The CV is your real estate that has to sell you on your behalf, it must sell so well, that you are invited to the next hiring stage.

12. Multi-Page Resume

According to the Saddleback College [31] survey above, most employers prefer a one-page resume, unless the position requires experience and detailed accreditation. If a potential job seeks an employee with extensive experience, you can and should include all of your applicable experience on your resume (although **most employers do not want applicants to include more than 10-15 years of past experience**). So it will be more than one page.

There are also certain professions that are exceptions to the one-page resume. For example, in academia, medicine, and international jobs, a **curriculum vitae** is often much longer than one page. There is also a profession whereby it is accepted to present a CV metric dashboard, Figure 8 page 43 accompanied by a full multi-page CV, that is of a Director.

Boards are often overwhelmed with candidates, limited in time to peruse the many applications for the role and thus heavily reliant upon a combination of tools. From the visual quick scan of a resume, to word of mouth and ATS, the board when they narrow down to a top 20, will then thoroughly assess a future Director's CV.

In this instance, we suggest using either a full detailed CV such as or using our next example, to accompany the CV for a dynamic 6 second scan that entices the reader to look at the candidate in detail if interested. It reduces the board's time and yours from applications that may not match the experience criteria that a board is seeking.

Dashboard Metric CV

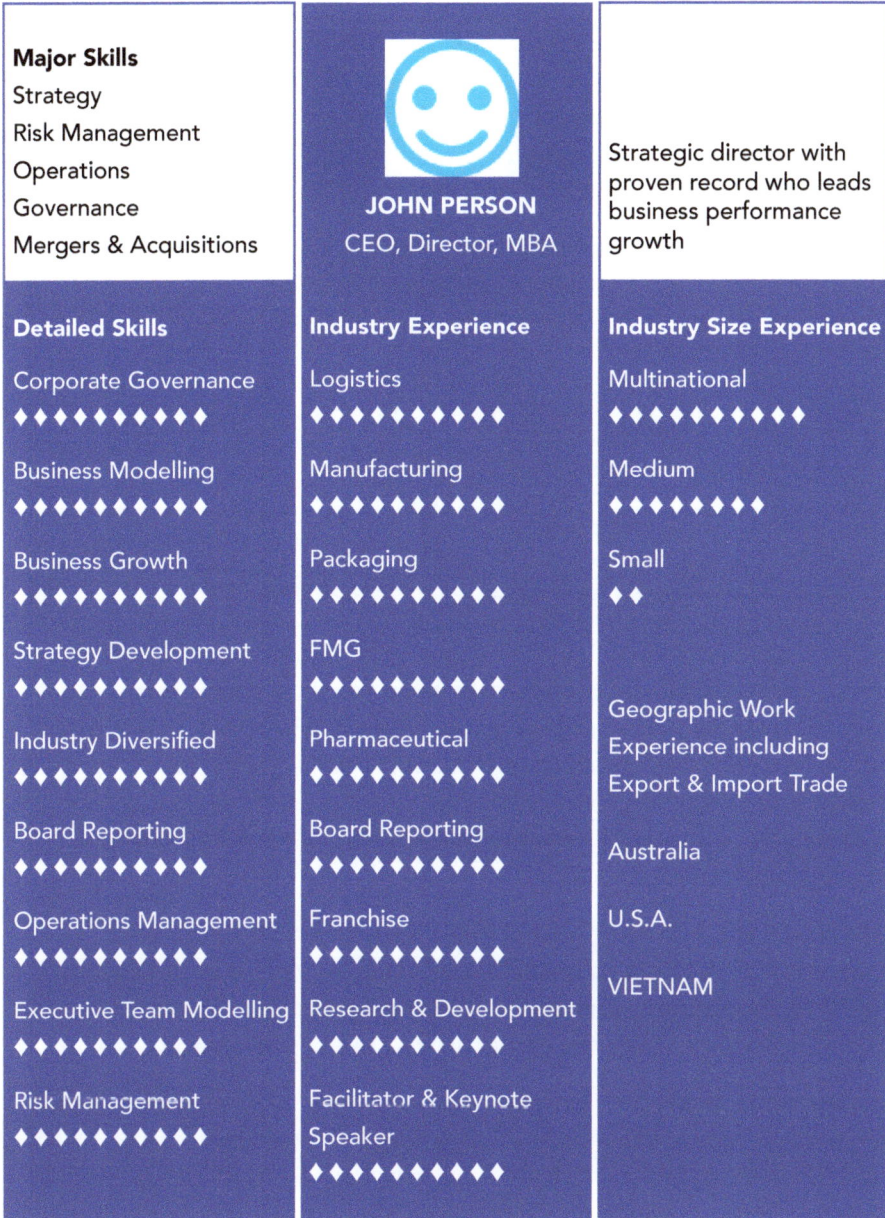

Major Skills Strategy Risk Management Operations Governance Mergers & Acquisitions	**JOHN PERSON** CEO, Director, MBA	Strategic director with proven record who leads business performance growth
Detailed Skills Corporate Governance ◆◆◆◆◆◆◆◆◆◆ Business Modelling ◆◆◆◆◆◆◆◆◆◆ Business Growth ◆◆◆◆◆◆◆◆◆◆ Strategy Development ◆◆◆◆◆◆◆◆◆◆ Industry Diversified ◆◆◆◆◆◆◆◆◆◆ Board Reporting ◆◆◆◆◆◆◆◆◆◆ Operations Management ◆◆◆◆◆◆◆◆◆◆ Executive Team Modelling ◆◆◆◆◆◆◆◆◆◆ Risk Management ◆◆◆◆◆◆◆◆◆◆	**Industry Experience** Logistics ◆◆◆◆◆◆◆◆◆◆ Manufacturing ◆◆◆◆◆◆◆◆◆◆ Packaging ◆◆◆◆◆◆◆◆◆◆ FMG ◆◆◆◆◆◆◆◆◆◆ Pharmaceutical ◆◆◆◆◆◆◆◆◆◆ Board Reporting ◆◆◆◆◆◆◆◆◆◆ Franchise ◆◆◆◆◆◆◆◆◆◆ Research & Development ◆◆◆◆◆◆◆◆◆◆ Facilitator & Keynote Speaker ◆◆◆◆◆◆◆◆◆◆	**Industry Size Experience** Multinational ◆◆◆◆◆◆◆◆◆◆ Medium ◆◆◆◆◆◆◆◆ Small ◆◆ Geographic Work Experience including Export & Import Trade Australia U.S.A. VIETNAM

Figure 8: Dashboard Metric CV

Everything you include in your resume must be relevant to the position, right down to your word choice. Why, you ask? Thanks to technology, many recruiters use an ATS [Applicant Tracking System] to screen job application materials, searching for keywords from their advertisement that are included in your resume.

Including the ATS **keywords** will increase your chances of making it past the first round of resume reviews, that will elevate your CV.

If you're struggling to trim your resume to a short form, start by creating an inventory of your accomplishments and work activities. List your responsibilities and your achievements in great detail. Your inventory document might span as many as three or four pages. Try to include a diverse spectrum of skills that have led to successes in each role.

Analyse each job that you are considering and circle the statements that correspond most closely to the requirements for that particular position. Piece together the most relevant statements into a shorter, targeted version of your resume.

Is your first draft too long? If so, try to eliminate statements that are of less significance when listing key achievements. Try to be as specific as possible with the information you list and be as concise as you can in your writing. Remember this is a list. Think of yourself as the end reader who has 50 resumes to read through in detail, allocating 5 minutes to skim over each. Your last role will be the first role read in depth, so make this one count, then lessen each one thereafter.

1.2 CV / Resume

Use a bulleted list and keep your job descriptions concise. Focus on your accomplishments, not your daily responsibilities.

Cut out any extra years. Even if you are an experienced candidate, you should include *no more than 10 or 15 years of experience on your resume.* The exception to this is if you have been employed in other countries, it is preferable to state this even if only a simple line item as in our detailed CV figure 6, p34.

Trim the education section. You don't need to include high school education or continuing education classes unless it enhances your candidacy or is requested.

Skip the references. It is not necessary to say "references available upon request" on your resume. It's understood that you will provide references, if required, as part of the job application process. This is up to you if you state this.

Provide Additional Information Online

Providing the option to view different information from that of your resume is a good idea to demonstrate and in some instances provide access to your portfolio.

Including links to your LinkedIn profile or personal website that will allow you to highlight your recent blog, post, article mention, award photo, business achievement, etc. If you do decide to do this, try to create your own personal url on Linkedin, rather than using the system generated sequencing.

We discuss LinkedIn in greater depth once you complete your Cover Letter.

To complete your CV, please check the 13 Greatest CV Mistakes below.

13 Greatest CV Mistakes

1. **CV Fraud:** pretending to be someone you are not. The truth always comes out and it will seriously jeopardise your future reputation and possible those thereafter.

2. **CV Accumulation:** the band-aid effect where the CV is added to over time with each new employer, position role, and activity. The issue is it doesn't read as if it flows, it needs updating and as your experience grows, your oldest roles need to shorten.

3. **Outsourced Titles:** Stating yourself as a 'Consultant', 'Contractor', 'Interim', or 'Designate'. Often, the employer interprets this negatively as you not having been worthy or couldn't find a permanent position and you are back again applying for this position. To address this call the positions 'short-term assignments' and explain the deliverables and outcomes of the project and why it was valuable to the business.

4. **Key Achievements not so Key:** Stating duties and responsibilities rather than stating the exceptional achievements that were above and beyond the role, Special Projects.

5. **Missing or unexplained gaps:** any absences in your CV. The ATS will readily pick this up and highlight it. Explain your gap in dates was due to leave, study, natural disaster etc.

6. **Spelling mistakes:** typos or poor grammar are easily avoided using spell checker, grammar checker and a friend's keen eye.

7. **Listing your roles chronologically:** Select a logic for the order you list and stick with it. Current to oldest order is standard.

13 Greatest CV Mistakes continued.

8. **Key Words omitted:** failure to include key words that match the job ad or job posting that results in the ATS excluding your CV.

9. **Mundane, procedural and irrelevant duties stated:** e.g. "Capable with Microsoft Excel and Word" – we expect that from students, but not from executives, it is irrelevant and you know the basics.

10. **Length of CV:** Too long or too short: The ATS will rate you poorly.

11. **Style of CV:** dull and boring lacking Iconography will see your CV left.

12. **Ego and slang words used:** Stating you are the "Go To" person or abbreviating words as if it is a text message is not acceptable.

13. **Reason for Leaving:** failing to add a reason for leaving; providing a story length reason; sounding ungrateful etc is not helpful. A simple few words that say how you were inspired to move to another role or another industry or country etc. is to be used.

You concentrated on your CV/Resume and you did a superb job, well done.

The Job advertisement may or may not ask for a Cover Letter to be uploaded separately. When asked to upload separately, always do so in pdf and note this tells us that the ATS will be in action to scan both.

What is read first by the Recruiter or HR Manager handling the recruitment of this position: your CV or your Covering Letter?

Clear Winner: the AMAZINGLY PERSUASIVE COVER LETTER: it is the gatekeeper that gets you through to the next review of your candidacy and your CV, so get your cover letter right.

Why is a cover letter requested? Sometimes it is to set the lazy CV submit to all by upload who can't be bothered writing a tailored cover letter from the eager best candidates, and other times, or in addition to this, it is to read the story about you and why you are applying for the role.

What sets the Cover Letter apart from your CV? Simply it is INVITING, INSPIRING and ENTICES the reader to want to look at your CV, it says you are the right person for the job, but it is also strategically created.

Is a Cover Letter Important?

Here is the dilemma: most candidates treat their cover letter as a formality, as a box they need to tick for their CV/Resume to be considered. But they're missing the point, your Cover Letter is your FIRST ENTRY POINT to the organisation that you are applying to.

Before the interview, your Cover Letter is the BEST CHANCE you'll ever get to tell your story. Think about it: when you walk into your next interview, those 2-3 people sitting in front of you have already scanned through your CV/Resume, and maybe even checked you out on LinkedIn. Although they have questions, they already have a pre-conceived notion about who you are and what you bring to the table. Your Cover Letter told them that and they are excited to meet you.

The whole reason you proceeded to the next stage of the interview process is due to BOTH your CV and COVER LETTER. You cannot afford to disrespect either, they are your selling tools, your job banner. You need to invest in both.

Your AMAZING Covering Letter

Try these Lessons and Criteria for your Amazing Covering Letter:

- Written Last
- One Page Only
- Address the Job Ad
- Express Great Interest in organisation and position
- Major Achievements
- Fun & Attention Getting.

Structure of a Cover Letter

Structure of a cover letter is paramount to *staying on track and achieving the key message*. When we consider story writing, there is a beginning, middle and end. The same can be said in relation to the layout for the cover letter but with more aligned structure to that of a job you really want.

Cover Letter Writing Style: Write the letter in 1st person, as you are writing directly to the reader. Avoid using buzzwords, avoid repeating "I" too many times and start each paragraph with a different word rather than "The" or "I".

Address the letter to the correct person, look it up, is it the Chair? If so, can you address to the chair with a name followed after this that exhibits you bothered to research who is leading the organisation; eg. To the Chairman, Mr Alexander Holtswarz.

The first paragraph is an introduction ATTENTION grab. The first sentence is critical to your letter. It will determine how the reader perceives you and how well you understand the organisation you are applying for. It needs to grab the attention of your reader. Eg of an ad for a CEO of a listed company in the pharmaceutical industry.

As an experienced CEO and Company Secretary of a leading pharmaceutical GmbH listed company, I understand and embrace good corporate governance and strategic vision in this high pressured research market.

What sets this apart? The KEYWORDS used that relate to the ad offering for a CEO, also add additional reinforced EXPERIENCE at a board LEVEL as a Company Secretary. This is further emphasised in the corporate governance that is required in a heavily regulatory industry and uses again keywords of governance.

Wording it to include the research market that is what can separate a standard pharmaceutical processor apart from a world leading provider of the first of a specific pain relief or vaccine is imperative.

Finally using words such as 'experience' and 'understand' tell the reader that you are up for and use to this challenge. Did you note a stock exchange was mentioned too? This further elevates your experience and aligns to the job.

Cover Letter 1st Paragraph: "I am writing to apply"… is an example of how not to start your paragraph, it is boring, and not creative. Inject some life and soul into your opening sentence.

TNT

The second paragraph highlights your KNOWLEDGE of the organisation. This paragraph recognises YOUR RESEARCH and UNDERSTANDING of the organisation and where it is headed. As you write this ALIGN the role and the organisation's plans back to your skillset.

ABC Limited is experiencing an exciting phase with an increasing international demand. Breaking into this market is rewarding if strategically planned correctly. My international experience has provided me with great insight and appreciation for how to win negotiations recognising cultural challenges. The knowledge and expertise housed in ABC Co's board of directors is inspirational to an enthusiastic CEO, seeking greater opportunities such as myself.

When reading this paragraph, we can see the alignment of experience and skills of the potential CEO candidate to that of where the organisation is placed. It also recognises good research conducted by the candidate of the direction the business is heading, that challenges will be faced requiring international and publicly listed skillsets and who not only resides on the board, but appreciates that the candidate is enthusiastic to work in partnership under the boards direction. A number of KEYWORDS have been included such as international, win negotiations and strategically planed.

Cover Letter 2nd Paragraph: Write with enthusiasm and excitement remembering to keep it professional and not over the top.

The third paragraph promotes the VALUE YOU WILL ADD.
You now provide a very short story of a proven achievement that ends with how this added value to the organisation. Think of what you have EXPERIENCED, what did you ACHIEVE, what was so great about this and how did it ADD VALUE. This paragraph and story again needs to ALIGN with the potential employer's industry and include KEYWORDS that highlight your skills as outlined in the ad. Our example CEO ad continues:

Harnessing the experience from my most successful Acquisition at a 30% lessor valuation than EOI, I would thrive at the opportunity to continue discussions you have commenced with Medcoprost to deliver a success story for ABC Limited. As a proven leader who practices blue ocean strategy, working with the board to take the business model into a technological transformation would benefit greater returns for shareholders.

Winning praise is what this paragraph has achieved. The combination of a current big move for this organisation and the dilemma it would face from ceasing the acquisition would stagnate growth but you are the beacon of hope, the added value who is experienced to see this through. You will then re-adjust the business model and review the products and services offered through a proven highly acknowledged methodology that many CEO's fail to administer is the other added value.

Respecting the end goal of returning shareholder wealth is a powerful statement. This is a little gutsy but there are no guaranteed ratios of returns or growth, and no guaranteed acquisition savings, just the commitment and focus of key organisational goals that you have researched in-depth will receive your dedication.

> **Cover Letter 3rd Paragraph:** Your added value is what makes you unique to other candidates being considered, so really think long and hard. If you were a CFO it is not making a profit, you are expected to always be managing profit, however it may be specific analytical skills, experience that will elevate you.

The fourth paragraph positively CLOSES out the letter. This can be a simple sentence that completes the letter. It is important that you end it with positive optimistic wording that says you are worthy of the next stage, the final candidates to make it to interview.

I look forward to adding value to ABC Limited during an exciting growth stage.

The POSITIVE words "I look forward to" emphasise the worthiness facts. This is seconded by "adding value". To then finish with the reminder that the candidate did perform research to see what stage the organisation was at "exciting growth stage".

> **Cover Letter 4th Paragraph:** Don't forget your salutation. Although this is personalised, it is always professional.

15. Social Media Portfolio

When we mention social media, you may instantly think of facebook, twitter, insta and LinkedIn. Yes these are the main types of social media but each has its place. A good rule of thumb is to **keep your personal social media separate from your work social media** at the time of writing this book. Let's examine these closer.

Facebook, insta and twitter will return anyone's tags or open accounts with photos to the recruiter or employer. If there is anything you would not like an employer, a stakeholder, a subordinate to view, then do not say, do not post, do not share it on any social media accounts, it will come back to bite you. When we advise this to our proteges they instantly grab their mobile or cell phone and start deleting.

Twitter is one where your promotion of particular movements that may be illegal or deemed as against your country's societal norms will return a negative view from your potential employer. Our actions are accountable.

LinkedIn on the other hand has become the go to for recruiters and employers to check not only your profile, but it shares a lot about your character, your likes and dislikes through any likes you have made in addition to your posts as mentioned before.

Richard Bolles[7] in "What Colour is Your Parachute" said "Almost all (91 percent) of US employers have visited a job-hunter's profile on social networks, and more than 69 percent of employers have rejected some applicants on the basis of what they found." That says that LinkedIn and Google are powerful search sites to check you out seriously for that new position.

Bolles warns "Things that can get you rejected: bad grammar or gross misspelling on your Facebook or LinkedIn profile; anything indicating you lied on your resume; any badmouthing of previous employers; any signs of racism, prejudice, or screwy opinions about stuff; anything indicating alcohol or drug abuse; and any – to put it delicately – inappropriate content, etc."

You now have an Award-Winning and Job-Winning CV and Cover Letter for the role you are applying for. Perhaps you created your template ready to tweak when the next attractive role presents itself.

Once your CV and Cover Letter have made it to the next stage, the employer and/or recruiter will look past what you provided, to that of your real life social media profile as mentioned above. LinkedIn whether you love it or hate, plays a big part in this. So let's understand what it is and how and to who you should connect or being LinkedIn.

We start with a quick health check of your LinkedIn starting with your profile. We expand upon each area in detail, but here is the quick list of what you need:

  a. LinkedIn Address

  b. Professional Headshot Photo

  c. Contact Information

  d. Headline

  e. About

  f. Experience

  g. Education

  h. Licenses & Certifications

  i. Volunteer Experience

  j. Skills & Endorsements

  k. Recommendations

  l. Accomplishments.

LinkedIn Address
Create your own LinkedIn address using your full name where possible.

Profile Photo

Your profile picture, or Business Media DP is a serious reflection of how professional you are. The wrong photo may cost you your next role. LinkedIn is a social media connection tool for business, and as such, it requires a business photo not a Facebook DP. HEADSHOTS are the recommended photo, taken by a professional photographer, conscious of background, lighting, shadows and distance.

The reason headshots for LinkedIn are recommended is that you do become a smaller image in feeds and pop-ups, so a photo taken full length does not do justice. Save the full length for your corporate about us page. As an executive or soon to be, it is not too much to invest in a private photographer to take your picture to get it right. Keep the photo updated every five years or risk appearing as someone who is not accepting of themselves as they age.

Imagine walking into an interview where they saw your photo prior that portrayed a 30 year old you, to see you have aged to 50. Embrace your wisdom and keep updated.

Unfortunately, the list of wrongs on photos is too long to list. There are no exceptions unless you are in the creative arts sector or it specifically relates to your role. An example of this is if you applied to Paspaley Pearls or Tiffany Jewellery, you could proudly display your prized pieces but again, as if you would wear everyday to work. Big and bling is not necessarily appropriate.

Contact Information

The easier it is for someone to reach you through email, phone and any social media will assist whilst you are actively seeking a job and to establish new connections.

Headline

Your title needs to be direct on target, or you may choose to be creative but remember this is about your PROFESSIONAL BANNER shown as a LinkedIn profile. The most important role you have is what your headline should state, where you have two roles such as those on Boards, your headline will depend on which you perceive to be the most valuable for the role you are seeking.

List the role you wish to be hired for first, if you are currently performing that role. Eg. Director position: Director and CEO. Eg. CEO position: CEO and Director.

John Petty

FCA FCPA AAICD | Chairman | Director | Strategic Growth
Business Adviser

Sydney, New South Wales, Australia · 500+ connections ·

Coachability

UNSW Australia

About

This is your story, your selling area that needs to be crafted well.
White space and dynamic content is needed. Make use of listing
your specialties here to assist being found by recruitment apps.
Include your industry and role type, an insight into your background
and add your call to action if you feel comfortable in doing so. If
you are still employed this may need to be reworded as you would
not wish your current employer to discover your call to seek a new
job.

In the next example it uses a grey wording of call to action of
a business partner, who can be internal or external. There are
many examples and we suggest you look at what your peers are
doing now, but here is one of a CEO seeking a Managing Director
position.

*With a background in the retail industry, I have been a results
driven CEO incorporating the Blue Ocean Strategy as my guide
to add value to the organisation. Leading such large workplaces
that span the globe has taught me that human capital is just as
important as technological transformation. This ambition has lead
me to introduce and develop cutting edge technology whilst
creating training programs that lead the floor staff into senior
management positions.*

*Reporting to the board for many years has allowed me to develop
and hone my corporate governance skills. My philosophy is to
continue to learn whilst sharing my knowledge and experience.*

MY SPECIALTIES
- *Shareholder Growth*
- *Strategic Organisation Plan*
- *Board Reporting*
- *Business Growth*
- *Strategy Development*
- *Executive Reporting*
- *Blue Ocean Strategy*
- *Business Model and Review*
- *Merger and Acquisition Negotiation Delivery*
- *GRI Sustainability Initiative.*

If you believe that I am your next business partner, Reach out today.

Experience
Your past 10 years is important for your work experience, whereas anything thereafter may be too old and become obsolete. Experience section is NOT YOUR CV but a **SNAPSHOT high level summary of the position** you held and who the company is that you represented. This section allows for each experience to add a url link and a logo, so make it visual and bring your experience to life. Limit it to 50 words or less and add the location.

Education
The order in which you place these is important. Your highest qualification should be first listed, then list your tertiary or university qualification. If you do not have any higher ed. You may need to leave this area blank.

For those attending workshops and upskilling this is a great place to include, but keep it RELEVANT and no need to list 50 that you did during a pandemic lockdown, rather just the top 3 most important that are relevant to your current offering.

Licenses & Certifications
This may be a particular regulatory license you hold such as an AFSL or REIV or may be a software license.

Volunteer Experience

If you have not volunteered then please give back. Voluntary work is the **most beneficial gift you can provide to those in need,** be it to a recognised registered charity for human, animal, welfare or environmental. If you have not joined, check out your local Lions Club. We use this charity example as they are one of the last remaining charities that give full proceeds to in-need worthy community causes, not to mention their Bunnings BBQ Sausages are great. There are many charities and local clubs that help others. Your current voluntary contribution will be valued and recognised through the ATS and your recruiter and employer.

Volunteer experience   +

                                                                ✎

Member FACC
Surf Life Saving NSW
Jan 2015 – Present • 6 yrs 1 mo

Member of Finance and Audit Committee
Anglicare NSW South, NSW West & ACT
Jan 2010 – Present • 11 yrs 1 mo

Skills & Endorsements

This area is how linkedin first started. Everyone was endorsing everyone for linkedin's AI suggested skills that you had not necessarily provided to your contact. Be careful and reduce the skills that others endorse you for, to that of those you want to be recognised for, that are meaningful to your current position and future position.

For example, receiving an endorsement for excel skills is not helpful to any executive whereas business modelling and business strategy are relatable required skills of a C-Suite executive. Delete what you do not need. This area breeds like rabbits so check it annually to keep it relevant.

Recommendations

This area is very important to the recruiter and employer. It should have independent unrelated appraisals of work you have performed for others. You can give and receive recommendations. If you have not received any, reach out to a client you provided work for, a past happy employer and ask.

Recommendations should include a specific result or a story of how you grew or impacted their department or organisation, subject to what it is that you would have impacted.

Accomplishments
We suggest listing here the upskill courses that are still relevant to your current role, and if you won any awards. Although if you have won an award that your future employer would be interested in, it is worthy of a big shout out on a post or blog. Awards may be directly related to your position, or maybe a community award for your service.

Interests
Limit your interests to those that are relevant to your career. We mention this in your CV section under interests. This area should replicate that of your CV.

Contacts
The number of contacts you have may be in the hundreds but it is the quality of the contacts you have that are external to your current role that matter. In addition to this it is external contacts that you have not been fellow employees at a prior workplace that matter. When we discuss quality we are looking at roles, levels, organisation sizes, industries, etc.

LinkedIn Posts and Blogs
Engage with others through posts and blogs on your LinkedIn of awards, achievements, success and interesting articles that are relevant to your position that you perceive as being of interest.

LinkedIn Likes
Danger! Warning! Your likes on a post or blog need to be thought out carefully. Although you may have a personal soft spot for a

cause, if this cause may be deemed as disruptive or contrary to your future employer's views, you risk not being selected for the role. This being said, you should never apply for a position with an organisation that you do not respect or do not value the way they operate their business. It is different with third parties as you can take a punt to influence a change to the business partnerships of those when you are hired.

The rule here is that LinkedIn is not your personal social media private platform, it is public and is for business use.

Connections

You may feel that 1000 connections is boast worthy, but what does that show you? It does say that you are keen on LinkedIn and connecting is a key focus for you using the platform, but until your recruiter or potential employer delves into who your connections are, their roles, their organisations and their locations, it may actually work against you.

As to be expected, LinkedIn will not tell you the negatives of over connecting, but the tool should be used for connections that are not in your organisation, or if they are working in your organisation, limit the number of connections. If they are past connections check these annually to ensure of relevancy to your career.

17. Inside Scoop on the Position and Competition

Before you apply for your next position that you see advertised, here's something you must do that gives you an edge over other candidates: Get The Inside Scoop (if you can).

To be FOREWARNED IS FORARMED.

You need to try to find someone who already works for the organisation or company or is a supplier or customer, and have a 15-minute conversation with them over a coffee (or even on the phone) to discuss your intentions to apply for a certain position, confidentially, of course.

Why?

Two reasons:

First, if appropriate, it allows you to include the following words in your application or Cover Letter: "After having a conversation with [insert name and department of person who already works in your organisation] about [insert company/organization name], I'm really excited about this role... etc. etc." This makes it more personal and gets you into the club.

This creates an impression that - rather than just looking for "a job" - you specifically want to work for their organisation.

Second, through that short conversation, you'll pick up on some of the lingo, jargon, nuances and acronyms people in the organisation use.

Use some of that jargon (sparingly) in your Cover Letter, and all of a sudden you're no longer a total outsider. From the point of view of the person reading your application or letter, it feels like you already belong there.

This is a huge attention getter that brings you potentially into the fold. However, there's a caveat to this strategy:

It takes time to research and then get in front of or contact this desired person to have this conversation. If they are not readily available or consciously avoid contact it may take time and delay your submission of your application: so make sure this tactic does not push you past the closing date for the application.

So you need to get in quick but understand that this strategy may not work or be feasible in all circumstances.

So it may only be a quick phone call or a brief passing coffee but that is better than nothing and submitting your Covering Letter and CV blind. If you take this recourse be sure to let your connection know that you are applying for the role and would appreciate any mention that shows you were keen and willing to reach out to connect, before you applied to align your interests and theirs. This may just win you appraisal.

Obtaining the insider knowledge on the previous incumbent and what happened to them is an important question and consequence. Your success to be interviewed, demands that you understand what happened to the previous incumbent and why this position has come up at this time.

18. Referees and Reference Process

Gaining and giving Employment References is a tricky issue. Especially the decision of who to ask or nominate for that Referee role on your behalf.

Would your current employer or immediate superior give you a glowing complimentary reference for you to move away from your current employer? Probably or maybe NOT.

The facts are your existing employer may not want you to leave, you are a valuable asset and therefore they would not provide a reference, especially if you have not resigned. However, after the dust has settled there is a tactic you can take.

Remaining in touch with your former employer every few months to say hello, and leaving it open for them to contact you to ask of things you may have been in the midst of completing, provides the platform for a future request, in say twelve months to request a reference.

You have received news that you have won the job and the reference checking process is about to commence: you now need to action and manage this well.

You will need to provide your new employer, the contact details of the referee and relationship. KEEP IT SIMPLE, as if you add too much high praise and the referee is not as obliging, it will not match. Simply provide their name, organisation, email and phone number.

The most important part is to choose referees that align with the industry of your new employer where possible and to provide three very different angles from three persons who value you to the point that they would re-employ you. This may be a:

- Former employer: a Director or C-Suite Executive
- A Current Mentor
- A Current Charity you are a member of.

The exception to the suggested referees is where you were retrenched due to a closure of an organisation, a natural disaster that was unsustainable economically to continue in or an organisational restructure. In these situations you will no doubt find that your employer will be happy to assist you to find a new role.

Contact with Your Referees prior to applying

Update your referees of the type of role you are applying for and where you can, of the organisation. Brief the referee of some ideas, comments and endorsements they could say about you, that are all true. Remember the truth will always be found. Always contact the referee PRIOR to submitting your application to ensure they are comfortable and as enthusiastic about your new role as you are.

If you are an employer or recruiter you may wonder how authentic the referee is and how to test this out. Ask, ask and ask as many questions as you need to uncover the truth of their employ and relationship. Try asking a sneaky question, 'Does candidate X like to play golf with you?'

The right Referee for you: We suggest that you ask the following question: "would you re-employ the candidate if they were to apply for their old position or a new position in your organisation." This is the best question from a HR and psychiatric viewpoint.

TNT

1.3 Connect

Cover Letter - CV - Attachments
As they say, it is all in the timing.

Whether you lodge your application early, on-time, in week 1, or in the last week, will all depend on the job ad, where and how the job is posted and how the Posting and Resume is requested.

Traditional recruitment utilised a four or five week timeframe as employers [especially the HR Managers] wanted to drag out the recruitment process to ensure that they had a wide, extensive and great team of candidates to choose from.

Two aspects were inherently wrong with that model:

1. It does not suit positions requiring immediate or quick fill: be it a special project or they needed the selected recruit to work in with a departing incumbent employee

2. Having taken so long, the desired candidate may have accepted another position by the time the whole process was complete, considering multiple interviews and reference checking.

If you are a candidate for a recruited position and if it is a traditional four week recruitment job post and interview program then the following is good advice on when to submit your job application [Cover Letter, CV/Resume and attachments]:

- **Not in Week 1:** you seem too impatient, have not properly researched the position and/or organisation, you had a CV and application ready on the shelf from another unsuccessful application, you do not have a 'real' job and are desperate and dateless [so to speak].

- **Week 2 is also too early:** it is timely if you want to show that you are keen and prepared BUT it is too early.

- **Week 3:** now is the time to start to make an impact and dust off your best suit. You have time to research, prepare for the particular position and organisation and present yourself in the best light. You may have a question or two to ask the Recruiter in advance of submitting your final submission; by week 3 they will be pleased and relieved to see your submission. Your submission has time to be customised to their job and the job ad and it takes this much time to get it right. Week 3 is PERFECT, it's not early and in time to be scheduled in for the interviews.

- **Weeks 4 & 5:** The Final days for the Job Ad closure. You submit your credentials but you are already fully employed: yes you are interested but you will have to be sprung from your already busy position where you are much valued and regarded. You show that you are well considered about your career but do show an interest to move up and on but it takes time to prepare your case and you are thinking deeply about the opportunity: yet not desperate or on the streets.

Summary: Do not be too impatient and that is what a Week 1 submission says. Take your time to understand and assess both the organisation, the position and its potential and consider the risks of jumping ship, if you are happily employed and well regarded where you currently are employed.

Our experience is that it certainly takes time to do that JOB WINNING CUSTOMISED CV and PERSONAL PORTFOLIO that is TAILORED to the particular job that you are applying for. In addition to this is the time to research the organisation and discover what happened to the previous incumbent and how this job may be advertised differently to any previous job postings – it all takes time and requires thought, research and consultations with others about your move.

Head Hunter Approach

What if the opportunity to move into this new position comes from a Head-hunters phone call and a request for you to consider this available position?

That may take you by surprise and you will have to think quickly to respond positively and professionally. Firstly thank the enquirer for thinking of you and making this call.

You could ask the following initial questions of the head hunter:

- Was the job advertised, if so where and when?
- What happened to the previous incumbent?
- Who was it who put your name up and what was it that the person thought of that made you suitable for the position?

- If you are interested or prepared to have further discussions, what are the next steps towards an interview and with who would that occur. You want to understand if you are a preferred candidate or they are just creating a field of candidates – this will tell you how excited you should be and then how much effort you would need to exert:

    - **What timing are they thinking of for interviews and then a decision being made**: you don't want to waste your time when it was an outside approach from the Head-hunter.

    - **A word of caution:** Head-hunters intention is to get as many potential names or candidates as they can as that makes them look good; get to the bottom of how genuine this job and approach is before expending significant time and effort.

Acknowledgement of Receipt of Your CV and Application

An important and professional step in the process of applying for a job and lodging a submission is to request that the organisation in their HR Department to which you are applying respectfully acknowledge receipt of your submission by providing an acknowledgement of receipt by email or some other form of communication.

You would expect an acknowledgement from a professional organisation so it is not an unrealistic request.

Why would you push this point and make it a formal request?

- You want to make sure that your submission has not been lost in the mail or gone astray in the ether.
- It shows that you are keen to be considered for the position as well as your professionalism in the application and how you administer yourself.
- You may not get this position however as a senior leader, you wish to build a professional and business like rapport with the recruiter and/or the organisation, they may even be influenced to create or offer you another position just to get access to your obvious talents.

20. Role Clarity Workshop [RCW]

In many cases when recruiting an employee, you don't just want a replacement but to take the opportunity to recruit a better and expanded skill for a position. This enables the business to develop its workforce and change its management team and gain additional skills in a changing business world.

This is best achieved by conducting a Role Clarity Workshop **before the position description is developed and the job posted for advertising.**

A Role Clarity Workshop [RCW] is conducted when an employer wishes to understand the high performance behaviours that are required for a particular position and in an appointed candidate and how these can be assessed and measured over time.

Conducting a RCW is essential if the recruitment of the best candidate is to occur – here the recruiter can bring added insight and capability to the recruitment process within the organisation.

Once the new CEO or CFO or CXO Executive, is in the job, conducting a RCW will help to evaluate the subordinates reporting to the CEO or CFO based on agreed behaviours for the particular roles.

If you are the candidate applying for the job, consider the RCW and ask the recruiter or employment manager if they have conducted such a workshop and if so, what were their findings as to the role, subordinates and org chart.

A Role Clarity Workshop may be supplemented by use of the AbilityMap Competency tables.

Role of AbilityMap Assessments

The critical aspect of a recruitment agency interviewing and assessing a candidate for a position is to assess their competencies required for performance in a particular position or role.

Unfortunately, traditional recruitment practices focus on identifying the underlying skills of candidates and then attempting to match them with the perceived qualities required for performance in a particular role.

In contrast, the AbilityMap starts at the other end of the equation by focussing on the competencies required for performance in the job and matching candidates to those competencies.

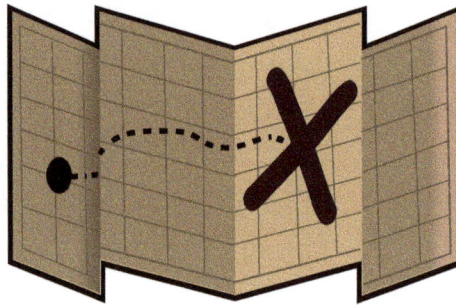

The AbilityMap Recruitment Diagnostic[1] is intended to MAP and MATCH the COMPETENCIES of the role with the SKILLS and APTITUDES of the various candidates to get the best Match of candidate for the particular position and the management style of the organisation. It is not about past performances but is exploring the best match for future engagement in the role and organisation.

This patented technology and resulting report is a summary of the role and outcome prepared by analysing the results from a number of managers. It will highlight the variability of expectations inherent in a manager's view of the role but at this time will help to iron out any significant individual variations.

To understand this technology better we have included an example AbilityMap for a CFO to explore the high performance competencies important for the position, refer to figure 10.

1.4 Research

AbilityMap Job Profile Report

Position: CFO   **Company:** Chandler Petty CFO Search   **Prepared by:** Kevin Chandler

Competency	Required Level for this Role	Behavioural Indicators of Competency
Good at solving problems	Highly competent	Is strongly motivated to anticipate problems and will find practical solutions, even before others realise there is a problem.
		Has the ability to tackle a problem by using a logical, systematic, sequential approach.
		Displays the ability to find effective solutions by taking a holistic, abstract or theoretical perspective.
		Builds a logical approach to address problems or opportunities or manage the situation at hand by drawing on one's knowledge and experience base, and calling on other references and resources as necessary: brings in help to solve significant and political problems.
Good at working with numbers	Highly competent	Is able to handle complex numerical information or statistical analyses quickly and easily.
		Recognised by others as being very capable working with financial or statistical material; good at scenario analysis and sensitivity analysis.
Good at managing resources: team and Corporate	Highly competent	Identifies "vital few" goals and allocates time and resources accordingly to achieve those goals when faced with competing priorities.
		Navigates quickly and effectively to resolve problems and obstacles, even when complex and unique circumstances occur.

Figure 9: AbilityMap Job Profile Report

1.4 Research

AbilityMap Job Profile Report

Position: CFO   **Company:** Chandler Petty CFO Search   **Prepared by:** Kevin Chandler

Competency	Required Level for this Role	Behavioural Indicators of Competency
Good at displaying business acumen and awareness	Highly competent	Driven to win in the business arena. Understands the organisation's strengths and weaknesses as compared to competitors. Understands industry and market trends affecting an organisation's competitiveness. Encourages and supports entrepreneurial behaviour in others. Is aware of the wider commercial environment and has the capacity to consider financial implications. Sees business success through financial outcomes.
Good at accepting personal responsiblity	Highly competent	Always feels personally accountable for their actions. Exceeds their commitment to others by frequently delivering work early; fast close and fast results. Maintains ethical principles even in the most challenging circumstances. Is a polished professional who exemplifies success and credibility? Inspires others to be more professional. Works whatever hours are necessary to complete assigned work.

AbilityMap Job Profile Report

Position: CFO   **Company:** Chandler Petty CFO Search   **Prepared by:** Kevin Chandler

Competency	Required Level for this Role	Behavioural Indicators of Competency
Good at building relations with customers	Competent	Asks questions to identify the needs or expectations of others. Will consider the impact on the external or internal customer when taking action, or carrying out one's own job responsibilities.
		Looks for creative approaches to providing or improving services that may increase the efficiency and decrease cost.
		Focus on 'Cost to Serve' as a performance measure.
		Has a focus on the customer and always seek to understand the customer's requirements.
Good at sharing and controlling information and knowledge	Highly Competent	Enhances the capabilities of the organisation by openly and effectively sharing their subject matter expertise with others.
		Shares knowledge freely and provide information to meet staff and customer needs.
		Develops Finance for Non– Finance Executives programs.
Good at working with teams	Competent	Enhances the capabilities of the organisation by openly and effectively sharing their subject matter expertise with others – especially for Finance].
		Shares knowledge freely and provide information to meet staff and customer needs.
		Develops Finance for Non– Finance Executives.
		Works with lower level operational staff on physical and financial performance.
		Works on capital expenditure program justification projects.

1.4 Research

AbilityMap Job Profile Report

Position: CFO **Company:** Chandler Petty CFO Search **Prepared by:**Kevin Chandler

Competency	Required Level for this Role	Behavioural Indicators of Competency
Good at leading others	Competent	Generates enthusiasm among team members for accomplishing shared goals. Seeks ways to improve their contribution and increase the level of responsibility of self and others. Expresses pride in the group and encourages people to feel good about their accomplishments. Shares information, advice and suggestions to help others to be more successful; provides effective coaching.
Good at influencing others	Competent	Generally influences others easily and has a very convincing style. Gain support and buy-in through generating multiple alternatives to meet stakeholder's needs. Provides understandable performance reports and helps develop actions and alternatives. Can achieve win-win outcomes that others can accept.
Good at operating independently	Competent	Enjoys responsibility for own area of work. Sets high standards. Works persistently and reliably without external motivation. Is self-reliant and confident in their ability to cope no matter what the circumstances.
Good at displaying high levels of integrity	Competent	Has integrity which does not vary according to circumstance or need. Confronts potentially unethical behaviour and reports indiscretions. Consistent and reliable. Seeks out and supports Corporate Social Responsibility [CSR] projects.

You have decided to either move on and out or up [within] with your career and current employer – GOOD ON YOU!

But you need to understand and appreciate that you are in a tough and competitive market and that future jobs will all come down to your SKILLS and CAPABILITIES and brand and the perceived value that you can add to this new position: should you win it.

As they say: "Beauty is in the eye of the beholder" – it all depends on whether the potential employer perceives and appreciates your BEAUTY as a future employee in this position.

Do they see that you can ADD VALUE and what is their perception of your respective skills and value to them.

But what if you are over estimating your value and skills and worth to your potential employer and your chances of success in this recruitment exercise and contest are less than you think? Maybe you have overrated yourself and you are selling yourself at the wrong level. Your perception and that of your potential employer are at different levels.

We see this far too often.

Potential candidates overestimate their skills and value to a potential employer or sell themselves very poorly.

They have not conducted a proper and realistic and independent review of their skills and value to an organisation or potential employer.

In this section, we show you how to conduct a realistic and impartial assessment of your Skills and Value to a potential employer: here is our Next 200 Days Self-Assessment and Skills Review / Diagnostic Checklist [refer to Figure 10 on page 74 then complete your worksheet located in the worksheet section]. Are you Ready?

It would be beneficial for you to perform our 200 Days Self Evaluation & Skills Diagnostic Checklist to honestly understand where you sit in this very competitive employment market.

1.4 Research

Self-Evaluation and Diagnostic Checklist

What are your Personal, Technical and Business Skills and Competencies that you have and should play to?

What do you offer the new employer? What is your brand and reputation? What are your distinctive experiences and proven abilities?

What will hold you back in this position? What are your lesser skills or deficiencies that will become obvious and you will need to address re remedial actions, training and development programs?

How do you rate as a Candidate for this Position? What makes you Stand Out?

In essence, you need to conduct your own personal SWOT POSITIONING ANALYSIS on yourself as explained below. Your PERSONAL SWOT is a Self-Assessment of Your Career and the Skills positioning in that Career Positioning Analysis.

What are your personal:

STRENGTHS – for the position:

WEAKNESSES – for the position:

OPPORTUNITIES – to fulfil the position:

THREATS – to fail in the position:

Figure 10: Self-Evaluation and Diagnostic Checklist

Complete your Self-Evaluation and Diagnostic Checklist worksheet on p292

For presentation purposes and to gain focus, you could present the results of the above SWOTíng of yourself on the SWOT PERSONAL POSITIONING MATRIX as described below:

SWOT: Personal Positioning Matrix

STRENGTHS	WEAKNESSES

S W O T

OPPORTUNITIES	THREATS

Figure 11: SWOT: Personal Positioning Matrix

Complete your SWOT: Personal Positioning Matrix worksheet on p293

This table will reinforce where you believe you sit now as presented or assessed by an interview panel and where your current positioning in strengths and weaknesses will provide further opportunities or threats to your successful employment in the future with your new employer.

In essence, the SWOT Personal Positioning Analysis will reflect on what you LOVE and DO WELL that ENTHUSES YOU against what DISINTERESTS you or you DO NOT DO WELL (or prefer not to do).

You SWOTing yourself is a great way to know or present who you really are and where you want to take your career.

This is essential homework in your First 100 Days of preparation of your 200 Day journey as you assess who you are and what you aspire to be in your career; where you want to go and what will assist you and what will hold you back in this journey.

Review Self-Evaluation & Diagnostic Checklist

Personal & Professional Feature	Your Assessment / Evaluation
What are you GOOD at? (your proficiencies)	
What are you known for or recognised for?	
What is unique about you?	
What are your greatest achievements?	
What are you POOR at? (your deficiencies)	
What personal developments do you need to enable you to be the person you want to be?	

Figure 12: Review Self-Evaluation & Diagnostic Checklist

Complete your Review Self-Evaluation & Diagnostic Checklist worksheet on p294

Complete your Self Evaluation & Diagnostic Review Checklist, located in the worksheet section on page 292, to then reflect on what it tells you about your capability to move on and up. Do you need additional training or personal development now before putting your name forward for that next job? What does this table tell you about your future actions needed?

Job Hunting – it's all in the TIMING

Job Hunting should be a FULL-TIME job or commitment requiring your enthusiasm. The two worst times to decide or be forced into a job hunt are:

- When you are out of a job or about to be out of a job and therefore desperately need one and when you are fully and;

- When you are deeply engaged in a great job that is taking all your energy and focus – but you know that you must move on and hopefully up, and you have been there over *three years.

We say *three years as by this time you should have exhausted all that you could in the role and be ready to experience bigger and better opportunities to keep yourself exposed to the most recent trends and changes in the industry.

Your career and next role requires the need for plenty of planning and structure as detailed in this book. Let's move onto your interview preparation.

NOTES:

Present

SECTION 2 - Present

SECTION 2

Winning your new role: The Interview
Departing Nicely: The Exit

Now for the really hard and personal bit: being interviewed for that position. It is tense and a lot will ride on your performance.

BUT ... CONGRATULATIONS! You receive the call as one of the SUCCESSFUL top ten candidates to be interviewed by a Selection team: based on your CV and COVER LETTER.

Perhaps at this stage it is only the recruitment consultant who will cull down ten [10] potential interviewed candidates to the final three candidates who will then participate in the final rounds of face to face interviews. This culling may occur through telephone interviews or by Skype, Zoom or other online interview means, so you need to have a good clear confident communication presence. This takes PRACTICE.

We have spent many hours coaching and training potential candidates through this stressful process: another contest to win.

We will now take you through the interview process, how to practice, tips and techniques for the interview, how to negotiate your remuneration package to finally how to exit gracefully. Firstly let's understand how the recruitment process works as you journey through each hurdle.

23. The Recruitment Process

This is a Last Man / Last Woman Standing Situation

Let's explain the Recruitment process as we see it and then you will better understand what you must do to be successful in the process to win that job … above the rest.

250 → 20 → 10 → 3 → 1

Our Experience – for any Executive position it is not unusual to get well over 250 candidates applying with 5% of those being from overseas. Applicants have various chances of success and possess and express various desires and credentials and values to the business. They will all be the best competitive band of contestants.

The Recruiter or HR Manager will wish to quickly reduce this field to a manageable 20 candidates which will be the 'maybe' list – the rest being rejected for whatever reason.

Now the SELECTION PROCESS gets more sophisticated and more intense; the task is to reduce 20 candidates to 10 candidates for either a face to face or detailed phone interview to assess the quality of candidates. The next and final stage of candidate elimination will be very intensive interviews with a selection panel that includes direct management and other influential parties on a selection panel with a view to selecting a successful desired candidate.

So the selection process truly is:

250 → 20 → 10 → 3 → 1

Yes you want to be the Last Person Standing. This is a commendable achievement.

We often consult to and meet candidates who were down to the last two or three candidates, had the final interviews, but missed out: dejected as they feel that they fell at the last hurdle. We have to say and mean it when we tell them it is very commendable to get to the interview stage and you should feel well justified to have made it that far in such a competitive market and process. Don't be dejected, get back up and try again when the next position presents itself.

We are asked by candidates who once having learned of their unsuccessful application, if it is feasible and advisable to request a DEBRIEF INTERVIEW or phone call from the recruiter or HR Manager, to ascertain why they were unsuccessful having made it so far into the process. This also provides for feedback and sometimes tips for improvements on any deficiencies that the interview process may have uncovered.

Our answer is always that it is a good idea and does not show you in a poor light and in fact may lead to further discussions or opportunities showing that you want to improve your performance and presentation. Most HR managers will be prepared to provide this advice, especially if you can give your feedback on the process from your perspective.

24. Job Interview Models

At some stage in the Job-Hunting and Recruitment process you will need to be involved in an interview: either by an online app, telephone or face to face: either as the interviewee or interviewer. There are various medians of interview and various audiences. The interviewer will be either the staff member that you would potentially work for or a preliminary interview with a HR Consultant or the HR Team.

There are also various types or purposes of these job interviews that you could participate in as either the interviewee or interviewer:

- **Interviews for Practice – Role Play**: set up an interview to help the candidate to relax and practice the meet and greet and then answering various model questions. This is normally done in a mentoring context and on certain occasions can be recorded and played back to the candidate to show any twitches or unusual physical movements or mannerisms that are distracting and need to be corrected or minimised. Focus on improving pauses in order to answer questions, avoid using umm and buzz social words like perfect.

- **Group interviews for one role**: to provide more information about the organisation to groups of candidates and examine how candidates can lead, manage, or react, to a certain scenario placed to them, competing for the said position. Sessions can be held live, or online and form another stage of the selection process.

- **Semi-final or the Final interviews:** to win the job are normally held confidentially with one candidate at a time.

The **JOB INTERVIEW STRUCTURE** needs to be thought through very carefully: here are the most common structures:

1. You are asked to arrive early for the interview BUT you must complete a scenario assessment [of a fictitious situation] and report back to the interviewer or interviewers then when the formal interview starts – it addresses how you handle pressure and whether you are decisive.

2. Formal interview with up to 15 questions finishing with the opportunity for the candidate to either present their credentials or ask questions.

Use and Practice on Skype and Zoom

Our experience is that at least half of all recruitment interviews, whether the initial preliminary elimination interviews are conducted by Skype or Zoom remotely. More recent trends have seen final interviews held remotely due to inability to meet live due to pandemics and natural disasters.

Our advice is that as a prospective candidate you should get yourself onto Skype or Zoom privately: with a private address for Skype or Zoom and then practice using it for these upcoming interviews. Check your sound and camera controls and learn how to adjust quickly and have a substitute headset as a backup. There is nothing more frustrating for both the interviewer and interviewee when you cannot be seen or heard when it counts.

25. The Interview Conversation

You want to leave this one hour job interview feeling confident and that you did well and put your best foot forward and acquitted yourself well.

How do you do that in reality? Two easy [when rehearsed] steps:

- MAKE IT A CONVERSATION where you are relaxed and come across well as someone who will fit the organisation and role.

- MAKE IT A 50/50 INTERVIEW:
  - 50% of you speaking to sell YOURSELF and
  - 50% listening to the interviewers selling THEM and their organisation and your potential future position.

By the time you are being interviewed, you are viewed as being already 'in the camp' – they want to know how you will fit in with their team. This being said, ensure your interview conduct it is not about, it is about US.

Here are some comments or questions for you to practice with:

"How do we measure success towards our strategies"?

"What does the organisation see as our greatest opportunities?"

You continue the concept of the interview being a conversation by suggesting that you would like to present your Personal Portfolio and give the interview panel the opportunity to review your work, ask questions and for you to explain your contributions to these significant improvements at your previous employer. This will be accepted well and engage the interview panel in a discussion.

Steer the Interview to how the Business will Benefit from the Value that you will Add

Your interview will focus on your past achievements and roles BUT you are being selected and employed for your FUTURE contribution to their business. It is an interesting contradiction that you must understand.

Your focus and direction at interview MUST BE to convince the Interviewers of your value and abilities for the future in their organisation.

26. Performance Pitch

At the Interview you want to make a **BIG** impression. You need to plan for this and take the opportunity: what you say in your big pitch to make a difference if given the position: this is your **BIG PERFORMANCE PITCH:**
- How will you make a difference [Your Approach] and
- What is that difference? [Financial and Non-Financial Outcomes]

Here are samples of some **BIG PERFORMANCE PITCH** topics that you could use or develop further, depending on the business or industry:

- Business Growth and Development: internationalising the business
- Financial Sustainability
- Innovation and being a dynamic organisation
- Customer Focus and Customer driven responsiveness
- Supply chain efficiency and route optimisation
- Technology driven or adept
- Ready for or to create Disruption.

Consider adding topics to your chosen big pitch such as:

- Corporate / Community Involvement; mentor, sponsorships, cadets, work experience
- Values Based Business Initiatives; charities, lobby groups, associations
- Customer Centric Service models; WAMIMS [Walk a mile in my shoes]
- Teams based management and performance driven management
- Innovation and driving business growth and diversification
- Supply chain management and efficiency
- Addressing compliance and industry and government regulations
- Commercial and business literacy programs for the organisation.

It is important to develop and use examples of past successes in these areas. Being prepared with considered topics for discussion will translate your dialogue through clear logic and persuasive responsiveness to important questions.

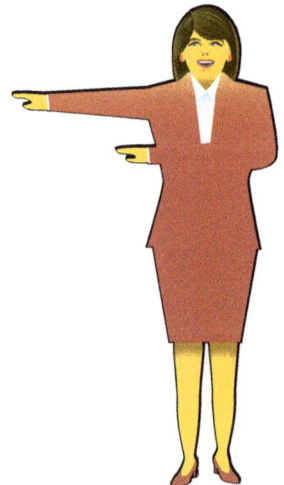

27. Greatest Candidate Attributes

Great and employable candidates exhibit: Style .. Skills .. Culture .. Leadership.

Use this Greatest Candidate Attributes T'n'T as a checklist for how you present yourself at interview and sell these features:

You are dependable and reliable

You are self-disciplined and well organised

You have a positive and commendable attitude

You have energy, drive and are enthusiastic

You are punctual and work long hours when required

You are project oriented and can pull together and work with a team

You handle people well and gain respect and regard

You like to solve issues and can adapt to the circumstances with creativity and strategic problem solving

Ability to write and present well and use appropriate language

You exude integrity

You are known for and have shown loyalty to your organisation, even though you are moving on

You value more than just money and bonuses

You are IT savvy and have great modelling and report writing skills and have honed your executive and management presentations and dashboard skills

You take advice and counsel from more senior, skilled and experienced mentors and counsel

You are respected externally by customers, suppliers, financiers, industry experts or groups and educational institutions.

You should review this Checklist and see which of these attributes you honestly cannot say YES to: if this is the case then you have work to reskill or develop your skills or an answer to present at an interview.

28. Initial Interview - First Impressions

The sayings **'FIRST IMPRESSIONS COUNT'** and **'FIRST IMPRESSIONS LAST'** are so true when it comes to career interviews.

Your initial submission with your Cover Letter and CV must and will make a strong first impression as we have already detailed. So too will your initial interview by phone or in person, also as already discussed.

Hence the reason for that very appealing and attractive personal portfolio which you present at the interview as detailed in the Section one: this portfolio says here is an achiever, someone very proud of themselves, competent, recognised, organised and able to present themselves professionally but with humility.

Now we get ready for your first personal face to face interview, that may and hopefully will be, the first of several interviews as you win over this contest and your desired new position.

29. Dress to Impress

Dress **APPROPRIATELY**. In fact, dress for the job you want and the respect and treatment you are seeking at the job.

Before your interview, you need to have assessed the appropriate dress code and how you dress for the interview: as an example is it tie and cufflinks, coats on or off, pen in pocket, smart looking briefcase in hand or presentation cache, with USB, laptop or IPad.

Traditional suits are still here, so tone it down a little and avoid bold pinstripes or squares, keep it *sophisticated*. Black, navy or grey suits are all acceptable. If you are an advocate for tight suit pants, ask yourself what am I selling? Is it my body or is it my knowledge, my intellectual capacity and my experience?

Ladies a simple suit or a business dress and again it is *sophistication* that is required, so please avoid the cleavage and any transparent clothing as it is no different for you as it is men when it comes to what you are selling.

Hair styles should be *professional attire* as if you were having a **PHOTO SHOOT** for the latest Annual Report. For all sexes we ask your jewellery to also fit within this profile and too often we see shoes that have missed the polish and appear as if they just walked an entire continent. Small things with big meanings of **how organised you are and how much pride you take in yourself matter**.

Colognes and fragrances that are too heavy may see your interviewer who suffers from hayfever or sinus, cut your interview short and not hire you. When and if wearing these, *subtlety is key*.

Roles for mid management up to senior executives and Board all demand the respect of the salaries awarded which is to accommodate a good, clean, crisp wardrobe.

Finally have your chosen wardrobe out ready, pressed and shone 24 hours prior to your interview. Why? If you find your clothes have shrunk, socially distanced buttons, or have a hole you just noticed, you have time to run out and replace or borrow.

Dress codes may be relaxed once you start work, but you have *not yet won the job*. This is **YOUR TIME TO SHINE**, to make that big impression. This being said there is an exception to the rule where you can drop down a notch to business casual as described next.

30. Decoding company dress

You might hear that a company has a dress code that is 'business professional.' What's the difference between that and 'business casual' and 'Casual'? How do you know what's too casual? You certainly want to get it right for your interviews and especially your first day on the job.

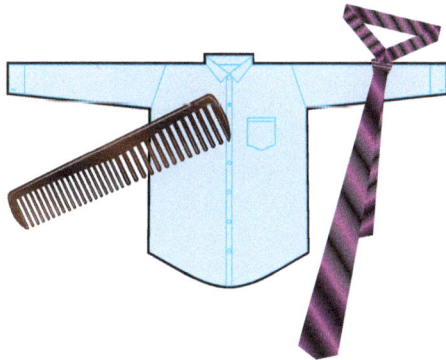

Here is our explanation for deciphering some of the most common office dress codes or terms:

- **Business professional**: In a business professional atmosphere, suits are the norm. Men may wear either a blazer or suit jacket, button down shirt, suit pants, a tie and dress shoes. Women might wear a skirt or pant suit with heels: hair for both is styled very neatly.

- **Business casual**: Forget the suit when you are told the interview is business casual: it is one step down from Business Professional. Men might opt to wear dress trousers or chinos, a button down or polo shirt, a belt and dress shoes. Women might consider wearing a conservative dress, or a blouse (or sweater) with a skirt, trousers or chinos and neat shoes or boots.

- **Casual**: When interviewing at a Casual office, it's still important to look polished and professional. (Save the jeans and flip-flops for when you actually have the job or the staff Christmas party or work planning day.) Men might consider wearing a long-sleeved dress shirt, chinos with a belt, and dress shoes. Women might wear a collared shirt with pants or a skirt or work dress.

Dress

- It is always better to be slightly or over dressed than undressed.

- Our advice is that it is better to dress up a category than dress down and regardless you want to show your real character so a professional dress seems more appropriate for a business interview.

- If you can wear it on the weekend or around home, then it is too casual for a job interview and perhaps work in general.

31. Standard Interview Behaviours and Questions

In the Interview stakes that are a tough competition for pole position, now is your big chance to make a **FIRST and LASTING impression.**

You may go first in the Interview phase and have to lead all the way by being memorable or come up later and be so refreshingly well experienced using your well researched insights, that you leave all of the other previously selected and interviewed candidates in a trail of dust, especially if they are interviewing up to six or eight a day.

A GOOD INTERVIEW IS A RICH CONVERSATION. This is our advice from Experience.

32. Interview Culling Process

Our coaching advice to help you step through the culling process toward that winning job:

1. **Practice** beforehand your Telephone Interview techniques:
   - Speak positively and powerfully
   - Listen and answer respectfully
   - Practice your responses to our pro-forma questions located in this section
   - Do not speak over the other telephone participants

2. **Prepare** for Face To Face Interviews:
   - Should you get to a final face to face interview, you should assume that you are down to the final three, maybe five candidates: so have confidence and show that at the interview and in how you prepare for that interview.

3. Ensure that you **address every member** of the interview panel by name and with an answer specifically addressed to them personally. Research the roles of the interview panel and also what their interests are to allow a direct respect and personalisation.

Proudly display your confidence that you have made it this far.

As they say, getting to the last 2 or 3 candidates is a great accreditation and achievement. You may not be selected but being able to say you got to the final two is a great credit and promotes your values to others.

DON'T BE DESPONDENT

I recently had a conversation with a coaching client who was despondent as he had twice got to the final two and missed out each time [one to an internal candidate].

I had to counsel him that he should be proud and elated and upbeat … not despondent … as reaching the final two was a great result and rewarded his preparation and presentation which was spot on, and that the next and better job offer was just around the corner.

I also said that he probably was never going to win the one that went to the internal candidate as they were may have been testing the market and it was a set up process – he felt better after hearing that counsel.

33. Pre-Interview Tips

Preparation and practice are key, and in doing so will help you on the day. Here's a few tips and techniques to be completed and practiced before the interview:

- **Ensure you have thoroughly researched the potential employer organisation:** visit their website, social media channels and news articles. Don't be afraid to ask for important information such as an organisation chart, annual reports or financial analysis by brokers or EquiFax report. This shows the interviewer that you are interested and taking this position and interview very seriously.
- **It's all in the timing:** you MUST NOT BE LATE. Always leave a time buffer to arrive early. Arrive an hour or two earlier, find a café nearby, rehearse, practice and then attend. At least you are already in the area to be on time, nice and refreshed.
- **Prepare yourself mentally:** ask the recruitment consultant or HR person the details of the job interview structure and process, who will interview you, for how long and how many candidates will be there. Particularly ask if it is a suite of candidates one after the other: that is a taxing schedule and where do you fit in the day's interviews.
- **Practice the common interview questions following:** also try to think of examples which describe how you have dealt with different and difficult situations as applicable to this business.
- **Query:** if you will be required to undertake a prior case study or scenario case study and report back with your recommendations.

34. During Interview Tips

- **Body Language**: Sit up straight, no fidgeting, hold eye contact and pay attention.
- **Never interrupt**: Wait for the interviewer to finish before you reply.
- **Listen actively**: Show respect and learn more about the business, the role and culture of your potential employer.
- **Ask questions**: Show enthusiasm and your intellect by asking interesting questions.

2.3 Interview

- **Speak Clearly and concisely**: if you have a foreign accent, watch to see if they can understand you and if they seem to struggle, slow your talking down ever so slightly.

- **Answer questions**: Fluently, confidently, in short (avoid rambling) and provide quantifiable facts through emphasising your greatest career achievements or organisational contributions. These answers will display what your VALUE ADD to the business was and to what financial or non-financial value. Use ratios if easier to emphasise the value.

- **Career achievements**: Memorise these and be ready to elaborate and have all the figures and stats recited.

- **Be enthusiastic**: about your career and what you have achieved – avoid unnecessary detail or waffle. Catch the interviewer's interest or attention with achievements and only the detail not included in your CV and Cover Letter.

- **Optimistic and Positive language**: speak highly of your past organisation and your career, showing loyalty and respect for past employers, bosses or colleagues. No matter how tyrannous they were.

TOWARDS THE INTERVIEW END: towards or even at the end of the interview, you will be given a chance to ask questions or add further comments on your suitability. Use this opportunity to sell yourself further and be assertive. Ask questions on topics like:

- Further elaborating on the organisation's structure, culture or attitude to training and career development for all staff, divert focus back to your leadership and support rather than on you and only your promotion.
- Expansion plans or repositioning of the businesses' strategic direction
- Changes in the business model or other exciting opportunities
- Competitive pressures and how the organisation proposes to keep its competitive advantage – ask in a positive manner.

35. Interview Etiquette

Knowing right from wrong is something you may think you have down pat, but it doesn't hurt to be refreshed in interview etiquette:

DO:
- **Dress to Impress**: refer to our how to dress section.
- **Meet and greet the interviewer (option 1)**: with a strong hand-shake but don't squeeze the hell out of them and have them in pain for the rest of the interview.
- **Meet and greet the interviewer (option 2)**: our current times as we write are in a pandemic, that is changing the hand-shake option to a temporary and perhaps permanent non option. Ask if ok to shake their hands if it has become the 50/50 each way bet, or simply smile, offer that end elbow greet and follow up with a happy positive 'It was so much easier with the hand-shake'.
- **Good eye contact**: and remember the interviewer's full name.
- **Address ALL interviewers**: as they all have a vote, respect all of them and show your ability to work a group or crowd.
- **Rehearse your CV**: details and focus on your major achievements and exceptional performance, and not the small stuff.
- **List your questions**: and bring them to ensure you cover them all as this show your interest in the job and the organisation through your thoroughness.
- **Let the interviewer convince you**: of the credibility of their organisation and the value of this position to the business.
- **Keep engaging:** the interviewer/s and **keep smiling**.
- **Answer questions quickly and concisely**: avoid dithering and long winded answers.

DON'T:
- **Be late** and keep the interviewers waiting
- **Interrupt** the interviewer
- **Smoke or drink before your interview** – the smell lingers on you
- **Volunteer your weaknesses** or show any negativity
- **Disrespect** your **existing** or any **previous employers**

- **Be boastful or arrogant** – you are joining a TEAM
- **Use profanities**, **slang**, **sexist or culturally offensive language**
- **Over use buzz words** - display your broader vocabulary
- **Raise the salary discussion**, win the job offer first, then negotiate
- **Seem desperate** or beg for the job.

36. Standard Interview Target Areas

Your performance at your face to face interviews will be greatly determined by your preparation and practice beforehand, especially with tricky or curly questions.

As a lot of focus will be put on cultural and organisational fit, a number of important questions will be posed around BEHAVIOURAL ASPECTS and COMPETENCIES to ensure or influence your or organisational performance.

So let's talk about interview preparedness and these interview techniques. Interviews are in their own form an exam but with more flexibility to answer. The best answered and also most suitable applicant **FIT FOR THE POSITION** will be selected, so practice is advisable.

The most logical and illogical questions which could be asked of you for the respective positions will see common areas questioned such as:

For the CEO position, the focus will be on:

- **Being Strategic**: driving performance to achieve the agreed board and organisational strategy, with examples.
- **Representational**: your ability to network and represent the business in various forums: industry leadership and government / corporate relations / stakeholder and shareholder relations.
- **Board relationships and style**: how CEO and direct reports relate to the board: domineering, conciliatory, leader, team player or team builder, collegiate, open/closed door or inbox available for comments.
- **Selecting, managing and appraising your subordinate team**: the senior Executive team.

For the CFO position, the focus will be on:

- See list specifically for CFO's in Section 4.
- More generally questions as to **relationship management with CEO** and Board and then downstream to divisional and activity managers.
- **Managing your team** of finance professionals and handling relations with Banks, Financiers and Investment houses: meeting Regulatory authority's requirements and your views on Corporate Compliance and delivering on KPI's for success.

37. Tough and Difficult Interview Questions

Interviewers on occasion have been known to exert their presence during an interview, sometimes aggressively in difficulty of the question asked. Being aware and prepared for this will assist you.

We start you with some tough but generic questions that you may be asked, and therefore best to practice:

- Give an example of a situation where you needed to be decisive. Explain how did you gather support for your position and that decision? What was the end result and was your position successful? What did you learn from that situation?

- What are examples of some probing questions that you ask of your fellow management to form your view in a difficult situation?

- How would you go about spotting talent in the team that you inherit upon taking on this position?

- How would you manage an underperforming staff member that you have inherited in your new position, that you need to manage out?

Here is one specifically for a CFO candidate:

How would you go about building a collegiate relationship with your CEO or Chairman of the Board? What is your management style?

- Is it closed door and pot of coffee?
- Is it a sandwich lunch from a brown paper bag?
- Is it off to the businessman's club or gym for a break during the day?

- Is it a dinner after work hours?
- Is it a social BBQ at home?
- Is it during travel with the CEO or Chair on your next combined business trip?

Remember that the interviewer often does not have a specific right or wrong answer – they just want to see how you respond and handle yourself and may go one step further to ask what your preferred style is.

38. Sneaky [Gotcha] Interview Questions

You have now warmed up on the generic questions, candidate response thinking mode is switched on, and you are doing well or know what you need to address. What about those sneaky questions, the ones that scream Gotcha?

You know at least one or two are coming with the interviewer's intent to test out your behaviour under pressure or under personal threat or even aggression. You will not enjoy them and they may [or are specifically asked] to UNNERVE you – so you need to practice and be prepared.

We provide you a few 'gotcha' questions, some are known but some not – be ready:

What is your biggest WEAKNESS? Please describe them for us.
If you say you are perfect or you have none, stop now…Seriously. Everyone has weaknesses even the most brilliant leaders have weaknesses, it is what defines us to improve.

What sort of a question is this? Think carefully about how you introduce or preamble your answer. Do you say "That's an interesting question" or "Well I have never been asked that before?" Perhaps you can try this answer, "That is a good question and one I do ask myself to try to critically assess my performance, recognising my weaknesses to address these" … and provide a few examples: you took a course on presentation skills, or negotiation skills or Conducting 360 Assessments or Black Swan Thinking etc. Practice your answer and be prepared.

The aim is NOT to focus on the weakness per se but to divert/turn the discussion around to your ability that will improve and overcome the weakness.

Tell us about your WORST FAILURE.

Failures are facts of every business but they result in learnings and make you better equipped for your future roles and performance. Failures may not be your fault or directly attributed by you, but we do learn from all forms of failure.

Similar to the above Weakness gotcha, if you say that you have not had any failures .. wrong answer. Work on one, be ready and make it a good answer with learnings showing strength and conviction.

Why should we hire you instead of anyone else?

The answer is you will be hired as you are the best and most suitable candidate because: [off you go - develop and practice your response of how you will add value to this exciting organisation]

Please give us some examples of perseverance and resilience in your career. Be prepared with an answer: express your approach to issues and challenges, your work effort and additional courses or degrees or accreditations: you may have taken on a special project at significant cost to your career because you know it would deliver transitional benefits to you and your organisation.

Tell us about yourself

A good practice for any question like this is to respond quickly within 30 seconds, think ELEVATOR PITCH. Have this answer prepared and cover all 4 of these points:

      a. Personal Goals

      b. Skills and Achievements

      c. Significant Contributions – what you are proud of

      d. Career Aspirations.

Eg. I play golf on Saturday mornings for relaxation, sit on my kids' school P & C Committee and introduced a new 360 Performance Review model in my last role.

Why *are* you leaving your current job? Or Why *did* you leave your most recent job?

WARNING! This is one of the most-loaded questions they will throw at you. There's one thing you must NEVER do or say—under any circumstances—is to disrespect your previous employer. Remember we told you this in our tips. A positive response would be that business is moving head office or a change in ownership or your desire for new challenges having been there five years and your superior manager is not moving on stagnating your career progress.

How would you handle a sexual harassment claim against you?
We are not a fan of this aggressive question but we have heard of some who ask. It is seeking to investigate either of: your ability to handle such a situation; pre-warning there may have been recent allegations made against other staff; your body language may be displaying flirtatious tendencies.

Further Interview Questions you may be asked

- What personal characteristics make you effective in an organisation?
- How would you describe your interpersonal skills?
- How would you describe your ideal career or employment role?
- How do you handle pressure?
- In what type of environment do you thrive?
- How would you describe your leadership style?

Turn your answers to their tricky questions into a positivity of understanding that you are not perfect and that you have addressed the question and the solutions with actions to provide in an interview.

39. Roadblocks To A Perfect Interview

Not all candidates have a "perfect" career track record: there is always something in the cupboard that could be an interview stopper, if it came out. What are those and how do you develop an answer and way forward.

You need to develop specific steps to quickly bypass each of these major roadblocks or inhibitors, as below, if they are raised with you at interview:

- You were retrenched or fired from a previous position or organisation
- You have a significant gap (or gaps) in work history
- You seem to stay in a position for twelve months then move on
- You have stayed with the same organisation for most of your career
- You have not moved from your role for over five years

- You have a series of short-term job stints
- You apply but come from a different industry
- You can't use an employer as a reference
- Age issues: either seem much too young or old to fulfil the role.

If any of these major roadblocks apply to you, you'll now be able to eliminate (or downplay) their impact... so... you will feel confident in your next interview... and... ready to land that job.

40. Answering Interview Questions - Poorly

Have you ever said something in an interview that got you into trouble?

Maybe you didn't even realise you said something wrong. Yet, suddenly, your interviewer seems a lot less interested in you, maybe even unhappy. Were you sexist, politically incorrect, derogatory, disparaging, negative, resentful, anal, small minded, flippant, clearly dishonest, disrespectful, etc.?

And, it looks like whatever you said, your chances for this job just went down the drain.

Well, even if you were **just worried** about that happening, here is a sample of the **6 most common mistakes** that you should absolutely avoid in your next interview:

Mistake 1. Length of Answer
The perfect interview answer should last between 20 seconds and two minutes.

That means two things: you should not answer a question with a simple yes or no. You need to share the critical details and should provide a thorough answer and great examples of how you operate, manage and lead.

When you feel like you've shared the highlights, cut yourself off, they don't need to hear your life story. If you feel compelled to share more, you can offer the information, "If you'd like I can also describe..." but don't be surprised if the interviewer turns you down.

If you've crafted your answers the right way, these time constraints are very manageable and effective.

2.3 Interview

Mistake 2. Not actually answering the interview question.

Now, some people think they are politicians and "cleverly" avoid giving a straight answer: which could be conceived as deceptive and evasive. More often, you may just be a bit confused about what the interviewer is asking.

If you are not 100% sure of the question or its intent, **ask for clarification.** Repeat the question back in your own words. Say something like: "So you wish me to explain ....?"

And, if you still don't know whether you answered the question, at the end of your response, say to the interviewer: "I'm not sure whether my answer fully answered your question. Can I further elaborate?"

Mistake 3. Speaking before thinking

At the interview, you will likely face an interview question that you're not ready for. Whether you sink or swim, depends on allowing for clear thoughts to answer. Pause, think and a deep breathe.

Your answer must be clear and strong, for example, "That's a really good question, let me take a few moments to gather my thoughts." If you're still not sure how to tackle it, break it down into pieces. Start by answering what you feel most confident about and go from there.

Remember each question is asked for a reason: consider the reason or angle and respond accordingly.

Mistake 4. Providing generic answers.

A good and attentive answer gives vivid examples. A borderline answer references yourself and the organisation.

A generic answer sounds like you had a list of general responses and picked wherever your finger landed. Generic answers include, "I'm a team player," or "I'm a big picture person" or "I'm really excited about the work you do here." Or "I like the culture of your business". You don't know this yet and you should not say it.

To avoid this mistake, you just need to prepare the right way.

Gather the key facts about the organisation and craft answers that **describe yourself effectively.** Present **how you would fit in** and cooperate in the organisation, talking **as if you are already there** in their organisation.

Mistake 5: Not creating a conversation

Any interview is in large part about **establishing a relationship between you and your interviewers.** That means you need to feel confident enough to be yourself and ask questions.

If it seems like they're just shooting questions at you in the hot seat, you yourself a disservice. So, when you have a question pop up during the conversation, ask it, for example:

If they ask you, *"what's the most challenging project you faced or worked on?"* at the end of your answer, you can follow up with, *"what are the kinds of challenges that staff or management encounter here in projects?"* Turn it back on them.

A good interview splits the air time **50/50** between the interviewer and the interviewee. Work on this technique and **time balance.** After all, you want them to feel that they have to sell their position and their organisation to you as well as you selling yourself to them.

Mistake 6: Interviewer's age intimidates you

What do you do, how do you react when you turn up for an interview and find that the interviewer is half your age or thereabouts? This is common and easy when you know how.

The interviewer has a job, needs a job and is doing the job they were appointed to do. You just need to get over the person being old enough to be your son or daughter: there is the answer – treat them as if they are your son or daughter and address and answer as if you are their parent and you have wisdom and experience and you are there to help and provide wise counsel and the value that experience provides.

You are now over their age and can proceed normally with your conversation and demonstrating what you have to offer from many years of experience and successes in various positions: you have much to offer this business and appreciate the excitement of working with a young and dynamic business and culture.

Express that your experience will be invaluable and they can rely on your respect and mutual sharing of experiences.

The Thirteen Greatest Mistakes Made at Job Interviews [What NOT to DO]

We have summarised the Biggest Mistakes for you in the following table:

1. Being evasive and not answering the specific question asked.
2. Being a Friend, Relative or Business Coach/ Associate. This is about you winning the job, not your parent gifting you a job. You risk respect for your exceptional skills.
3. Criticise or bad mouth your previous or current employer.
4. Raise the issue of salary or when you could expect to be promoted.
5. Arrive late, rushing or disorganised.
6. Fail to remember the names of the members of the interview panel, or fail to address all interviewers, only addressing one.
7. Use of inappropriate language, swearing, profanities or culturally offensive references.
8. Too long to answer a question: rambling and dithering.
9. Talking about yourself constantly or in third person, and bragging about achievements rather than emphasising the value you can add for this new organisation.
10. Raising any poor or troublesome CSR or legal issues that may be facing your potential new employer, rather than being informed, positive and understanding.
11. Begging for a job, being desperate. You made it to the interview that proves you deserve to be heard and evaluated for the role, so no need for negatively appearing desperate.
12. When asked if you have any questions, you reply incorrectly with No. You must have a few questions prepared to show an interest, your research and respect to the interview panel.
13. End the interview with a whimper, saying nothing. You want to end the interview well on a winning note, reiterating your great interest in the position and that you hope to receive a favourable approach as you thought the interview went well.

41. Extra Interview Question Practice: Be Prepared

To assist you further in your practice, we compiled some questions from various professional recruitment experts that they say are the GREAT QUESTIONS that GREAT CANDIDATES ASK and the GREAT QUESTIONS TO ASK GREAT CANDIDATES.

Firstly, the GREAT Questions that GREAT Candidates Ask
this may seem in reverse order but go with it as it works better this way.

Jeff Hadon[18] of INC.com has **five great questions** that he says the GREAT candidates ask:

1.What do you expect me to accomplish in the first 60 to 90 days in the job?

Great candidates want to hit the ground running. They don't want to spend weeks or months "getting to know the organisation."

The potential candidate wants to make a difference - right away. They ask for the expectations of the organisation and the interview panel and hopefully their immediate bosses.

They want to prove that they have a '**Can Do / Will Do**' approach and also are results focused.

2. What are the common attributes of the top performers in your business?

Great and insightful question. Great candidates also want to be great long-term employees. Every organisation is different, and so are the key qualities of top performers in those organisations. The candidate wants to know what the organisation or interviewers think makes the top performers stand out in this business and corporate setting.

Maybe the top performers work longer hours. Maybe creativity is more important than methodology and compliance. Maybe constantly landing new customers in new markets is more important than building long-term customer relationships with existing customers. Maybe it's a willingness to spend the same amount of time educating an entry-level customer as helping an enthusiast who wants high-end equipment.

Great candidates want to know, because:

1) they want to know if they fit, and;

2) if they do fit, they want to be a top performer also.

3. What are the key deliverables that really drive results for the company?

Employees are investments, and every employee should generate a positive return on his or her salary, [Otherwise, why are they on the payroll?]

In every job, some activities make a bigger difference than others. You need your HR staff to fill job openings, but what you really want is for HR to find the right candidates, because that results in higher retention rates, lower training costs, and better overall productivity and profits.

You need your service techs to perform effective repairs, but what you really want is for those techs to identify ways to solve problems and provide other benefits-in short, to generate additional sales or new product opportunities.

Great candidates want to know what truly makes a difference in this particular business. They know helping the company succeed means them succeed as well. It is all about driving success and key deliverables achieve this: the interviewee wants to know what the interviewer thinks these key deliverables are so they can more readily make their decision to join the business.

4. What do employees in your business do in their spare time?

Happy employees:

1) like what they do and;

2) like the people they work with.

Granted, this is a tough question to answer. Unless the company is really small, all any interviewer or company representative can do is speak in generalities about support for community service or staff welfare: e.g. see Corporate Social Responsibility section.

What's important is that the candidate wants to be sure of having a reasonable chance of fitting in-because great job candidates usually have options and a fresh approach to community involvement.

5. How does your organisation deal with difficult situations and pressures?

Every business will face a major challenge or several over time: be it technological changes, competitors entering the market, shifting economic trends, changing business models, corporate or social change.

Great candidates don't just want to know what you think or do as a company; they want to know what you plan to do-and how they will fit into those plans. The real issue is whether you are an out there responsible organisation.

Here is *another list* of Questions headed **'Seven Questions Only the Great Candidates Ask'** by Jeff Hadon of INC.com: asked slightly differently.

1. "What do you expect me to accomplish in the first 60-90 days in the job?"

Great candidates want to hit the ground running. They don't want to spend weeks or months "getting to know the organisation." They don't want to spend huge chunks of time in orientation, in training, or in the futile pursuit of getting their feet wet. They want their senior management interviewers to set expectations and to discuss desired outcomes.

They want to make a difference - and they want to make that difference right now.

2. "If you were to rank them, what are the top three traits your existing top performers have in common?"

Great candidates also want to be great employees and work in a great team. They know every organization is different culturally - and so are the key qualities of top performers in those organizations.

Maybe the top performers work longer hours. Maybe creativity is more important than methodology or compliance. Maybe constantly landing new customers in new markets is more important than building long-term customer relationships. Maybe the key is a willingness to spend the same amount of time educating an entry-level customer as helping an enthusiast or committed customer who wants high-end equipment.

2.3 Interview

Great candidates want to know, because:
 1. they want to know if they will fit in, and

 2. if they do fit in, they want to know how they can be a top performer.

3. "What really drives results in this job?"

Employees are investments, and you expect every employee to generate a positive return on his or her salary, often referred to as Human Capital.

Great candidates, especially executives want to know what truly makes a difference and drives results in your organisation, because they know helping the company continue success is what they can drive from day one, then they can expand the results into areas you highlight.

4. "What are the company's highest priority goals this year, and how would my role contribute?"

Is the job the candidate will fill important? Does that job matter?

Great candidates want a job with meaning, with a larger purpose - and they want to work with people who approach their jobs the same way. Otherwise a job is just a job.

5. "What percentage of employees were brought into the business by current employees?"

Employees who love their jobs naturally recommend their company to their friends and peers. The same is true for people in leadership positions - people naturally try to bring on board talented people they previously worked with.

They've built relationships, developed trust, and shown a level of competence that made someone go out of their way to follow them to a new organisation.

And all of that speaks incredibly well to the quality of the workplace and the culture.

6. "What do employees do in their spare time?"

Happy employees 1) like what they do, and 2) like the people they work with.

Granted, this is a tough question to answer. Unless your company is really small, all you can do is speak in generalities. [Or you can pick out a few people and describe what they do outside of work - and if you can't even do that, you don't know your employees nearly well enough.]

Great candidates want to be sure of having a reasonable chance of fitting in on a personal level as well as a professional level because cultural fit is extremely important to them. It may be a sporting club or a charitable endeavour but this outside work endeavour is a great team spirit creator.

7. "What do you plan to do if...?"

Every business faces a major challenge: technological changes, competitors entering the market, shifting economic trends, changing customer preferences, or changes in government policies.

So while some candidates may see your company as a steppingstone, they still hope for growth and advancement. If they do eventually leave, they want it to be on their terms, not because you were forced out of business.

Say I'm interviewing for a position at your ski shop. Another store is opening less than a mile away: How do you plan to deal with the competition? Or you run a poultry farm: "What will you do to deal with rising feed costs or changed animal welfare policies?"

Great candidates don't just want to know what you *think*; they want to know what you plan to do and how they will fit into those plans.

42. Questions for the Interviewer

Questions to Ask Great and Not So Great Candidates

These are the 'out of left field' questions of candidates to test them out, catch them unawares and sense their capability to respond to adverse situations.

John Brandon[8] of INC.COM says he puts these questions to candidates into two buckets. The **first** bucket is all about their **credentials**. He goes through a typical set of questions about background, education and experience. This is obviously helpful in determining if the candidate has the right skills for the job at hand.

Then, he asks questions on a **second** bucket list that are a bit more unusual. The goal is to find out untoward issues and feeling. Here's just a snapshot of these **unusual questions:**

1. What are the top three (3) factors you attribute to your success in employment and/or in business? [Factual and see what the candidates think is the main reason for their success]

2. On a scale of 1 to 10, how lucky are you in life? [Wait for interesting answers to a very interesting question. Learn what they think this question might have to do with their career]

3. Tell me about a time when you were at a company/business and disappointed someone. What did you do next? [About recognition of wrong or sub-optimal performance and redemption through intentional actions]

4. Tell me about a time when you were at a company/business and someone disappointed you. What did you do next? [About your management style for accepting and managing underperformers]

5. Tell me about a time at a company where you felt your values or beliefs were being compromised. What did you do next? [About your ethics and principles and what you did next]

6. If you were starting a company tomorrow, what would be the top three (3) core values for that company? [Obviously about ethics and culture]

7. Did you build any lifelong friendships while in past roles or teams? Please elaborate. [About your personal style and rapport with the business or outside with customers or industry groups]

8. Tell me about a time when you've wanted to quit, or did quit. Why? What did you do? How did you handle it? [About your breaking point or tolerance level]

9. Tell me about a time when you witnessed company culture go bad. [About how perceive culture and appreciate it]

10. Tell me about a mentor or coach you've had in the past and how they helped you. [Shows your acceptance of help and guidance.

43. Questions for Candidates to Ask at the Interview End

Towards the end of the interview, the Candidate will normally be given the opportunity to ask questions of the Interviewer, either as to the organisation or the position or maybe the process and issues around the existing incumbent's progression or the position becoming available for this recruitment etc.

Harness the opportunity to show your interest, perception and potential contribution to the organisation.

Perception and understanding through the style of questions you can ask in relation to the organisation or the market position of the organisation in its industry are good to practice, for example:

- What does the organisation believe are the possible growth directions and projections for the industry or this organisation?
- Are there any new technologies which will be impacting the business both as an opportunity or threat to the business and how will the organisation take these opportunities or mitigate these threats?
- Are there any significant strategic plans or intentions that would impact on the business's position going forward?
- What is the perceived quality and appreciation of the team that I would be inheriting?
- Do you think it is feasible to have a 100 Day Plan or what other counsel would you give re the rate of progress in achieving my goals in the job as I have explained?

Now, if you sometimes find yourself in a similar position, and you genuinely don't have any questions about the role, here's an easy fix:

Take a question they asked you, and **turn it around** so that it's now about the role. For example, if they asked you what your biggest strengths are, you can ask them: "What do you think are the most important strengths needed for the role?"

You can pull this same "trick" or technique with almost any question.

You MUST ASK QUESTIONS if given the chance … show your interest!

44. End of Interview Wrap Up

Towards the end of the interview, you will be offered the opportunity to ask the Interviewers questions or clarifications about the organisation or the position being recruited or the process being undertaken to select a final successful applicant.

Without being presumptuous, you want to **clarify** the following points about the selection process and how the job offer will be managed. This is acceptable and understandable.

If you are at near final interview stage you can afford to be rather aggressive about seeking clarification of when a decision can be expected. Back yourself and let them know you are being pursued elsewhere.

Try these three points of clarification:

- When may I expect to hear from you with an answer or offer? – will it be another round of interviews or a decision and offer immediately?
- How long before any decision is made or an offer received – do you have a preferred internal candidate or a selected choice?
- Do I need to meet any other senior executives in the organisation for a decision to be made – if they say NO then you pretty well know the answer.

If your sentiment is that you are not the No.1 choice, then you may see no disadvantage in asking the following question:

"Well I put my best foot forward, could you give me an honest assessment and feedback on my presence and presentation and your views on where my further career development might take me or any suggestions on what other roles or career development I need to undertake to reach the level of the position I was applying for".

As you leave the interview

Often we note an awkward moment as interviewees leave hastily or not knowing how to wrap up. Try these tips after thanking them as per the above wrap up:

- Pack your briefcase or bag of all items and then stand to leave.

- Offer a strong handshake or an elbow(as in the pandemic distancing style). Be sure to attention every interviewer.

- Thank them again for the opportunity to meet and their invaluable time

- Smile, smile, smile and smile authentically. The nerves are gone and genuine happy smiles speak volumes.

Within the first 24 hours, whilst your influence remains at the forefront of the interviewers mind:

- Write a short personal thank-you letter to thank them for their time and reaffirm your interest in the position and hope you get called back for further discussion.

- If your application is unsuccessful, don't be afraid to call and ask for feedback on the interview and your CV and submission as you wish to improve your personal development and do better in the next round of interviews.

45. Waiting for the Job Offer

You had the interview and you formed a view of how it went: maybe great and you were confident or maybe you were a little tentative and you did not sell yourself enough: maybe you could have done better. You can't change that now.

However, you can still keep in the game and keep yourself in front of the organisation and the selection committee.

Here is what we recommend you can do after your interview: depending on what type of interview it was, you can do the following:

If a **PHONE INTERVIEW**
Email after your phone interview and say:

Thank you for the opportunity to meet (if only by phone) and discuss your capabilities for the position.

You enjoyed the time with them and felt it is a great business and career opportunity. Add that you liked the feel and culture of the organisation.

You are very interested in the position and the company. Mention any relevant projects that you had worked on that gave you insight and experience for this position and affinity to their business

If a **FACE TO FACE INTERVIEW**
If a face to face interview, you will have a more personal affinity and rapport and you can email after the interview to say:

Great to meet you face to face and the other interviewees [your team].

You had gained a greater insight into the business and the great opportunity that was this................. position and the goals and directions for the business that you can relate to very much.

Say you can see how you could fit well into the business and your particular Skills, culture and work ethic would place you well for the position.

If then no reply, then email to remind the recruiter/interview person that you are still very interested in the position.

Should you try to ring the interview or selection panel representatives? Absolutely Not. This is viewed as inappropriate.

46. When to Discuss Salary

NEVER – repeat **NEVER mention salary** at any recruitment interview – especially the FIRST interview.

Yes it is difficult to know when the recruitment phase has finished and the job negotiation starts BUT wait until you are offered the job and are THE candidate that they want to the exclusion of all others.

We understand that it is difficult to get excited and to put your heart and soul and all that effort into a recruitment when you don't know what the salary or remuneration package is going to be, but you must wait and you must use other means to get a gauge on the salary range. They may advertise and say the salary is "commensurate with the market" - that's fine as you can establish the market and they won't get you for less than you are on now and what another employer thinks you are worth.

When you are told that the organisation want you, and in fact all others have been officially told that they are unsuccessful – then is the most powerful time to start to talk and negotiate your package.

Of course the new employer will be pushing to try to work out your value to the business and hence whether they can afford you, that is only logical.

You could indicate a range which starts with your current salary, inflating it for the cost of performance bonuses that you will inevitably forgo by moving on and accepting their offer.

Your final salary should be impacted by two factors:

- Your worth to the business – how you can add value, bring new skills and introduce new business or relationships, and;

- The respective salaries of the employees above and below you.

2.4 Negotiation

You now know the answer that you must do the **research** to be able to **assess**, **negotiate** and answer the two aspects below:

1. Do a Value Assessment of your role and of you performing that role: calculate the Value you can add to the business - cost savings on consultants and additional revenue and investment opportunities.

2. Assess and know the salary ranges for the employees who will be reporting to you and the other executive team members, including the CEO and board members. It is a simple table:

Person Below You Earns:	Person Above You Earns:	Your Salary Should Be:
$	$	$

You should also suggest use of an independent salary search firm to VALUE THE POSITION and give a job relativity assessment.

In the end, your new employer should appreciate that you are not going to leave a great secure position for less than you are on now and that you will be forgoing significant bonuses or executive performance arrangements, which must be built into your new employment contract for it to be attractive for you to leave where you are and join this new employer.

Most importantly, you must not say absolutely you are accepting the new employer's offer of employment until the final salary starting price and benefits are agreed and documented, provided to you in a formal written contract offer.

The final consideration should be in the detail of the employment contract. We suggest you check:

- **Restraint of Trade terms:** as this may restrict your next role, especially if in the same industry and sector. CIO's are poorly restricted in these to the point that many contracts restrict a CIO from working anywhere until the restrain time has lapsed.

- **Skills training:** irrespective of your C-Suite role, the ability for you to stay in the lead with your skillset and external regulatory changes and technology changes is paramount to the success you can bring to the organisation and yourself. Further mentoring does not come cheap, so include a $5-$10k per annum with rollover if unused, expiring upon departure.

- **Membership payment:** another relevant but forgotten area is your annual subscriptions to your professional body.

47. Police Checks for Employment

You are in an employment interview and it is going well. You think you are the preferred candidate and an offer is pending.

You are then asked if you would agree to your potential employer conducting a FORMAL POLICE CHECK for employment purposes.

What would your reaction and response be?

You should be prepared for that request and have your answer ready to respond immediately:

- **YES**, of course, I have a clear record, and 'I know that you would want to do that as a formality: I appreciate the thoroughness or your search, Yes GO FOR IT'.
- **NO,** it is too early in the recruitment process

Understand the impression that your answer may give to the interviewers.

Police Checks are conducted through the AFP [Australian Federal Police] National Police Check system at www.afpcheck.com or www.nationalcrimecheck.com.au – it is an easy online service and covers criminal record. Immigration, citizenship, visas. If you are in a different country they should also be applied from your national police headquarters.

Organisations that are governmental or in the education sector, ordinarily require a full AFP check that is both foreign and national focussed including criminal convinctions.

However, a standard organisation may only require a general police check which is much cheaper, quicker and is more national focussed.

Your Passport is normally required for executive and board positions as a matter of security considering you are in an influential position. They also make it much easier for HR to arrange your international business travel. You are well within your rights to question the secure storage whereabouts and process of such information.

2.4 Negotiation

48. Workplace Personal Limitations

What if you apply for a job but knowing that you have certain personal limitations, disabilities or restrictions that could impact your performance or fulfilment in the job?

You want the job!

You won the race fair and square and you are their preferred candidate BUT..What if for certain personal reasons, you have limitations or need special conditions on your availability to fulfil the position, such limitations may include:

- Parental or children's special needs
- Inability to travel overseas or interstate for whatever reason
- Obligations to complete a special education or tertiary course, such as an MBA or Directors course or a personal development program
- Defence force or military reserve commitments
- Community or social positions, roles and commitments.

How and when do you raise these limitations deserves special and thoughtful consideration.

Each of these arrangements say that you are a special and thoughtful person and employee and add to your credentials and value to an organisation. The only issue is how to accommodate these special circumstances without adversely effecting your ability to do the job. However, they must be raised at some time in the interview or application process and that is the subtlety to do so such that it does not exclude the candidate for that reason: play it safely and wisely.

49. Risk in Executive Recruitment Selection and Appointment

In today's competitive, uncertain and rapidly changing business environment, the future is unclear and certainly not assured.

Likewise in recruitment, the interview panel is faced inevitably with two types of candidates:

- **A safe pair of hands:** a tried and tested performer
- **A risk taker:** who will test the boundaries and help create and manage change

Which of these two types of roles is the organisation advertising the position and which is your proven style or mode that you will push to demonstrate in the interview process?

Proving in your answers that you understand risk, can and have managed risk and that you view risk as an opportunity for the organisation and you in the role.

If based on your past roles and current expertise, your selection would be viewed as a risk, then you must have answers as to how the organisation would/could mitigate that risk to make your appointment worthwhile and beneficial.

Your answers would involve strategies and comments like:

- retention of current expertise and skills in a transition period.
- development of formal risk management and risk mitigation arrangements with senior management and the board.
- develop and explain your first 100 days in the job program: clearly demonstrate that your risk position and approach will be moderated until you are well into the role, reassuring no hasty risk decisions would occur from Day 1.

Understanding who your predecessor was and if and why they moved on or were moved on will help you understand if the 'safe hands' or 'risk taker' is envisaged for this position going forward – your research for this position will better inform you of this and then you can structure your credentials and interview answers accordingly.

The employer and candidate should aim to be matched using a RISK PROFILE to avoid unnecessary inappropriate recruitment hire. The employer should specifically address risk criteria before the recruitment and selection process begins.

Risk is important for all parties. As a candidate do your due diligence to assess any current or outstanding legal issues of the organisation that may result in the organisation collapse, closure or bad reputation, thus transferring via your CV.

Matching You and The Organisation

Reflecting on the MATCH, of you and the organisation ... In all of the emotion and excitement of applying for this new position and if a new employer, it is critical to assess the MATCH of you and this organisation;

- Does their culture, philosophies, style, ethics, loyalty, training, career/ succession planning, promotability etc match yours?

- Would taking this role best move you to where you want to head in your career and personal development?

- Is the industry and the size of the organisation in alignment with your career roadmap?

As some point amongst the enthusiasm and interview pressure, you must step back and assess whether there is a cultural and personal fit that will ensure that this new role will work for you and the organisation.

We see it so often that too much effort is expended in the hype and effort to win the job and not enough on whether this job is the right job for your ultimate career journey and destination.

Remember that accepting a position that proves unsuitable or troublesome or creates brand damage will set your career journey back at least one and probably two years whilst creating a hole in your CV that you will be forever explaining.

2.4 Negotiation

50. Offer Negotiations: Negotiating Your New Package

CONGRATULATIONS! You won the hard influencing stage of the job and received your offer. The offer needs scrutiny especially the more senior you are. Negotiation stage is the next step to securing your talent in this wonderful organisation.

How do you negotiate a new job offer and package to your advantage?

No matter how badly you want this job, they are rarely offered to you completely on your ideal terms. Following a successful interview, a job offer may be up your prospective employers sleeve, so what do you do when the package is not exactly what you expected? They will start low and want to negotiate.

Your choices are:
1. ACCEPT the position on their terms;
2. NEGOTIATE the offer with the aim of a better bigger deal and accepting;
3. or you may DECLINE.

The steps for job offer negotiations and tips to help you get the most out of your next big role:

- **It starts with the salary talk.** Essentially, negotiating a job offer begins just after the interview process and the selection announcement when the discussion of salary expectation takes place. At this beginning stage, you are already letting your prospective employer know what you think you're worth, so always go into this discussion having researched current industry salaries, *refer prior chapter Section 2- When to Discuss Salary.* That way, when you hopefully receive a reasonably remunerated job offer, you'll know whether it's realistic and reasonable, industry comparable and what your credentials deserve for the position. The next chapter, the **Jack Chapman** [9] **Salary Negotiation** method may provide you further techniques.

- **What to do when you receive the formal offer.** When considering a job offer, it's easy to get caught up in the excitement and just accept on the spot, however it's important to let your prospective employer know that you need some time before giving an answer. You need to evaluate the t's & c's and discuss with your partner and/or mentor to then confirm your decision within 24/48 hours.

- **Evaluating the job offer.** Even if you want the job, make sure you take into account the entire compensation package, not just the salary. While remuneration is important, you may feel that certain benefits and perks outweigh a lower salary. Before you make the decision to accept the position, consider how the position will affect your daily life including travel time, work hours, company culture and other commitments. And other benefits such as super, family leave, overseas travel, children's education support, relocation payments, if relevant, etc.

- **Evaluating the job offer from a big brand name.** Temptation to accept a reduced salary for the trade-off of a big brand name on your CV, needs to be evaluated without the excitement of the initial emotion. Perform a cost benefit analysis considering also the compensation package items.

- **When you decide to negotiate.** After a thorough evaluation you've decided that you'd like to negotiate a better offer. Before asking for higher pay or more benefits, be sure to politely thank your prospective employer for the offer and express your excitement about the position.

When raising a counter-offer, be aware that your expectations may not be fulfilled. Remember, negotiations are two-way. Showing that you're willing to compromise will stand you in better stead for the future working with this company. If you're stubborn or intransient, the employer might just offer it to someone else and you lose out. This is your judgement call. If proceeding to negotiate you may wish a plan c, whereby you could consider suggesting a larger bonus or increase at year one of employ if your plan b counter-offer was knocked down and you are adamant your worth in the market is greater.

Knowing who has the ultimate authority to approve your package/remuneration and knowing as much as you can find out about executive bonus' paid to other executives in the organisation will help you tremendously during this negotiation stage.

- **When you decide to accept.** If you've accepted a job over the phone, it's a good idea to write a job acceptance email or letter to confirm the details of employment and to formally accept it. This is your insurance policy

Your email or letter should be addressed to the person who offered you the position and include:

- An expression of appreciation for the opportunity
- Your written acceptance of the job offer
- Basic terms of employment, based on your phone discussion (salary, benefits, bonuses, working conditions etc.)
- The starting date of employment
- Duration of any probation period and period of notice

- **When you decide to decline.** Similarly, when declining a job offer, you should write a polite email or letter that is brief and to the point, and which avoids giving any specific reasons for your decline. You may feel the pay was not enough to make ends meet, or the hours would have driven you into the ground, but for the sake of parting on good terms, do not mention it.

51. The Jack Chapman Salary Negotiation Method

Was referred to as "The best guide to salary negotiation I've found is ***Negotiating Your Salary: How to Make $1000 a Minute.***" In it, career coach Jack Chapman [9] offers five rules for negotiating your salary:

1. **Postpone salary negotiations until you're offered the job.** Let your potential employer decide whether you're the right candidate, and then talk about money.
2. **Let the other side make the first offer.** As in the Smith-Wenkle Method, your goal is to allow the employer to suggest a salary. Lots of people find it awkward to evade direct questions about salary history and expectations: but you must not.
3. **When you hear the offer, repeat the number — and then stop talking.** Chapman calls this *"the flinch"*. "The most likely outcome of this silence is a raise," he says. This technique buys you some time to think while putting pressure on the employer. Often, they will come back with a higher offer – but you must play the silence card.

4. **Counter the offer with a researched response.** Your counter-offer should be based on what you know about yourself, the market, and the company. This is why it's vital to do some research before the salary interview so that you know a reasonable salary range for your position and for yourself: especially what the staff above and below you are earning.

5. **Clinch the deal — then deal some more.** Your last step is to lock in the offer, then negotiate additional benefits, such as extra holiday days or a company car or finance assistance with further professional studies. This is like agreeing on the price of a car before you negotiate the value of your trade-in, and it's a great way to get a better compensation package.

Most hiring managers don't automatically try to low-ball salary offers, but they will usually start with an amount that is lower than what they are willing to pay, because they assume the candidate will try to negotiate upward. Negotiation is a skill you can hone, but it's up to you to get what you want and what you deserve.

52. Negotiating Executive Performance Contracts

Negotiating Performance Contracts including KPIs and Bonuses at Risk

For most senior executive employment contracts there will be a base salary and then a performance bonus which will be "at risk" depending on the performance of the employee according to some agreed KPI based performance assessment scheme or model.

These 'At Risk' Pay for Performance contract provisions are structured to top up a base salary which is assured with additional consideration such as:

- Business and revenue growth development
- Profitability improvement
- Market value improvement
- Brand recognition and vale added
- Social, ethical and community recognition
- Staff morale and cultural fit engagement
- Customer satisfaction engagement.

These Executive Performance Contracts can be very lucrative to the new executive, if structured favourably and are not overly ambitious or aggressive. However, they can seriously affect morale, motivation and executive behaviour if set too tough and are not achievable or create the wrong or counter-productive actions by Executives that adversely affect the organisation.

Selection of the right and positively reinforcing KPI's is crucial and critical to the success of these Executive [AT RISK] Performance Schemes.

Further packages of Employee Share Schemes [ESS] are not only subject to your achievement of KPIs, but the ramifications of being taxed on up-front schemes that you have received, but not yet exercised a sale, must be considered as to their true net worth. On the positive side, for an organisation that you see you can add value to, and easily drive high performance growth, ESS might be a good option.

Also worthy of consideration is the voting rights received with the ESS offer, if any, in addition to the discount given, timing of receipt and ratio holding that may test the eligibility for taxation concessions. In some countries ESS is simple however in Australia it is more complex.

The difficulty for you as a candidate is determining the likelihood of achieving the targeted benchmarks – that they are realistic and have been honoured and paid in the past.

This part of the negotiation and offer acceptance takes time, that is well worth your attention.

53. Job Probation Periods - for the Employer and Employee

Most job offers have a probation period attached, to protect the employer if they find they have made a mistake in the selection and/or there is lack of compatibility between the employer and employee. This difficult situation is further compounded by candidates who inflated their experience, to having been in the role for three months, showing their true experience.

You must decide if you will accept an offer of employment, subject to a probationary period. Do you leave a well-paid and secure position for one where it is probationary and not secure and subject to a period of reviewable probation?

The bottom line? Don't necessarily rule out probationary employment, it's common practice, but be aware of the potential risks:

- If you're hired on a probationary basis, ask how you will be evaluated and what happens when your probation period ends. Ask if others have worked or are working on probation and what happened to them upon probation expiry.

- Discuss pay and remuneration up front once you are offered the position. Understand if you will be paid less than the full-time rate while on probation and whether you will get other benefits.

- Know your rights. Most probationary workers have very few. Consult a recruitment lawyer to understand your legal rights and your rights between full-time and contract workers and the probation period offering.

Probation Periods works both ways but can be a little controversial. The employee may get a start that they otherwise would not have got. The existence of a probationary period just tipped the employer to say OK we will give you a go and see how you fare and your performance. That is a positive.

Employers can test out the new employee, see the skills and talents and deficiencies and quirks and yet still not have a long-term legal commitment. However, the cost to recruit executives, managers and directors tends to outweigh negative probationary periods. Our message to you is once you are comfortable with answers received re the period, do your best as you would do otherwise.

If you are not satisfied with the probationary period, you can always try to negotiate to decrease it, reminding the recruiter that it is you who will be sacrificing a current stable role to join this employer and as such you will perform your very best.

54. Your Acceptance Letter

STAY or GO? You won the contest.

They recognised your capabilities and the contribution you can make and they want you on their team …

CONGRATULATIONS!

Most candidates who win receive a phone call to tell you that you won and the formal offer is in the mail or on an email.

Excitedly you recognise that you will have a **BIG YEAR** in front of you and your First 100 Days in the Job will be critical and is about to start. You must manage your exit from your existing employer who presumably will be sad to lose you.

What if your existing employer ups the ante and offers you more to stay? You need to be prepared for this option or situation and understand what your position will be should this eventuate. You must make a decision to then progress with one line of employment ONLY.

How do you **ACCEPT** their offer of the new job and **NEGOTIATE** your package? What if there are significant differences in your and their view of the value of the position and **YOUR WORTH** to the new organisation?

If you decide to move on, it is these steps in order that we suggest you follow:

1. It is time to negotiate your future package
2. Receive confirmation to agreed negotiated package
3. Forward your Acceptance Letter.

It is now common place to have Performance Contracts which have significant 'Pay for Performance" or "At Risk" payments which can masque the real salary package being offered: be prepared for these as you are leaving a steady known package for a potentially significantly lower guaranteed salary but with significant upside potential for performance [however measured].

2.5 Accept

Here are some suggested comments and initiatives for your ACCEPTANCE LETTER:

- Accept graciously

- Suggest your agreed and guaranteed commencement date

- Set a benchmark for remuneration and employment conditions [eg. Your governance or masters course or your bonus methodology]

- Include the negotiated package version or date

- If you have an in-place holiday booking or some other commitment which really cannot be avoided, then specify it up front and suggest how this can be accommodated and managed.

Next, we show you a sample job offer acceptance letter, Figure 13 page 129 that you can tailor and use.

Sample Job Offer Acceptance Letter

Your Name   )
Your Address   )
Your City, State, Post Code   )
Your Phone Number   )
Your Email   )
Date

HR or direct report Name   )
Their Title, eg CEO   )
Organisation name   )
Address   )
City, State, Post Code   )

Dear ....

Thank you for offering me the position of .... with ...*(name of new organisation)*.... I am pleased to accept this offer and look forward to starting employment with your company on ...*(date)*....

As we discussed, my starting salary will be $240 000 plus superannuation and health and life insurance benefits will be provided after 60 days of employment. The bonus and employee share scheme that have been amended per our final agreed version 3, is also attached.

Thank you again for giving me this wonderful opportunity. I am eager to join your team and make a positive contribution to the company.

If there is any further information or paperwork you need me to complete, please let me know and I will arrange it as soon as possible.

Sincerely,

(Your signature)

...*(name)*...

Figure 13: Sample Job Offer Acceptance Letter

2.5 Accept

Ethical responsibilities when accepting a job offer

Your acceptance of a job offer is binding so it is important not to accept the offer until you are sure of your decision. Backing out after you have accepted the position is considered highly unethical and will become public knowledge very quickly.

Reneging on an accepted offer will not be considered 'good form' and those you have wronged may make a call to your current employer to advise of such.

Where you have more than one offer and also that of your existing employer, be honest as you can only keep them waiting for so long, as you negotiate the best deal and make a decision with one that is accepted. Always notify the others as soon as possible. There is a saying, it only takes six degrees of separation for your secrets to be unearthed.

55. Giving Notice Graciously

Great you won! And now you have decided to move on. You took your experience and reputation and outbid the strong field to be the preferred candidate and you accepted and negotiated your future position and direction. That feels good.

Now you need to exit your existing position and organisation with grace and with your reputation and credibility intact.

The critical point - you do not have to give reasons for resigning and moving on or to disclose your future directions or employer but probably most misunderstood information in this disclosure will appease any contentious issues about the reasons for resignation or any future roles which may be seen as conflicting with your existing employer.

Should you have been at your current position for a considerable time and built up a strong brand and rapport and service period, it will come as a shock and many will want to know why your decision to move on.

How you handle this disclosure and the exit period will be a **MEASURE OF YOUR SUCCESS** as a transition manager, and **HOW YOU WILL BE REMEMBERED** as an ex.

There is a very apt saying, 'don't burn all your bridges' - staying loyal to your past and your heritage is important and will be a reference point should your current move not prove as successful as you would have hoped and you are again in the market for a job and your **last most successful reference is with this past employer.** Yes, you want this referee for your next role after this newest one.

Notice Period

You need to negotiate your Notice Period and/or work-out period and this will be a very political situation.

There is a saying, 'the grass is not always greener on the other side'. So tread carefully. You may be back in the employment market sooner than you think or wish. In some instances, your replacement may not work out and your prior employer may ask you to return, offer a better package and if you are not happy in your new role, you may just take them up on this.

You should have organised a media or internal staff communication process informing your peers and immediate reports of your decision to move on. How you spin the move and depart graciously is up to you, but be **GRACIOUS, PROFESSIONAL** and with **HUMILITY.**

Most importantly, your existing contract or performance agreement will inform you of your notice period which you should expect to be held to. This may change when your present employer learns of your departure. The big issue is whether, due to your past service and loyalty, you can **NEGOTIATE** a shorter NOTICE PERIOD or you will be kept to stay on for the FULL work out period.

If you are moving to an industry competitor or conflicting role, your existing board or management team may decide it is better to march you out that day. That is not a negative reflection on you, rather it is good risk management by your former employer. You need to at least plan and be ready for this possibility.

We see a number of executives who have extensive notice periods or restraint of employment conditions put on what is called "Garden Leave" as they work out their notice period. Should this occur, it is a legal restraint but does give you time to sort out your personal affairs, and recharge fully prepared to hit the ground running in that new position.

Once you have accepted the new job offer and resigned from your current position, you should *formally withdraw* from the job search market and notify all agents and potential employers of your decision and success.

Giving Formal Written Notice

A simple Resignation Letter is just that. You do not have to give reasons or inform your employer as to your new employer. Rather you can present as humble, gracious and warm, thanking them for past opportunities and give encouragement to management for the future of the organisation.

Informal, friendly and yet appreciative for your employ, this example of a notice of resignation is a typical Notice Period compliant letter of resignation and probably as informal as a formal letter of resignation should be.

Other choices of Letters of Resignation will be less chatty, more formal and direct.

The following page exhibits our Sample Resignation Letter, Figure 14 on page 133.

Sample Resignation Letter

Your Name

Your address
Your email address

Dated ....
Att: .....(Manager)...
Organisation ....
Org. address...................

....

Dear ....

        NOTICE OF RESIGNATION: Your Name

Please accept this letter as my Notice of Resignation from my position as .... at ......*(location if your organisation has more than one)*.......................

In accordance with my employment contract, my last day of employment will be ....*(dated)*..... unless you wish otherwise.

I received an offer to serve as ...*(new role)*...... of an ASX 200 company(change to suit you), and after careful consideration, I realise that this opportunity is too exciting for me to decline.

It has been a pleasure working with you and your team over the last ...(number) ... years. Your organisation is poised for continued growth and I wish you much success with ...*(add a major project, merger or acquisition or deal)*...

I would like to help with the transition of my duties so that systems continue to function smoothly after my departure. I am available to help recruit and train my replacement, and I will make certain that all reporting and records are updated before my last day of work.

...*(first name of person whom you have written letter to)*..., thank you again for the opportunity to work for ...*(name of organisation)*. I wish you and your staff all the best and I look forward to staying in touch with you. You can email me anytime on my private email at ...*(your private email)*.... or call me on my mobile on ...*(your mobile number)* ..

Yours Sincerely,

 (your name)

Figure 14: Sample Resignation Letter

56. Cleaning Out Your Desk and Office

It is time to move on and leave your office, your desk and your files in the best order possible.

If there are corporate awards or other historical documents which reflect well on your service there, you may decide to take a copy, photocopy and bind them but leave them where they rightly and they legally belong.

Three issues that politically need to be addressed of who gets or owns:

1. Awards and Certificates for the organisation but with your name on them
2. Corporate Certificates or Awards
3. Your personal Reference Books library and other Manuals and workbooks   that you have developed during your time in the organisation.

Develop an agreement with your existing management or HR personnel as to what must stay and what you can take, or even copy. This discussion and decision will be determined by where your next employment position is, such as the competition.

Equally relevant for decision are the strategic plan formats, performance reports, spreadsheets and reporting formats and special project reports that you have developed and published for the organisation. Are you able to copy or duplicate for your private portfolio?

YOU MADE IT! Congratulations on your new accepted job offer … BUT … if you have not prepared a full 100 day calendar, you are not yet ready. Read On as we prepare you to step into day one of your new journey. You will be judged by your new employer during the crucial first 100 days in the job, where Performance matters.

Perform

SECTION 3 Perform

57. Success Rates

You WON the job from your award winning overall performance, including your CV and cover letter where your employer learned of your capabilities. Busily in your wardrobe you were selecting the first days impactful dress-to-impress attire to wear. Now you begin your new start, but how well you perform will be determined on how quickly you hit the ground learning upon arrival and how well prepared you are.

Statistics from various sources are generally agreed that at least 50% of new chief executives or finance executives appointed fail within the first 18 months on the job and up to 10% fail spectacularly. Why?

Watkins M. "The First 90 Days" [34]: Boston: Harvard Business School Publishing, 2013 stated "Over 50% of new leaders fail to meet or exceed expectations within the first 18 months of their assignment because they fail to successfully leverage their first three months on the job." What is the strong message: the First 100 Days – in the Job – after the Precursor 100 Days Interview, CV, portfolio – IS CRITICAL.

We have been taking you through how to win that great CxO position: but the last thing you want is to win the role and then fail within 18 months or more to fail spectacularly.

We need to learn more about why these obviously very talented and revered Executives [selected from a tough team of aspirants] fail in the new job and how companies and appointees can stop or avert this failure before it begins.

The statistics are alarming and the disruption to the organisation in addition to the personal and corporate brand damage, with added costs of re-recruitment and morale are such, that we must get it right first time and avoid this recruitment disaster.

Research by the Corporate Executive Board [32] conducting over 2,600 in-depth qualitative interviews with Fortune 1000 executives, found four common traps that well-intended executives in a new job unwittingly step into, and hence why they failed.

Interesting results and the name catching terms say it all, as below:

1. The Mandate Bait
2. Stakeholder Blindness
3. Altitude Distortions
4. Power Failure

Top Four reasons for Failure:

1. The Mandate Bait

Many newly appointed executives arrive with a perceived mandate to repeat their past successes such as; did it before somewhere, so can do it again; just watch me and follow me. Rather than looking realistically at the current situation and corporate culture, these executives reach back to their bag of tricks that 'worked before' and begin slapping those formulas on the new environment without contextualisation. Rejection sets in as the leader's diagnosis turns into an indictment of the culture inadequacies.

The organisation more firmly resists and begins resenting the executive's ignorance of what will and won't work. To avoid this trap requires deep knowledge of context, and an ability to read it quickly, adapt to it and show a sense of humility and respect for the organisation they now lead up, rather than their past successes elsewhere.

You should adopt a new slogan such as "Hit the ground learning, not running." Show humility and empathy, not arrogance and self-centered blindness. You are a leader of choices NOT the ultimate decision maker.

2. Stakeholder blindness

As the new incumbent, you will be in deep relationships with new peers, former bosses, new direct reports, sometimes previous peers, and new bosses who are the most critical at the highest levels of the organisation.

Yet there may be a personality problem; the successful candidate won and wants to exert their authority and self-directed management style; they say they are a powerful individual and distinguish themselves through individualism; they painfully underestimate how much they need others when they get to the top. It can't always be "My way or the highway".

Forming mutual partnerships with those who most hold the keys to your success and whose success you can influence, is critical. You must understand who all these stakeholders are and how to respect and engage with them. Stakeholder blindness will blindside you and potentially knock you over.

3. Altitude distortion

Holding the title of the new big boss needs to be handled with care. How your messages are sent and received by others, and how messages arrive to you, changes dramatically when you near the organisation's top.

Assume figuratively that you have a megaphone strapped to you 24/7, and everything you say and do is amplified and open to interpretation, which may be far from your intentions. Similarly, information you get is now sifted. People syphon data and tell you what they think you want to hear, unfortunately.

It is now different at the top and you may not get the appropriate and most perceptive information to make proper management decisions.

To counter this situation, executives revert to a different and possibly more protective or authoritarian management style, which was not how or why you were appointed to the position as a senior executive.

That bold leadership style that the Interview Committee saw and liked, transitions to a very different style that is now perceived as an autocratic and unbending management style that is not working. You now seem to be in conflict and your management style is the cause of this conflict and a destructive corporate culture that has developed under your time at the top.

Simply, you have proven that you could not lead and it is too great a stretch for you and your management style, personality and capabilities to be successful in the job.

4. Power failure

Most executives struggle with the larger sphere of positional, informational, and relational power afforded them by bigger jobs.

For Executives stepping up to a bigger position, they are so fearful of wielding power that they avoid using it, especially when the risks seem high. Indecisiveness, accommodating mediocre performance, co-dependent relationships with others to hide behind, and irresponsible use of confidential information are just some of the symptoms of a leader who has abdicated their power. They are fearful to make decisions, especially the big ones and hence are judged to be ineffectual and lose the respect of those who appointed them with great anticipation and acclaim. This approach is a fast road to conflict and disenchantment with the board and other senior management.

When the rumour mill starts and the confidential reports start to leak like a sieve, the newly appointed is on a slippery slide out the door. Self-protection, not self-service, is often the driver behind such fearful leaders and it was not what they promised to deliver.

According to a recent study by the Centre for Creative Leadership, nearly 40 percent of new chief executives fail outright within their first 18 months on the job, and even more of them fail to live up to the expectations of those who hired them. This could only be the result of a flawed process of leadership hiring, wrong choice and then failure of on-going support for the successful appointee.

Let's face it, great organisations are not set up to support their leaders well, nor are they clear about expectations of the acceptable behaviours and actions related to that new leadership role. It is more like, 'well the winner won so let's let them manage the situation'. We see this model fail so many times, and stats report 50% of the time.

Hewertson, author of **"Lead Like It Matters … Because It Does"** (McGraw-Hill, 2014) [5] named five major reasons that new leaders are unable to perform successfully in the new job:

1. **Over or under-confidence**. Most new recruits, whether they're in a leadership position or not, know what they'd like to see in a boss. They often feel confident that they could rise to the challenge and become that boss if they had to. When it comes time to act, though, this can be a little more difficult than expected.

   Once in the new role, however, people often forget what they know and get a bit full of themselves, or are so unsure of themselves, they become ineffective and purposeless.

2. **Approaching leadership with the wrong expectations**. It's one thing to be a team member, it's another to lead those team members. Leaders are frequently unprepared to deal with the realities of managing a group, so they either ignore problems that arise or react poorly to them.

   "Rarely do new leaders have a clue about what they are really getting into," Hewertson said. "For many of them, it's not what they expected, or had the desire or competencies to do well."

3. **Lack of training in the right skill set**. You need many different competencies to master the discipline of leadership. Managers must learn how to lead well, and the skills and motivations needed to lead may be the opposite of those needed to be an individual contributor. It's no longer about just you: You only succeed when your people succeed, and many new leaders don't make this shift gracefully. Instead of focusing on tasks, leaders need to support the other people doing the tasks, so those people are successful and contribute.

4. **Ignoring the need to build relationships**. Leading is all about relationships; growing trust, building teams and utilizing excellent interpersonal skills. Leaders pay a high price for ignoring the important process of building healthy relationships. To create these relationships, leaders need to pay attention to their teams, keep learning and never assume anything.

5. **Failure to listen**. Leaders tend to think they have or need to act like they have all the answers, they don't have all the answers, and they shouldn't act like it. Hewertson said. "Listening is not a strong suit for many new leaders, and too often they jump in quickly rather than listening, learning and building on what they see."

In her book, Hewertson described four categories of skills that leaders must master to succeed:
- personal mastery (self-awareness)
- interpersonal (communication skills)
- team (harnessing group dynamics)
- culture/systems (organisational assessment).

Of these four "core tenets" of leadership, personal mastery is the one leaders need to focus on first and foremost in order to avoid becoming a statistic of leadership failure.

"Without first being self-aware of one's strengths and weaknesses, it's very difficult to manage one's own behaviours, or to be aware of others or to manage relationships effectively," Hewertson said. "It's essential to know your own purpose, values and vision, [and] how you are perceived by others, including what's working and what's not working for you. Then you can take that knowledge and apply it to gain and enhance the skills needed to be a highly effective leader."

The fact that up to 50 % of executives fail during their first 18 months is a disaster, calamity and regrettable. But why is it so high?

There can only be one reason they fail? It's not because of technical incompetence. It is the wrong executive - wrong job. In other words, the shoe did not fit yet they tried to wear it anyway.

It seems obvious that the one significant way you can avoid becoming another member of the 50% Failure Club is to become sufficiently AWARE OF YOURSELF: your **strengths**, **limitations** and **passions** and how you **relate and respect people**.

Many executives, however, suffer from the delusion that they are multi-talented, versatile and highly adaptable, which translates into the management mantra - I can do anything I put my mind to. Management gurus from Peter Drucker to Jim Collins to Marcus Buckingham will tell you otherwise and from our experience of coaching and working with hundreds of executive, we agree.

Your old approach simply may not work in the new organisation: watch, look, learn and adapt: a sensible management approach for the new leader.

If you want to be successful - "Know thyself." Socrates had it right. So no pre-described leadership or management model and adapt as you go … quickly and decisively.

58. Transition Action Plan

At your recruitment interview you discussed your FIRST 100 DAYS in The Job – you showed your thoughtfulness and preparedness that you knew you had to have such a plan and be prepared to implement it.

Now you are the **WINNER**, it is time to effect this plan and program with great aplomb and gusto and commitment.

You will already have prepared a One Pager on your style or orientation and then an Action Plan for the First 100 Days in the Job.

No doubt, you may have been appointed to a Probation Period of Three Months, so you need to be mindful that the clock has started ticking and you need to start kicking goals but in a reasoned and strategically planned manner.

If you do have a Probation Period then you need to clearly understand the Performance Criteria of how you will be assessed as being either successful or unsuccessful at the end of that First 100 Day period.

Let's detail a **SUCCESSFUL TRANSITION** into your new job.

That Successful Transition starts from when you accept the position and you enter into what is called "the job change and countdown process and period."

We start with the expectations of your new employ and the pressures you will face.

59. Pressures and Expectations

The WARNING: Leadership Consultancy FIRST 100 at www.First100.com says recent studies suggests that upwards of 40% of newly appointed leaders struggle to make an impact in their early period in the job. Is that because they were unprepared or could not step up to the job or there are other factors which inhibited their performance?

You don't want to become *another* of those statistics that did not make it past their first anniversary of their appointment as a CEO or CFO or CXO. **The First 100 Days**[17] will be a vital milestone and judgement point of your leadership capability to develop the trust of the organisation past your baptism of fire and achieve the capacity to stamp your mark and lead on.

The First 100 Days will be full of challenges:

- Time pressures, conflicting demands and an intense learning curve.
- A sense of being overwhelmed, putting out fires, minor issues and inability to get to the real strategic issues and priorities.
- Forging new stakeholder relationships and building new networks; you will be a new representative for the organisation and need for your authority to be recognised.
- Dealing with unfortunate legacy issues from your predecessor.
- Challenges in inheriting a team that may not be to your liking or resentful of your appointment, especially if there are other internal candidates for your job who may have missed out.
- Avoiding the early political or cultural gaffes.
- Getting the balance right between moving too quickly and moving too slowly.

Your **First 100 DAY FOCUS** should include three critical words:

- Strategy

- People

- Results

Know what they are and how you will impact and come to be judged on how you influence and manage these three vital aspects of your initial corporate management.

Get a very quick understanding of your businesses' organisation chart or Landscape Map and look for **KEY PLAYERS** or **INFLUENCERS** who may not be listed on that organisation chart or map. These are the important outliers who have not been brought into the camp but can and will have a critical impact on your success and ability to influence or change in your First 100 Days. Outliers may be the former Chair of the board; the founding patriarch; the corporate marketing or brand ambassador; your Senior Audit Partner; etc.

Writing your First 100 Day Plan BEFORE YOU START and updating it as you go is a very good plan and practice.

60. Leading CSR Role

Your role in the C-Suite should also include accountability for **Corporate Social Responsibility [CSR]** and you should establish this very early in your tenure, having discussed this at your interview for this role, and knowing this is an expectation.

CSR or as it was previously called TBL – Triple Bottom Line or Sustainability Reporting, is now critical to the success and long term future of your new employer.

The concept of a 'LICENSE TO OPERATE' is reaffirmed by the organisation being able to show or prove its sustainability credentials. In many cases, an organisation [especially the bigger Corporates] will not deal with smaller business unless they can prove and report on their own sustainability practices, such as packaging, recycling, waste, energy utilisation, employment practices, such as human trafficking and slavery, bonded labour, child exploitation, sex exploitation, diversity, affirmative actions, carbon emissions, community involvement, donations but to name a few. There are literally thousands of measures that can be requested.

The Candidate at interview must be able to describe how their previous team participated in and helped manage the performance and reporting of the organisation's **Sustainability Report** for both internal management and external reporting purposes. If your organisation was not of the capacity to afford such a large costly report, your awareness and informal measures of your CSR will be commanded.

61. External Specialisation Utilisation

We previously recommended that the newly appointed Executive seek the support of a seasoned business coach or mentor to help guide and counsel them in the new role.

Other influential parties who are specialists and external/independent to the organisation are:

- External auditor and/or tax partner specialist
- Chair of Board sub-committees: FARM/CARM, Audit & Risk, Governance & Remuneration, Ethics Committee
- Former Organisation Directors
- HR Consultants
- Strategic Planning consultants with experience in the industry or the organisation.

Consider other formal professional industry bodies that you can join or gain accreditation from such as the AICD, AIM, CAANZ, CPA, AHRI, Governance Australia, ICAEW, WITSA, IIMP, etc.

62. Well researched and Informed

Will you make a **Winning Transition** to your new position and organisation?

The measure of success in taking on your new role asks: have you engaged with the organisation such that when you arrive on the first day, you are already accepted, anticipated and part of the perceived future of the organisation?

What a great result that would be. This will be a real measure of your success in winning the job and then being accepted into the role, having the authority to make a difference.

How do you make a difference in this new role as you transition?

FIRST IMPRESSIONS COUNT!

The attitude you adopt as the new person and leading the team, the communication protocols you establish, and the priorities you formulate and communicate will lay the groundwork for your success. Planning is key to your success and so to is engaging with the organisation BEFORE your first day on the job.

The saying, **'Start before you start'** is so apt. Being well informed, understanding, thoughtful, well researched and engaged before you start is what you are able to do.

You must read and know as much as is possible about your new company and the role, your team, your customers and your services and have considered and digested many of the following:

- Annual reports for at least past three years
- Industry News Reports
- Research papers affecting or reviewing the industry and your new employer
- Know the website backwards – understand its customer contact model
- Products and services offered
- Social Media platforms used
- Locations and distribution networks
- Read all the board and committee papers for the last 12 months [if available to you as a new C-Suite member]
- Assess all the board's major issues and strategic directions and options
- AND THEN prepare your own Landscape Map [also called a Mind Map] that depicts all the issues, challenges, directions, pressures, themes, specialties, and operations etc. for the business. This is a critical document which you will update during your FIRST 100 Days: what new messages or facts have you learnt? what new issues have emerged? what new pressures or issues to contend with? Also what suspicions have been confirmed?

The First 100 Days in the Job is and will be considered as an early 'PULSE CHECK' on your selection and leadership performance.

You won so now prove it.

Meet your peers before you commence
Coffees and informal meetings before you start will assist you to understand the issues and areas on focus with all the 'right' people

Having completed as much research and familiarisation as you can before your first day on the job. Now you must turn up at the office, park the car and walk into the premises and presumably your office.

Today is all about absorbing as much information as you can, so use the 90/10 Rule: your goal is to listen 90% of the time and talk 10% of the time: with most of that 10% should be asking questions. Let's say that again ... **ASK QUESTIONS.**

Take lots of notes of new information and varying views and suggestions. It is important to jot down names, views, suggestions and something memorable about your first interaction with each person. This is a BIG message.

Who likes to go skiing, who is a football tragic and of what code, who is a wine fanatic, who is a senior at their local church, who is doing a post graduate course, who is away from home and their family for an extraordinary period due to your company's work commitments, etc., etc., etc.

What did you learn or now better appreciate from each person you met today?

Your next round of meetings will be with your subordinates or immediate reports and they will be as important as that initial interview with those who awarded you the job.

Some of these immediate reports may have applied for your role but missed out, so you need to be particularly sensitive to this situation. Get good intell on any job losses, their values, views and intentions.

You will meet so many people today and make a lasting impression – positive and negative. Your presence will spread like wildfire across the organisation, prior to you meeting everyone. It is a huge day. Be warm, be natural, be yourself and be symbolic, but most importantly, you want to learn and the make reasoned decisions.

Be PREPARED for your first day and BRING your RESEARCH and FINDINGS:

- Organisation chart
- Your themes and areas of focus
- Know what you intend to say at that first meeting with:
  - Senior Staff
  - All staff below immediate reports
  - Customers
  - Suppliers
  - Board members
  - Community Groups
  - Stakeholder Groups

You will meet so many people all at once, in your first day, first weeks and month.

How do you remember their names? Here are two hints that will help you.

1. **Ask for their business card** – pause and note the name and official position. All these cards will look alike but you can jot down a message on the back to remember or note something special about the person or their role. For example – just sold $1 million project or likes a certain football team. An effective way to associate with a staff member is to enquire as to a special project that they are working on at the moment to benefit the organisation: e.g. a Corporate Social Responsibility [CSR] project or the upcoming Group Conference.

2. **A technique to remember a person's name** when introduced to them is to say their name back to them and repeat it in the conversation at least five times: Jim, hi Jim, nice to have you working with us Jim, Jim what are your major issues, Jim really great talking to you Jim. Then try a word association: Jim is a fitness fanatic as he is always in the gym. Look at Jim at the Gym and see a fit person.

FEEL CONFIDENT

You should have already worked out what your 'brand' represents: why did you get the job and what does your immediate superior [Board or CEO] want or expect of you. This will shape your initial messages and demeanour.

Meeting the Boss:

One of your most important meetings in the C-Suite is with your immediate superior, your boss. The other important meeting is with board members.

Obviously your first handshake and half hour discussion with your new boss will be critical. Will this meeting be a closed door or open door discussion? This provides a strong message.

Will you take pen and paper to take notes [some might say instructions]? Do you scribble down notes on your IPAD or Post-It notes? How do you emerge from this meeting, smiling or serious and who and what do you do next?

You really are now well into your **FIRST 100 DAYS IN THE JOB**!

64. First Week on the Job

You worked through your FIRST DAY. Time now to assess and plan your FIRST WEEK. Who do you talk to in this first week? Obviously:

- Your new boss / bosses – any influencers or board members
- Your immediate staff / reports
- Your business support managers
- Any Customers proving or providing special relationships
- Any Suppliers of goods, services, technology, leads and introductions

If not by the end of the first day, then absolutely by the end of the first week you must have had a meeting with all key players across the business. This will be upwards of twenty staff or external parties and these persons will be both internal and external to the business and within your responsibility centre.

Drawing a **LANDSCAPE MAP** [otherwise called a MindMap] is a great way to document and understand the 'lay of the land'. It helps you to sort the important relationships and connections that exist to steer your influence into the organisation, management team, board relationships and make your mark in the business.

Your landscape map should list name, position, likes of authority and/or communications and reflect their effect on your success in this new position. If they are an **INFLUENCER**, you want them to know that you recognise and regard their opinion.

A WORD OF WARNING: Beware of disregarding or disrespecting anyone in the management team and / or at the Board of Directors. Understand their particular views on Corporate Governance and how you serve or support those views. Remember all C-Suite and management are to serve the Board and Shareholders.

Your goal in this first week is to establish relationships and understand those that exist, to enable you to work effectively with the team as you develop your role's objectives that require your urgent attention, and begin to set those key targets.

Critical External Stakeholder Engagement

By the end of the first week, you need to have assessed and made arrangements to meet with all of the important external stakeholders of the business, such that those meetings will be finalised within your first month on the job.

You surely will have offended your external stakeholders if they know you have been appointed, you are on the job and you have not made contact or arranged a future appointment with them by the end of your first week on the job.

This involves specific **PLANNING** and **SCHEDULING** reliant upon you understanding *who is important*. Your objective in these meetings is to listen, liaise, understand their issues and talk of your new organisation's direction and performance under your control.

Include joint venture partners or important supply chain partners who will be looking anxiously for your style, focus and your direction which will have an impact on them.

3.2 First 30 Days

Community groups, employment associations, and unions [if relevant], industry bodies, sponsors or marketing partners or associates etc., will comprise your list of influencers.

Please refer to Figure 15 on page 159 for your Convocation model and diagram.

65. End of Week Two

By the end of Week Two, you should have formed a view of the issues, challenges, personalities, directions, impediments etc. that will or are SHAPING YOUR ROLE and ability to contribute and to make a difference in the new position. You will be assessing how you will tackle your new role and what management approaches best suit you and your new employer.

You will have reviewed the strategic plan in place and applied this against your new learnings of how well it is being achieved with respect to your role and start the process to determine if adjustments need to be made in order to achieve the strategic plan.

Talk to your Predecessor?
Now for a touchy subject BUT one that MUST be broached.

Do you have access to and should you talk to or seek guidance from your predecessor – if they are available to you?

In some circumstances this will be easy and advisable as your predecessor has moved upwards providing you opportunity as a useful counsel with direction and support to help ease you into this role. Remembering all the while that you have your own style and leadership in the role.

In other circumstances, the previous incumbent may not be available or held in good regard or stead by current management and the Board, so the issue of seeking advice or counsel may be a more difficult one. In such circumstances your inherited lower level staff may be a better place to enquire and learn about past issues and directions, past conflicts or past poor relations with other senior management resulting in that persons' demise or removal.

You want to know what went wrong and what lessons can be learnt. Discovering what actions your predecessor took that were deemed as unpopular and possibly caused their demise, are those you wish to assess quickly, avoid repeating and turnaround.

66. End of The First Month

A month has past and no doubt quickly. It is time for you to reflect, assess and survey your current and future troops, customers, the marketplace, processes, reports, board conduct, executive teams collegiality, and any potential serious challenges, and great business opportunities etc.

By the end of the first month in the job, you can and should form a **'State of the Nation' assessment [SON]** of the business and build this into a presentation which you can deliver as needed. It would probably be 3-4 pages with slides, which you can whip out to lead a discussion on where the organisation has come from, what's working and what still needs further attention and your determined focus. Tell them all about your vision and immediate steps or areas of focus and how you need their help and input: how **TEAMS** work, **T**ogether **E**ach **A**ccomplishes **M**ore.

Being asked 'What is your assessment so far of the organisation and its issues and future directions' will be asked so be prepared. Have a professional looking presentation ready, perhaps a **SWOT** refer [Appendix A4] or your own tool that will see you well positioned to respond, gaining invaluable respect. Whichever tool you use, be sure to use your organisation's templates and logos if they exist.

You may have been invited to attend a board meeting or be allocated a board position such as Secretary or Director. If there are sub-committees it would be advisable that you monitor and enquire of positions available. You have now been through a month end close and 'Results' presentation and met all influential persons in the business, ready to start to influence, direct and lead future progress.

There are many tools and techniques to suit specific C-Suite roles and we have included a few of these tools you will need initially in Section 4 subject to the role at hand and a few in the Appendix.

Optional '**DISCOVERY SURVEY**'

After a month, you can conduct a discovery survey with your subordinates and peers to understand and calibrate against your initial thoughts of what the staff feel are the organisations':

- Strengths
- Weaknesses
- Achievements to date
- Challenges
- Priorities – present and in future
- Value proposition and value deliverables

The title of this Survey is important. You wish to DISCOVER aspects [messages, relationships, values, specialities, deficiencies etc.] that you don't know or did not appreciate but now want them to be explicitly discussed and considered for future actions.

The Discovery Survey says a lot about your **management and executive style**, that when not only reading the results of the survey, you create a **Discovery Action Plan** to ensure you address and action both the negatives and positives.

The Discovery Survey sends the message: YOU ARE HERE AND YOU ARE LISTENING.

Success in your first 100 days requires **Stakeholder Engagement** and **Stakeholder Management**, involving:

- Managing the various stakeholder expectations and stakeholder contact
- Supporting the Board: understanding their Big issues to receive their support and accreditation and involvement
- Partnering with Family Members [if a family business]
- Driving the CEO's vision [unless you are the new CEO]
- Leading Business Unit Managers reporting to you directly and indirectly.

We know that you won the recruitment exercise and now you are kicking goals in your First 100 Days, but a word of advice. You should not consider yourself beyond learning and gaining insight from another set of eyes and thoughts as you progress your career in new directions in this new role.

Do not be afraid to seek help from a trusted and wise mentor or coach who can help you through the maze of your first year in the job. Wise counsel and a sounding board is always a good investment in time and reflection as you adapt to this new position and organisation; or potentially new industry or marketplace. Be a sponge and access all available information and industry trends.

Engaging with Your Inherited Team
Now to your management style as you meet and greet and work with your key personnel and team.

You get to meet and synergise with and assess your TEAM.

You are a team player and manage as a team leader: you need to quickly meet with and assess the capability of your team: understand any deficiencies and develop an action plan to compliment any resource requirements. Or manage out if one or two existing and inherited personnel / immediate reports are not suitable or not collegiate for moving forward positively and constructively.

3.3 First 100 Days

It is certainly our experience that up to 20% of these existing and inherited staff will not be suitable for your future directions and team roles.

You will have to perform some serious personnel suitability reviews and take some serious decisions on who stays and who goes: but that is management and is to be expected.

We like the idea of a **Personnel Skills Audit** (as recommended by Harvard Business Review [HBR] – see this in later section.

A few generic questions that as a senior manager, you can ask and discuss with your team and especially your immediate reports:

- What is your role, what do you do and what is your contribution to the organisation and our department?
- How could we do it better, if we had the facilities or approval to change what we do?
- What do you consider are the best and worst aspects of our performance as an organisation or team?
- What do you think we should change immediately to improve our performance or working conditions or service delivery?
- What do you think should be my priorities as CxO in the first 100 Days in The Job?
- What help, guidance, resources, training, direct input do you need or I can approve to help your team perform your role better?

68. Strategic Planning Involvement and Direction

It is very important as a senior manager or executive that you stamp your mark and this means having significant involvement and direction in the **Strategic Planning Processes**, **Formulation and Direction** for the organisation.

A strategic plan should already exist in addition to a mission statement, value proposition statement and a series of strategic projects for the business. You would have learnt and assessed their relevance and achievability as part of your preparation for the initial interviews and forming your views of the appropriate way forward for the business.

In these initial formative weeks, you will be consciously assessing whether the in-place strategic plan is relevant, ambitious, achievable and/or how you can contribute to making it happen or whether it deserves a complete make-over with your future participation and tutorage.

You know about and can facilitate a Blue Ocean Strategy Workshop and that it is an important strategic positioning tool that needs to be conducted on behalf of your new organisation or conduct a facilitated LEGO® SERIOUS PLAY® Methodology[27] workshop that takes a different interactive pathway to work through solutions and strategically explore directions the organisation had or had not considered.

Whatever the workshop you choose, your strength to lead or take a prominent role with the development, the action plan and management of implementation, will hold you in high stead.

Considering any staff that may have missed out on your position and their group of friends within the organisation, is one to keep at the forefront of the way you approach during these first 100 days. Being involved in strategic positioning assessments and strategic / tactical planning is an essential focus and concrete contribution to your new organisation.

69. Innovation for Business Development

Innovation is key and as the new C-Suite, you must foster and support such innovation across the organisation as a culture within the whole organisation. The organisation needs to create and then measure and report innovation, new business development and the results and outcomes of innovation. It is a measurable goal and achievement for you to foster and support.

Business Growth and Development is invaluable in growing shareholder value and you need to encourage, facilitate and accommodate the development of new ideas and business opportunities. Growth is a strategic driver for future success in our competitive markets – stand still and you will go backwards and contract.

As the new Exec recruit, you should bring to the Executive team, a knowledge and practical working experience of **Blue Ocean Strategy** and the **SWOT 3x3 Strategic Action Model**.

These techniques can bring significant focus on new business directions and working on those projects and programs where you now assess the business has competitive advantage or must move to gain or implement a distinctive competency that differentiates it from its competitors. As Jack Trout wrote in his award winning book, **'Differentiate or Die!'**, [30] that if over time you do not differentiate your business and its business model to move to a differentiated offering, your business will be a Me Too and die.

Think about how you can help the business to DIFFERENTIATE its presence and you have a driving force in this new organisation or your new position to initiate this direction.

The Conundrum in your new role, will be... Do you GO EARLY AND MAKE YOUR MARK with a pre-established public and conscious strategy to bring about CHANGE ... or SHOW PATIENCE and LOOK and LISTEN and be more conservative in your response?

The Leadership Group counsels on the First 100 Days: "Senior Executives get to top positions because they are bright, decisive, talented and experienced and they should have a clear idea of what they are expected to deliver. But the First 100 Days are a surprisingly short time in which to make a mark and build those vital new relationships." We hear this sentiment expressed so often.

The Leadership Group approach to planning and coaching the new CEO during their First 100 Days starts and involves the following issues and approaches:

- Key stakeholder and relationship mapping [refer "Convocation Map" Figure 15 on page 159 – then action
- Winning people over – assess and address all interested parties
- Generating quick wins – and doing it
- Unravelling the politics – be politically aware and smart
- Defining priorities and focus creating the desired climate
- Focus on a Successful transition.

Complete your Convocation Map located in the Worksheet Section on p295 with major stakeholders and influencers relevant to your position.

CONVOCATION MAP

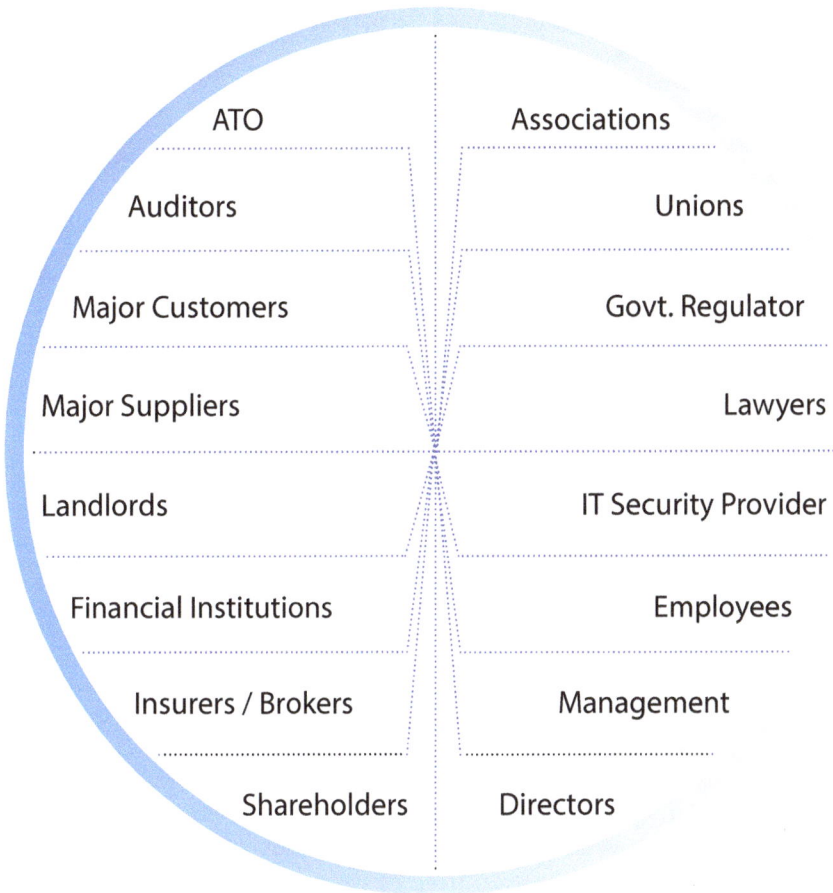

ATO   Associations

Auditors   Unions

Major Customers   Govt. Regulator

Major Suppliers   Lawyers

Landlords   IT Security Provider

Financial Institutions   Employees

Insurers / Brokers   Management

Shareholders   Directors

Figure 15: Convocation Map by a CFO

Paul Pressler [29] – CEO of THE GAP said *"My First 100 Days are all about listening and learning. The last thing you'll get from me is a grand vision in the First 100 Days. You need to **give yourself time to be a sponge**."* A nice sentiment.

Robert Hargrove in his book ***"Your First 100 Days in a New Executive Job"***[19] takes a more confrontational role to stamp your authority as a new chief executive. This is a much more aggressive but maybe risky approach that could get key players off side. Hargrove talks about a measure of leadership dynamism and a bell weather of leadership effectiveness with the key idea of *"to go for **'quick wins'** that establish a virtuous circle of increasing credibility and help avoid a vicious circle of decreasing credibility."*

He suggests four practical down to earth tips to immediately apply in your new leadership style:

1. Have a story ready for day one, as key stakeholders look for signals immediately; take symbolic action within 72 hours of arriving.

2. As you take control develop a 'teachable point of view'; this is a story of how you intend to win in this business.

3. Build a team of 'A' players; get the right people on the bus; assess the internals and get externals on the bus, get the wrong people OFF the bus.

4. Declare an Impossible Future that unites warring tribes.

You can see the conflicting and contrasting management approaches in the above discussions and approaches. These need to be seriously considered in the context of your organisation and your appointment. How will you play out the role in your new organisation and under the direction and support of the Board who just appointed you?

70. 'Walk A Mile in My Shoes'

As the new guy on the block, you want to get out and about and be seen, not just as the executive but as someone who wants to understand the business, its key drivers and how the business in total, including other functions, may or may not be supporting the business.

You want to know what others in the business do and how your decisions and edicts impact on them – examine as if you walk in your customer's shoes.

For the new appointee, this concept is important to foster and an eye opener. Experiencing what customers and suppliers experience from your staff in requests for attention or lack thereof, and for information, reporting deadlines and delivering products or services.

We share with you a brilliant relatable story about customer service and staff attention that was recently told on a daytime radio show, with the company being named and shamed for their poor service

A customer selected their desired garment and approached the counter to pay and have it wrapped as a present, a service offered by the garment group. Unfortunately the two sales attendants were having a conversation about inane things, such as the kids schooling and weekend endeavours etc. as the customer stood back and waited .. 10 minutes without service or being served [yes she spoke for qo minutes] .. when the sales attendants decided to serve and say 'Next Please' the customer said NO THANKS and please have your store manager ring me on this number. Unsurprisingly no call was received as the manager was no doubt never advised.

What did this tell us? **Customer attentiveness**, **customer retention** and **customer service** are critical.

Walk a Mile in My Shoes means MANAGEMENT EXPERIENCES WHAT CUSTOMER'S EXPERIENCE: good and bad services.

71. Managing Your Team

As well as being a senior executive needing to have great working relationships with other senior executives, you are a manager of a HIGH PERFORMANCE TEAM: whether as CEO, it is the whole organisation or as the CFO it is the Finance Team or other executive positions. How you instil team SPIRIT and COMMITMENT with your team as the newbie will be important, especially when one or two of your staff may have aspired for or applied for your position and missed out.

Addressing your team and how you relate to them will be important, this topic would have been addressed at the interview and presents itself again now, needing you to apply it as you are in the position.

You must meet and discuss your expectations on performance with the senior members of your team. As the CxO Executive, you will need to hold a serious heart to heart discussion with all of your immediate reports to cover off the following:

- Your initial perceived expectations
- What they aspire to achieve for you and the organisation
- What help and guidance do they expect you to provide
- Specific suggestions on your working relationship
- What will be your communications model down to them and then up to the Executive team and the Board.

72. Promotion within your First 100 Days

Rather than moving out, your next move may be within your existing organisation as you move up the management and executive tree to a more senior position. If you move internally within your organisation and within the First 100 Days, you must assimilate into the new position, influence a new team, leave your old team and create the right culture in your new team. You will need to **impact both upwards and downwards and review your business strategy**. This internal move involves the same process of researching, applying, winning the new role and moving on, but in the same organisation.

You already know a lot about your existing organisation, and you have a **personal brand** and lots of **corporate knowledge** that should help, but you still need to apply and win the job. Assert yourself by walking about in your new role with your new team and take your current corporate knowledge and adapt it to your new role.

Review the tools and material we have presented earlier about the First 100 Days for a new executive, as this is a similar situation with respect to your promotion, but you already have the leading insight as to the internal relationships and stakeholders, giving you a leg, rather than a foot in the door.

It is important that you develop your **One Page Plan** for your First 100 Days in this new role and step up a cog in your performance and representative roles.

73. What Not To Do in The First 100 Days

Professor Jack Zenger from the University of Massachusetts conducted a study to determine that it is the following leadership failings that hold leaders back in their First 100 Days and thereafter:

1. **Humble Bragging:** bragging about themselves behind a mask of self-deprecation. Be yourself and do not show false or outlandish traits.

2. **Being too serious:** being too passionate, too focused, appear aloft, remote and not friendly. As a leader you should be a people person and engage.

3. **Not asking enough questions:** you should stop and listen and don't be an 'I AM' or an 'I will tell you what I think' as 'I AM the new boss'.

4. **Emotional hijackings:** do not play the emotions card, especially the negative one. Control your emotions and you will stay in the driver's seat.

5. **Whipping out your phone:** don't do it! It is disrespectful to any conversation you are having face to face.

6. **Name dropping:** it is good to know important and interesting people but using every conversation as an opportunity to name drop is pretentious.

7. **Gossiping:** you will look negative, spiteful and unprofessional if you gossip.

8. **Having a closed mind:** as the new person on the block you must have an open mind. No one wants to talk to a new boss who has already formed an opinion and is unwilling to listen.

9. **Sharing too much, too early:** over sharing comes across as self-obsessed and not prepared to hear, learn and take on other people's views. Patience and time to reflect are important traits.

10. **Sharing too much on social media:** research says that people who overshare on social media crave for attention and acceptance. Using social media needs to be done thoughtfully and with self-control.

The above are importance lessons for a senior manager and executive starting well in their First 100 Days.

3.3 First 100 Days

Reflective comments and Counsel from our experience are for you to **Be yourself**.

Understand the challenges and pace yourself.

There are 5 key Issues or Areas of Focus that you must address or follow:

1. You must COMMUNICATE
2. You need a PLAN of Action and a GOOD plan
3. You must Confirm or SELECT your management team
4. You must communicate your STRATEGIC themes and directions
5. You must define and then produce RESULTS

Let's examine these in detail:

1. Communications:

- Create a platform of mutual trust through communications
- Communication is leadership
- Tell all interested parties how you and they are going
- Share your findings and conclusions but keep your doubts to yourself
- Admit if you do not now, saying "I do not know at present", but undertake to know thereafter
- Inform your superiors of your progress as you survey and garnish more intelligence.

2. A Good Plan of Action:

- Understand all components of the business you have taken over: business model, how you make money, apparent risks and sensitivities
- Interview your key management team, fellow executives and key staff
- Meet with key stakeholders; internal and external
- Meet with the board and key investors
- Conduct 'Back of the Truck' or 'Café' meetings to understand where you really sit in culture and future challenges

3. Select your managemnet team:

- The Big issue is between existing team loyalty and a new broom
- Best team is a combination of:
    - Old and new people
    - Internal and external resources
- Consider a Different leadership style
- Combine younger and older leadership styles
- Select wisely as you need loyalty with ability to constructively criticise.

4. Communicate Strategic Themes:

- Everyone knows you are new in the job but expects you will stamp your mark and have been selected to bring about improvement, change and will have a detailed action plan to effect this change.
- You need to think through your strategic direction and initiatives and how you will implement them in your new organisation.
- Consider who else can help to develop and implement strategy: it does not have to be just you and yours; that in fact is dangerous and not collegiate.

5. Produce results:

Don't forget you have a role to perform, people to lead: servicing customers, running operations, and keeping talented staff motivated and enthused.

Showing results in the transition period is a must.

Show you can deliver.Understand where bad results or news flow from and how to handle and communicate these.

These five areas are the positives of moving forward as the new transitional senior leader; strong, purposeful, deliberate, reflective, considered, consultative, strategic, people manager, respected industry leader, team player and team builder, etc.

3.3 First 100 Days

NOTES:

SECTION 4

Profiling the **C-Suite Executive roles** for the first 100 days is important for those of you stepping into this role and those who have been in the role but may find this information of use.

The previous three sections discussed and provided industry and skill wide commentary and advice on preparing to move on in your career. We also discussed how you could assess your skills and competency, any training required, and get yourself ready to apply for and win that dream position, moving into your **First 100 Days in that Job**. These three sections were written and scoped to be generic in nature and could be applied in any position in the organisation.

In this section we will take these principles and techniques and expand them to apply to the predominant roles in an organisation that make up the C-Suite – the primary Executive Positions managing and directing the organisation.

We appreciate other C-Suite roles exist in medical, science, mining and agricultural sectors but to name a few, however we have limited our expansion of roles to that which are repetitive in the majority of organisations.

In this way, readers can get the general principles of Transitioning their Career Progression over the Next 200 Days but then it is supplemented by specific skills, tasks and resources necessary for each of the C-Suite Executive Positions.

CEO	[Chief Executive Officer]
CFO	[Chief Financial Officer]
COO	[Chief Operating Officer]
CHRO	[Chief Human Relations Manager]
CIO	[Chief Information Officer]
CTO	[Chief Technology Officer]
CMO	[Chief Marketing Officer]
CSO	[Chief Sales Officer]
CRO	[Chief Revenue Officer]
CDGO	[Chief Development Growth Officer]
CGO	[Chief Growth Officer]
CPO	[Chief Procurement Officer]
CSM	[Chief Supply Manager]
CLO	[Chief Logistics Officer]
CSO	[Corporate Sustainability Officer]
BxD	[Boards]
DIRECTOR	[Director of the Board]
CHAIR	[Chairperson of the Board]

A broad spectrum discussion is needed before you delve into your specific role, that being of your leadership and management style.

75. Management Style for Effective Leadership

What to do in the First 100 Days – that piece called the "TONE AT THE TOP".

You must self-evaluate, consider the history and characteristics of your new organisation and appropriately develop your TONE approach. You will explain and sell it at interview and now must affect it in this role.

Sam Aruti of of CIO magazine[2] suggests that there are three ways to start your First 100 Days in the Job colloquially, it is up to you which you choose or choose all:

1. Spend time figuring out what you have got yourself into - **INVESTIGATE**

2. Go right in and fix everything – **FIX IT**

3. Continue 'business as usual' – **HANG BACK**

So let's discuss these three leadership / management styles which are quite different: consider and work out which suits your circumstance, the organisation and your personal management style. This is a conscious and reflective piece of work.

1. INVESTIGATE – become an observer: become a student of your new environment – STOP and LISTEN. Don't try to fix what isn't broken. Have meetings with your subordinates and their subordinates to understand what is good and bad and to develop a go-forward strategy. Discover what they do, what are their skills and what they think is right and wrong. Make meetings personal.

Once you know what your team think, it is then time to talk to your clients or customers. Talk to your business unit leaders and get their recommendations as to which of their staff you should talk to.

Harvard Business School Professor Michael Watkins [34] in his book "The First 90 Days" suggests one critical question to ask each person you meet, that question is "*If you were me, what would you focus attention on?*" Watkins suggests you use this question and take the answers you receive to provide you with a starting point for prioritising the things you need to do, the things you want to do and those that you do not touch or change.

Wall Street Journal article by Carol Hymowitz says new business leaders becoming CEO ask the following five questions of their staff:

  a. What do you want to keep?

  b. What do you want to change?

  c. What do you want me to do?

  d. What are you afraid I'll do?

  e. What else do you want to ask me?

Using the example of a typical approach by a CEO for the INVESTIGATIVE mode, we highlight three key points:

I. **Listen to critics:** most will have legitimate concerns that you are inheriting and their views may be irreversible but you will need to deal with them. Ignore them at your peril: even if they are squeaking gates, you must oil them and remove the noise.

II. **Commit from the beginning:** to act on what you learn and to give a formal response, even if you have to change the look and feel of the organisation.

III. **Don't try to win arguments about debates or decisions that occurred in the past:** rather show them the future so they can focus on what is important.

2. You may be asked to "just go in and **FIX IT** fast" in your new role. We caution you using this approach, even when asked to fix it quick, as fixing hurriedly before you understand what works, may look impressive at first, but the wheels may fall off the cart as it trundles down the road, leaving you, the new executive responsible. The Fix It transition style:

FIX – the board employed you to Fix their problems, so you will have to form views and fix the important ones. Go deep to understand issues, attend meetings that you would not normally attend, work closely with the hands-on team, use all your expertise to analyse the situation and make decisions.

Take copious notes. Assess what policies and procedures are in place and how they affect outcomes. Review what other policies are needed to enforce and conduct the business in an efficient manner? e.g. travel authorisation policies, new recruitment procedures, refined and updated staff evaluation and salary reviews, expenditure authorities and limitations.

The danger of the Fix It approach is that you are perceived as a destructive Rambo style and that is not an appropriate statesperson type perception. You will not win friends or disciples if you don't do something to fix it. No actions means you will be viewed as lame and ineffective, which you do not want the title for. Unfortunately, you may have boxed yourself in, but you sold yourself at the interview as being capable of action and decisiveness, and you won the contest. What to do?

Consider this positioning: A combination of 1 and 2, Investigate and Fix It seems very logical and appropriate.

Now to style 3 that comes with another warning label to be careful and cautious as it may not suit, and may not be what you were appointed to do.

3. **HANG BACK** – "Business As Usual": if the people that hired you wanted more of the same, you probably would not have won the job. Therefore, this is not a likely approach. It is not as challenging and not as rewarding, if you are an action-type person.

The dilemma is which type of possible approach you select to change management. Perhaps you have your own style altogether that trumps these, and if so, and you are confident it works, then run with it.

It's now time for you to delve into your specific role, to explore your first days, weeks and 100 days on the job. The roles for CFO and CEO are lengthier as a reflection of our expertise in these areas as mentors, prior positions, managing as directors and recruiters.

76. CEO [Chief Executive Officer]

You are the newly appointed CEO.. Congratulations!! You won the race so how will you follow through in the position?

One approach in stamping your mark as the CEO is to **meet individually** with all board members **before your first board meeting:** but not before you start on the job. Presumably you get your feet under the table as the CEO and before the first formal board meeting; about four (4) weeks after you start you must have met all the board members and have a heart to heart, discussing among other things:

- What are their issues, concerns, strategically important directions and imperatives [from their perspective].
- What will your style be and how will that interact with their thoughts, requirements, and governance model.
- How the Board Committee process works at present or may change in the future under your CEO'ship.
- The Board meeting agenda and possible improvements and modifications.

Board dynamics are so important for a newly appointed CEO.

As the newbie on the block and if on the Board, you must understand and respect:

- History and precedent; traditions and strategic partners
- Personal interactions and power positions or voting blocs
- Critical strategic issues, directions and key success factors
- Board members 'pet projects' or areas of focus and expertise
- Directors' representational positions; that is, **who directors are aligned to** or are representing, serving or focusing on.

This discussion about the CEO meeting with and understanding the individual board member's position and focus is very important. If you are going to adopt or work with best practice corporate governance, it is essential to clearly understand and resolve the respective board and management arrangements and authority to consider how this will be played out under your new position as the CEO.

Exploration of the current issues and arrangements need to be explored early in your initial research of the new board, management and CEO team:

- What is the working relationship, reporting and authority between the CEO, the Board Chair and the Board, and board members individually;
- Which decisions fall to the ambit of the Board and which to the ambit of the CEO: you need to develop and have accepted the Delegations Policy which the board and CEO intend to operate under and the Board Charter;
- What is the power and authority of the respective Sub-Committees of the Board, the major ones [but not limited to] being:
  - FARM [finance, audit and risk management]
  - Audit and Risk
  - Remuneration
  - Sustainability
- Resolve the Board Calendar and monthly Board paper/protocols/format and timing for distribution etc.

These protocols must be quickly developed and agreed across the organisation.

As the new CEO…**Set the Tone!** Like a new President or Prime Minister would do: First 100 Days and now here is how we will operate going forward.

What would you say you would want to achieve in the FIRST 100 Days? This involves terms like:

- State of the Nation
- Tone from the Top
- Lead the Team
- Change Management
- Stakeholder Engagement
- Sustainable Market Positioning
- Transformative Models

These words become part of your management and leadership style and nomenclature.

A Key Imperative for the nearly engaged CEO: **Understand the Finances and Financial Imperatives Quickly.**

Work with your CFO immediately as you enter the job, to prioritise your understanding of the financial status of the organisation. Focus on:

- **The Balance Sheet:** the gearing, credit position, working capital, and financial capability and debt obligations; what is the net equity or net worth of your business; what asset, liability and borrowings do you have to play with?

- **The Profit and Loss Statement:** Revenue sources, Gross and Net Margins, bottom line: funds available for dividends and EPS earnings per share, or needed to be retained in the business.

- **The Cash Flow position including dividends and loan payments:** funds from operations, funding and borrowing capacity, and the next twelve months forecast.

A critical issue and understanding for the newbie is the financially sustainable business model: how do we make money and how to protect that position. You must be across this issue very early in your new tenure, should it be necessary to move quickly to change or reinforce this issue of attaining an appropriate financially sustainable business model.

This focus on your financially sustainable business model considers such issues as:

- How do we make money or more importantly do we make money?
- Who are your profitable customers and which are unprofitable and why? What are you going to do about this situation?
- Who are your major and necessary product or services suppliers? Are we getting the best deals? Can we guarantee supply in the long term?
- What is our break-even position and marginal cost advantage?
- Do you expand or contract to find the 'right' business size and right overhead structure?

- Are you using your business capability optimally?
- Can you outsource or insource? What are you good at as a business and what must you get right?
- How does your current technology or operational assets stack up with competitors and do you need a significant re-capitalisation of your business?

Answers to these questions will have you thinking and questioning in the right direction. Once you have the BUSINESS MODEL you think is correct, ask your CFO to develop a TRANSFORMATIVE BUSINESS MODEL. The ability to be sustainable through external factors that may be market or technological enforced, will see your organisation able to withstand as you already factored in greater use of asset sharing, but to name a few of the key 6 elements of a successful transformative business model.

Defining the role of the CEO is one that you may think is a given, obvious, but not necessarily so as you will learn when a dual role of a board position is included. We will now expand upon the role of the CEO, that will influence and guide you how to operate in the First 100 Days in the Job.

Role of the CEO

Despite being the head of the organisation's senior management, your role will vary as to the size of the organisation. The main dilution of this role is seen in smaller size organisations where you may be involved to the point of wearing a number of C-Suite hats.

For the purpose of simplicity in this chapter, we will be assuming the CEO example has a position in a mid-tier to large size organisation, with delegated authority from the board that provides for the roles and duties as outlined in a standard organisation constitution. You may wish to read the other C-Suite roles if you are stepping into a smaller organisation.

The CEO role embraces two primary tasks:

1. **Set and direct the organisation's strategic direction:** create and reinforce the organisations 'Flags on the Hill' and provide a culture and environment to challenge subordinates to strive to achieve these goals and aspirations; provides a context for motivating managers to collegiately strive for organisational excellence.

2. **The face and brand as the front of the business:**
representing the business in all regards; public profile and
stakeholder relationship management.

Further roles of the CEO:

- Lead and manage the organisation through delegated board
authority
- Responsibility for the organisation's day-to-day operations
- Uphold the constitution of the organisation
- Create the vision for the organisation
- Governance relations
- Managing the organisation's resources.

The many responsibilities for a CEO are:

- Business Model review and implementation
- Organisational business plan development and implementation,
as approved by the board
- Implementation of all forecasts, budgets and strategies, as
approved by the board
- Recruitment control for executive management
- Extraordinary requests submitted to the board that exceed the
threshold parameters [eg. financial, capital, leasehold]
- Conduit of communication for all legal matters, regulatory
matters, brand awareness including damage matters, high
risk level employee misconduct matters, product or service
contamination or breaches that may cause harm to public
person/s, union strikes, business interruptions causing cessation
of operations, threats of terrorism to the organisation, external
disaster impacts, etc.
- Risk mitigation, strategies, control and management for inherent
risks and material risks including reporting of material risk to the
board
- Overall nexus to the board of the organisation's affairs, financial
health status, explored growth areas, major wins and loss of top
customers and suppliers, major project milestones, operations in
general at high level and business development.

- Management, review and control of the organisation's processes and procedures
- Full transparency to the board
- Provide all reporting to the board on a timely basis and by the due timelines.

CEO with a Dual role as Director

There is some confusion for the CEO as to the requirement to be a Director in addition to their role. There is no actual regulation in Australia and New Zealand for a CEO to be a director, however it is recommended for efficiency of board meetings that the CEO is provided such a seat at the table to enable ease of briefing of the organisation's performance and operations each meeting. The interchangeable title of a CEO holding a board role is MD [Managing Director].

It is discouraged to have a CEO holding a dual role as Chairperson of the Board. Good risk management would see such a person not hold so much power as it provides for inability and difficulty to manage the CEO especially when removal of the CEO is required.

The Difference between CEO and Chairman of the Board

While the CEO directs the operational aspects of a company, the board oversees the company as a whole, and the leader of the board is called the CHAIR of the Board.

The Board appoints the CEO and the Board is the ultimate authority and is said to be responsible for the Corporate Governance of the organisation. The board has the power to overrule the CEO's decisions, and the Board, through its Chairperson sets the terms and conditions, authority and powers of the CEO.

Board meetings are chaired by the Chairperson. The CEO normally reports to the Board in a formal and structured Board Report to the Board. In some cases, the Board will meet without the CEO [called a Private Session] where aspects of the organisations progress or the CEO's performance are discussed in the absence of the CEO. This private session shows the power and presence of the Board and the Chair, relative to the CEO as the Chief Executive Officer.

Wise counsel by McKinsey & Company

McKinsey and Company in their McKinsey Quarterly provided "A Guide for the CEO Elect – the first days, weeks, or months and 100 Days".

In this study Kevin Coyne and Bobby S. Y. Rao[13] say "The days, weeks or months between taking the job (accepting the offer) and assuming power are precious. Put them to good use".

This is **BEFORE the First 100 days** of the "Next 200 Days in the job" which are critical.

They say "Experience shows that getting a good start is essential. Much has been written about a CEO's First 100 days, but what about the weeks and months before the job even begins." This is the vital period between *taking the job* and *taking the reins*. ***Our message to you is to make use of the period.***

McKinsey's say that a newly designated CEO can accomplish a great deal before actually assuming the post: "Taking as much advantage as possible of the period between their designation and their ascension can make the difference between success and failure."

A warning by McKinsey: "Within three years of the appointment of a new CEO, one third of all CEOs chosen to guide US companies are gone," you are not assured success.

Other advice from McKinseys includes:
"SEIZE THE DAY" they say, "The golden time between winning the job and starting it differs for every prospective CEO. But it is a time to *learn* and *gain insights* even *before* your public announcement. Once your appointment is announced it is all different. Many demands from the many and varied stakeholders and your behaviour and mannerisms become more closely watched." Brilliant insight! ***Win before your appointment is announced.***

A CEO designate may take their work-out period to tidy up loose ends at the old job but should try to take the *one-time advantage* of the opportunity to prepare for the new position.

"Identify and attack areas of Weakness" McKinsey says many studies suggest that addressing **weaknesses before you start or in the first month will have a disproportionately important impact on your success** and outcomes as the new appointed CEO. Address the gaps before you start and develop swift actions to be seen to be decisive in the areas where observers know action is sorely needed.

Hit the Road Running with the Board

"Get to Know the Board" McKinsey's advice is that the CEO-designate should go out of their way to meet and familiarise with each board member on a personal level as early as possible.

To be a successful CEO candidate, the process of understanding the board [and its members] must begin even before the job interviews, and to continue after appointment to the CEO position, with each board member. These discussions are vital to build a rapport but also to understand such things as how the board operates, why a previous CEO or CFO failed or succeeded, what the board sees as its main threats and opportunities and any unsaid critical success factors or the 'Elephants in the Room'.

Zenger of MIT says "Have a story ready before Day One." Stakeholders and those who appointed you will be looking for important signals *immediately*. Internal audiences, the market and media will be looking for messages about your **winning plan**. You will be asked about your long-term strategy for the company and how you will get there. Be prepared for that question, but it is too soon to preach it.

What makes a good story for Day One?

Good leaders recognise this story shouldn't be too detailed too early in the process. Also recognise that each constituency should know or hear that the CEO recognises [and cares about] their presence and point of view and will work hard to develop and communicate a direction that will give them all confidence under the CEO-Elects' direction.

All of the above reinforces why the period before Day 1 in the Job is critical in formulating a positive statement that inspires confidence in the new leadership.

McKinseys provide three great pieces of advice on the style as a new CEO:

1. "**Get Help for the Unpleasant Tasks**": Inevitably as the new CEO steps up, there will be casualties as other senior members of the management team either do not shape up or they were contenders for the top job, missed out and now it is time to move on or be moved on. The new CEO does not really want a reputation as a toe-cutter or malicious successor, but there will be a need for certain regeneration of personnel.

   A good approach is for the incoming CEO to bring in a Management or Team Consultant to conduct a Team Effectiveness Review and to make recommendations on gaps and overlaps in team composition. Any unpleasant tasks are best managed through a consultant's report and actions.

2. "**Find a Confidant**": it is lonely at the top and having a reference point or wise counsel will pay many returns. To be able to discuss a few ideas or alternative options before making them public, has merit.

3. "**Beware of Civic Duties**": as the new CEO you will be swamped with quests to take up corporate, civic or industry representational roles. But this will come as you know you need to spend enormous amounts of time just getting yourself across the nuances of your new business and/or new role. As attractive and personally satisfying as these invitations may seem, it would make sense to put on a 'wait and see' approach for the first 12 months of your tenure in the new job. You could say, '*Thank you very much, I appreciate the compliment but my employment contract does not permit this at this time*'.

Managing Your Team in the First 100 Days

Congratulations on receiving the prestigious role as CEO that along with it comes great rewards, satisfaction and responsibility. As well as being a senior executive with working relationships with other senior executives, you are **managing a high-performance team**.

How you instil team spirit and commitment with your team as the newbie will be important: especially when one or two of your staff may have aspired for or applied for your position and missed out.

Addressing your team and how you relate to them will be important – it would have been addressed both at the interview and then needing to be affected now that you are in the position.

Meet and discuss your expectations on performance with the senior members of your team. As the CEO, you will need to hold a serious heart to heart discussion with all of your immediate reports to covers off the following:

- Your initial perceived expectations
- What they aspire to achieve for you and the organisation
- What help do they expect you to provide
- Specific suggestions on your working relationship
- What will be your communications model with the Executive team and Board.

Churn

Two BIG Issues are CHURN: Customer Churn and Employee Churn.

By the end of your First 100 Days, you should have understood the measures of success and failure for your organisation's CHURN: both for Customer and Employee.

Having had prepared a report on the facts and actions to address this CHURN will have you well placed with all senior management and the Board.

Churn is a great waste: whether customers or employees.

Customers: You inherit great and loyal customers on your books, know what they buy, your business relationships with them and know that they do not need to be won – you just need to value and retain them. CEO's should create a corporate philosophy and message that **Customers are King** and that the organisation must deliver excellent customer experience that is second to none.

As CEO, you must appreciate and demonstrate the **VBIF [Value of Business In Force]:** the inherent value of customers won, retained and relationships in force that you may have disregarded of late. Customer churn costs organisations. This is a **value measure** that you can lead and champion as the CEO.

Employees Your biggest assets are your loyal and trusted staff that have received a lot of investment through training and care. Again, any churn will result in further recruitment expenses including staff training which is expensive and disruptive. You need to quickly assess which staff:

- are invaluable and need retention.
- need further development and will ultimately be valuable.
- may not suit the long term direction and culture of the organisation in your new climate.

The CEO has a valuable role to demonstrate the intrinsic value of employee skills, retention, morale and developing that intangible value that is the KNOWLEDGE MANAGEMENT within your organisational staff: across the whole organisation.

CEO Tools

As CEO there are a number of tools that you will use to drive performance growth in the organisation, that may be used by you, by the CFO or collaboratively as you work together in business partnership. The tools [refer to appendix] suggested as the most important within your first 100 days to grasp where the organisation currently sits in order to build your strategic plan are:

- Business Model
- SWOT
- BCG Growth Share Matrix
- Was / Is / Will Be

Once you have developed these tools, you and/or the CFO can present these to the board, your senior executive team and department managers, along with your strategic plan of the next 100 days of changes you are considering or will implement. These tools create feedback from your team so allow this to happen in order to learn of other issues that you may not have considered.

FIRST 100 Days as CEO

The First 100 Days will be crucial to your success as CEO in the role and to that of your organisation than you now lead. To be effective in your FIRST 100 Days in the Job, consider the following Ten key areas of focus or lessons as the CEO:

1. Take time to understand your new role: have a good feel for the organisation and what drives its performance.

2. Work out the real priorities and what you can achieve as a success.

3. Recognise the **importance** of your FIRST 100 and 200 days: ensure your expectations and the Boards' are in sync.

4. Celebrate early WINS: get something working well; foster confidence as a team, be that a new contract or product line or improved process.

5. Avoid early gaffes or wrong decisions. Keep close to your Chairperson who will help with the political landscape and help you avoid ill-considered decisions.

6. Do not try to exert your authority prematurely: show patience, wisdom and willingness to make sound well based judgements.

7. Build coalitions of support and effective relationships: think always **Stakeholder Management:** how do you engage and get support from *ALL* stakeholders.

8. Build trust and support with the Chairperson of the Board.

9. If this is a turnaround or troubled business, ensure effective communications with staff, suppliers, customers, funders etc: even to buy you time whilst helping to build rapport and confidence in you, your approach and strategies.

10. Plan to get to the end of the FIRST 100 Days in the Job and have your SECOND 100 DAYS all planned, ready to go.

Remember your FIRST 100 Days in the Job is a two-way street: both listening and speaking.

It is important that you understand the **Corporate Governance structures** for your new business: how the board operates, how individual directors contribute and can help influence your change agenda.

Do not be afraid to seek mentoring or developing a good sounding board from your Chair or other board members: especially as to issues or priorities.

In summary, as CEO in your FIRST 100 Days, scrutiny will be intense and you need to be prepared and have a model/program like that explained to move forward appropriately.

Let's Summarise: **BE VISIBLE: spend time in the business working alongside management, staff and clients to understand the core problems and how you can develop strategies and approaches to solve them, focus on core strengths and understand the steps to VALUE CREATION.**

As the CEO, keep the Board informed, appraised and supportive of your strategies and directions. As challenges or major issues emerge, be quick to disclose, discuss and seek appropriate timetables to address and resolve.

The First 100 Days in the C-Suite will be head down, many meetings and assessments and bringing to the fore your expertise in strategy, finance, customer focus and business management. You will want to make a difference and stamp your mould on your organisations team or at the board and the executive level.

As we get to the end of the First 100 Days in the Job, you need to demonstrate your calibre as a STRATEGIST and how you have the skills and techniques to help position the organisation not only in the Present but also for the Future.

You must be strategic and be seen to be the strategic partner.

Critical will be your willingness and ability to participate in or facilitate a Strategic Planning session on behalf of the business: both at the Group and then Business unit levels.

Key to this will be the following three programs or areas of focus or techniques, that you can use these models to facilitate strategic planning in your new business.

77. CFO [CFO *formerly* **Chief Financial Officer**]

The Chief Financial Officer CFO is one of the top three senior executives in a business with a specific mandate and background around financial, commercial and business management.

You are the newly appointed CFO, a great honour and win, so how will you follow through in the position?

One approach in stamping your mark as the CFO is to meet with the CEO first and foremost. Reliance upon you by the CEO and being instrumental to driving the CEO's vision requires a superlative business partnership with the CEO. We then suggest you meet individually with all C-Suite executives and your finance or CFO team. Where it is possible to meet with board members, we strongly encourage you to do this; they have the insight and direction to guide you in the organisational goals they strive for.

When do you meet, before commencement or in the job? Reach out to the CEO a week or two before you start. Try to arrange a lunch, get to know the CEO and their style. Discover why your successor departed and what they did well and didn't do so well. The CEO if they have time for your meeting will regard this as an enthusiastic new injection into the business. There is no harm in requesting an introductory lunch.

So presumably you get your feet under the table as the CFO and before the first formal board meeting – about four (4) weeks after you start you must be **across the current reporting requirements**, ready to produce but not yet change reporting as it is premature with your limited knowledge of the organisation's workings.

What would you say you would want to achieve in the FIRST 100 Days? This involves terms like:

- Business Partnership
- Tone from the Top
- Drive the Vision
- Stakeholder Engagement
- Sustainable Financial Position or Model

These words become part of your management and leadership style and nomenclature.

A Key Imperative for the nearly engaged CFO: **Understand the Finances and Financial Imperatives Quickly**.

As the CFO, a priority for the immediate start in the role is to understand the finances of the organisation. Focus on:

- **The Balance Sheet:** the gearing, credit position, working capital, and financial capability and debt obligations; what is the net equity or net worth of your business, and what asset, liability and borrowings do you have to play with?

- **The Profit and Loss Statement:** Revenue sources, Gross and Net Margins, bottom line: funds available for dividends and EPS earnings per share, or needed to be retained in the business.

- **The Cash Flow position including dividends and loan payments:** funds from operations, funding and borrowing capacity, and the next twelve months forecast.

A critical issue and understanding for the newbie is the financially sustainable business model: how do we make money and how to protect that position. You must be across this issue very early in your new tenure: should it be necessary to move quickly to change or reinforce this issue of developing an appropriate financially sustainable business model.

This focus on your financially sustainable business model considers such issues as:

- How do we make money or more importantly do we make money?
- Who are your profitable customers and which are unprofitable and why? What are you going to do about this situation?
- Who are your important and necessary product or services suppliers? Are we getting the best deals? Can we guarantee supply in the long term?
- What is our break-even position and marginal cost advantage?
- Do you expand or contract to find the 'right' business size and right overhead structure?
- Are you using your business capability optimally?
- Can you outsource or insource? What are you good at as a business and what must you get right?
- How does your current technology or operational assets stack-up with competitors and do you need a significant re-capitalisation of your business?

Answers to these questions will have you thinking and questioning in the right direction.

CFO relationship to the CEO

The CFO relationship has been described as the **Pilot / Co-Pilot** relationship, an analogy that works very well. Both have their respective specific roles in navigating and flying the plane [and your organisation] but sometimes the pilot needs to sleep or use the amenities and the co-pilot takes control of the plane.

At other times, they together need to address major issues with the performance and safety of the plane or issues thrown at them from outside the plane. They work through these as a team with their respective backgrounds and expertise.

The pilot and co-pilot need to work out their relationship as to:
- Control and command
- Authority and representation
- Relief and replacement
- Direction and decisions:
    - The CFO needs to build a strong supportive relationship with the CEO and determine when a CFO takes over or takes a back seat.
    - Building honesty, trust and reliance will be important as is mutual respect for each other's skills and competency.
    - Develop a plan of how to support each other in your various roles without competing and with mutual respect.

The market wants to see a **united and collegiate relationship team** between the CEO and CFO.

On many occasions, the CEO and CFO will do a tag-team presentation to the shareholders, the financial and analysts market, community or industry groups, further emphasising the need to understand their respective talents and involvements to sing from the same song sheet.

A critical issue revolves around who is responsible for STRATEGY and how Strategy is determined and communicated across the organisation.

Depending on the person who holds the position of CEO, the CFO can either be the leader or facilitator of the strategy determination for the organisation.

As the CFO you should bring to the Executive team a knowledge and practical working experience of Blue Ocean Strategy and the SWOT 3x3 Strategic Action Model [discussed in the Appendix A4] in addition to your other strategic tools used.

Role of the CFO

Best described in the journal, CFO: The True Meaning Behind the Title, by Sandra Oakley[28] and John Petty, the role is defined as "**the conduit of information between the Shareholders, CEO, Board, C-Suite and Management that harnesses their skillset in one of the most important roles as the gatekeeper and information strategist**."

The CFO has three elements to their role that are; to identify key drivers to create the Strategy, to Develop channels and manage the processes to then Execute the strategy and processes to drive growth. This is a high level summary of the role. Read on as we expand further into the many responsibilities of the CFO.

CFO Style

Korn Ferry[24], the international recruitment house said in an article reporting on a new survey in the International CFO Magazine, under the heading "New CFOs: the First 100 Days", surveyed the new style being taken by CFO's upon a new CFO position, **"Put away the spreadsheet and get out of the office"**. This is an interesting and correct style the CFO must take.

The survey which collected responses from 183 recruiters worldwide commented, "in a new executive's 'First 100 Days' at a company" and said that **"a strategic outlook and interpersonal skills are the most important indicators of success"**. "The new Finance Exec needs to get off to a great start, have a plan and not falter." Korn/Ferry's financial officers' practice said when a new finance executive stumbles, "it takes three or four months to get back on track".

The most common mistake of the new executives of all disciplines, according to the Korn/Ferry survey is:

- failure to establish strategic priorities (23.5 % of respondents)
- committing cultural gaffes or "political suicide" (16.4 %)
- waiting too long to implement change (15.8 %)
- not spending enough face time with subordinates (14.2 %)

People skills (cited by 44.3 % of respondents) and **cultural compatibility** (38.3 %) were considered the most important items in a new executive's toolkit.

In terms of style and focus on the big-picture tasks, the following was the top of the to-do lists of new executives:

- 25.1 % said new executives should first assemble and solidify a team
- 24.6 % advised articulating a statement of vision and goals
- 15.8 % recommended understanding what is most important to the CEO and the Board
- 13.7 % encouraged adapting to the new company culture

Note that Micro-level goals were held in much lower regard: only 4.9 % thought new executives should first achieve several quick successes, and only 3.8 % advised new executives to turn immediately to fixing obvious, nagging problems.

The Message for CFO's: Finance Executives were well advised to *avoid a micro-level focus.*

The Korn/Ferry study say to the newly appointed "don't try to execute 25 things in your first 100 days". Many new executives fall into this trap after being overwhelmed by dozens of requests. Instead, sort through everything that lands on your desk and identify the three most important tasks — then do them." This is the Pick the BIG 3 supported by McKinsey in their First 100 Day Paper. And reinforce again the point – and achieve them.

Now a BIG personal message!! Newly appointed Chiefs should focus on moving forward instead of dwelling on their experience and past successes. Appreciate that it's a new company, a new situation, a new position and a new team. After all, no one wants to hear the constant refrain, "Well, at my last company, we did it this way…"

CFO duties

More specifically, the relevant areas of focus for the CFO and Finance Team will include the following technical areas of competency:

- **Statutory and Financial Reporting**: including design and details for the Statutory Report to ASIC and the Annual Report to Shareholders.

- **Management Reporting**: to the senior Executive team and Corporate Board as well as downstream Divisional and Business Unit reports: focus on Financial and Non- Financial Indicators [NFI's].

- **Treasury Management and Funding**: compliance with funding/banking covenants, ensuring cash management is efficiently managed, longer term solvency, capital management and corporate gearing: dealing with current and potential funding and banking sources.

- **Risk Management**: support to the Audit and Risk or FARM Committee to ensure proper planning and management of all financial and commercial risk of current and future funding of the business.

- **Effective Budgeting and Forecasting** of performance.

- **Business Analytics** including product and customer profitability analysis.

- **Organisational Taxation structuring and compliance** and all other legal custodial matters.

- **Cost management and cost control** through expenditure authorisations.

By the end of the First 100 Days in the Job, as CFO you need to have assessed whether you have the RIGHT STRUCTURE within your Finance team possessing the skills and capabilities required by your team members. You may need new blood and you must specify these requirements, implement new management and operating team member structure for your finance team.

Your focus on your team, the finance or CFO team will need to be considered as we outline in the next few headers to:

- Coach and Mentor
- Manage
- Churn
- Counsel
- Deliverables
- Efficient Processing

Finance/CFO Team Focus
CFO as the Internal Business Coach and Mentor

A privileged position in your new role is to help your Finance team to optimise their performance and arrange formal training. In addition to this as a C-Suite executive, you can mentor managers at a lower level in a generic nature on commercial, business and even finance performance and competency in their departments.

Mentoring and coaching others in better report interpretation and reading, amongst other generic practices such as risk management increases their competencies whilst enabling a better workplace in the organisation.

The Finance for Non-Finance courses mentioned later are a great help: to explain to operational and technical managers what finance is about and the rules and conventions that accountants and finance teams must apply. Accountants as well as understanding cash and cash management, must also report under IFRS [International Financial Reporting Standards] or if you are in the U.S.A. it is GAAP [Generally Accepted Accounting Principles] and accounting and auditing standards. This can be very confusing: not only for accountants but for the management of the businesses they are accounting for.

As the CFO, you should help senior non-finance executives to be able to read their monthly financial reports and to ask the right questions about the financial performance of the organisation. Most importantly, to be able to match the financial and non-financial reports and underlying drivers of the business will improve performance growth.

Assisting managers to understand that financial reports are historical and that the **hidden detail** to assist their departments' performance, is often in the **non-financial information**.

Remember, that the Financial Reports should be a mirror [in $ terms] of what is actually happening in the business operationally.

For example, if you lose a major customer, your business will suffer financially with lower sales volumes and contributions.

Another example is; to achieve increased production output targets you have to take on extended overtime at penalty rates, your expenses will dramatically increase and probably your margins will be squeezed and downgraded.

What physically happens ends up in the financial reports. The reasoning as to why you lost the customer may be in the non-financial reports, such as DIFOTis and NPS.

This discussion between finance and operations is an important internal business coaching role for the finance team. You must be up to this as the new CFO.

Managing Your Team in the First 100 Days

The position of CFO is one we know only too well and one that as you are a senior executive, you are also the co-pilot to the CEO. Instilling confidence with other senior executives as you rely upon their harmonious working relationships, whilst managing a dynamic high-performing team.

How you instil team spirit and commitment with your team as the newbie will be important, especially when one or two of your staff may have aspired for or applied for your position and missed out.

Addressing your team and how you relate to them will be important – it would have been addressed both at the interview and then needing to be affected now that you are in the position.

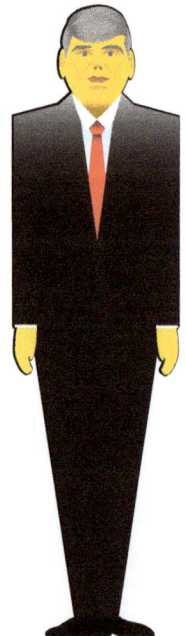

Meet and discuss your **expectations on performance** with the senior members of your team. As the CFO, you will need to hold a serious heart to heart discussion with all of your immediate reports to covers off the following:

- Your initial perceived expectations
- What they aspire to achieve for you and the organisation
- What help do they expect you to provide
- Specific suggestions on your working relationship
- What will be your communications model with them and up to the Executive team and Board.

Churn

Two BIG Issues are CHURN: Customer Churn and Employee Churn.

By the end of your First 100 Days, you should have understood the **measures of success and failure** for your organisation's CHURN: both for Customer and Employee.

Having had prepared a report on the facts and actions to address this CHURN will have you well placed with all senior management and the Board.

Churn is a great waste: whether customers or employees.

Customers: You inherit great and loyal customers on your books, know what they buy, your business relationships with them and know that they do not need to be won – you just need to value and retain them. CEO's should create a corporate philosophy and message that **Customers are King** and that the organisation must deliver excellent customer experience that is second to none.

As CFO, you must appreciate and demonstrate the **VBIF [Value of Business In Force]**: the inherent value of customers won, retained and relationships in force that you may have disregarded of late. Customer churn costs organisations. This is a **value measure** that you can demonstrate to your new business as the CFO.

Employees: Your biggest assets are your loyal and trusted staff that have received a lot of investment through training and care. Again, any churn will result in further recruitment expenses including staff training which is expensive and disruptive. You need to quickly assess which staff:

- are invaluable and need retention.
- need further development and will ultimately be valuable.
- may not suit the long term direction and culture of the organisation in your new climate.

The CFO has a valuable role to demonstrate the intrinsic value of employee skills, retention, morale and developing that intangible value that is the knowledge management within your organisational staff: both for your finance or CFO team and across the whole organisation.

The McKinsey's 'CFO First 100 Days in the Job' research reported that many CFO's in their First 100 Days had spent time 'on the road' with sales reps understanding the key customers' needs and how their organisation was or was not servicing those needs. Many CFO's confided that they learnt many important messages or information that nobody in the organisation had appraised them of.

External consultant for counsel

As you commence evaluation of your finance team and the standard of accounting in the organisation you may wish to have a meeting with the current or previous audit partner, to understand:

- Past contentious accounting or reporting policies or issues and how and why they were resolved as they were;

- Any dubious or contentious accounting policies or treatments that need further discussion: such as impairment provisions or provisions reversed;

- Concerns about the quality of staff in your Finance team, possible any legacy issues with staff;

- Need for further training or professional development of the Finance team staff;

- Suitability of the basic accounting and other operational systems, ERP hurdles and reporting tools;

- Quality of accounting reports and transaction processing passed across for audit purposes;
- Additional areas recommended for further audit review or attention;

Any other areas or concerns that the incoming CFO should be aware of.

The Big 4 Deliverables for a Finance Team

Choosing which Deliverables to roll out as the new CFO is a matter of prioritising and timing. Which ones you choose and how to establish, progress and commit is a review McKinsey's took to provide some wise counsel.

The Big 4 Deliverables approach and focus can be used for all functions and roles as an executive transition to a new role.

McKinsey's advice was to pick 3 or 4 BIG ACHIEVABLES, PROJECTS or INITIATIVES at end of First 100 days to **make a difference** as the Finance Team and **implement** these in the Second 100 Days of your Tenure.

These could be from the following list:

- Progress Finance Function processing efficiency, including accelerated month-end reporting
- Improved and Focused Board and Management Reporting – including focus on Key Drivers and Critical Success Factors
- Customer Profitability Analysis and focus on Cost To Serve for particular customers or Customer sectors
- Capital management and capital project evaluation
- Adequacy of IT and CRM and Decision Support systems and current and future architecture: a big $ ticket item
- Move to Rolling Quarterly Forecast [RQF]
- Adoption and Reporting of organisational CSR [Corporate Social Responsibility]

Developing a Company Wide program and rolling out a customised Commercial Skills Training Program for Non- Finance Executives and Business unit Managers [without Financial Training] is called a Finance for Non-Finance Managers and it is essential to improve the Financial Literacy and Competency of the organisation.

Coachability.net.au can advise of relevant training courses for your organisation.

In the next section, we examine a number of aspects of CEO and CFO responsibilities and performance in the new job where you must make a difference and perform and achieve in and past the First 100 Days in the Position.

Efficient Transactional Processing
A roadmap to Best of Breed Finance Teams

One of the key messages of the IBM Global CFO Study [20] was that CFOs must move towards what was called "FINANCE EFFICIENCY": in other words conducting the transactional processing of accounting, finance, business, and commercial relations in an efficient and seamless manner: imposing minimal requirements on operations which have better things to do.

One of the key focus of the CFO in their First 100 Days in the Job must be to **assess** how efficient the finance team is operating and to **develop** a program to process map and then **improve** their **finance efficiency** within the first six months of taking on the role.

Finance Efficiency here covers:

- **AP [Accounts Payable]** – paying your accounts to suppliers
- **AR [Accounts Receivable]** – prompt and accurate invoicing and collecting revenue/debts/receivables and credit management
- **Payroll** – paying wages and all other government charges, super, taxes, FBT; compliant and on-time and accurate processing
- **Asset management** – control and register of assets including depreciation, stock control, security and logistics in and out of premises
- **Cash flow management** – budgeting and forecasting, banking relationship and treasury management
- **Monthly month end reporting** to management and the board and downstream to operational management for control and pricing purposes and efficient resource and labour utilisation
- **Quarterly** Reforecasting of year end results and on a **Rolling Forecast** basis.

The CFO will need to assess the appropriateness of any accounting software packages in use across the group and any business intelligence software used for extracting and presenting information and reports to management and the Board.

In particular the new CFO should lead a complete redesign of your current board pack and ensure it provides the relevant information that the Board requires – conduct a **Board Reporting Review** with all board members to question and understand their particular requirements and 'likes' in discharging their respective corporate governance obligations and providing the KPI's that tell the management and Board the vital information on progress and performance.

To the extent that the Finance team is assessed as not being at Best Practice in its transactional processing, the CFO will need to introduce a project to map the processes with a view to introduce process improvements and cost efficiencies in data management. A new focus on digital processing will come to the fore here.

CFO Governance and Compliance

We soon head into your first 100 days and the tools that will assist you to assess your positioning to make well informed decisions within this period. Before we go into the more technical side, there is the matter of compliance and governance that fit into your style.

We are now working through what the CFO must pay attention to and address in the First 100 Days in the Job.

CFO as the Chief NO Officer

Now that is an interesting title. This is often the approach and contention of the CFO and especially a new CFO who wants to create their credibility and territory as the overall Financial Controller of the cash and expenditure management of the organisation.

As the CFO and as the protector of the organisations' **Capital and Financial Credibility**, it is acceptable and in fact, incumbent for the CFO to say NO to certain financial or investment proposals; and certain excessive expenditures or programs, where a return cannot be clearly demonstrated or does not reach the organisations agreed hurdle rate for investment.

Tight budgeting, realistic forecasting and stronger capital project justification are a clear way to exert authority as an incoming CFO: it will be well accepted and respected if done well and with professionalism and demonstration of the benefits to the organisation.

The CFO has been described as the **Guardian** of the ORGANISATION'S WEALTH AND FINANCIAL POSITION and so it is necessary for the CFO to be involved in and recommending of all investments and strategic arrangements that could impact on the Financial Viability and Solvency of the business. We often see the role of the CFO described as being responsible for the **Financial Sustainability** of the business.

Dealing with banks and financiers are the purview of the CFO.

It is better for the CFO to say 'No, that is not an appropriate use of our resources or capital value' than to allow a value eating proposal to proceed.

The Board and CEO look to the CFO to be one such guardian and to strike down such inappropriate proposals. The CFO will introduce a **capital investment evaluation regime and model** whereby only capital projects that meet a desired hurdle rate will get the green light. The funding and the projects are ranked for approval and then the funding will proceed.

As such, you can see why the CFO is sometimes called irreverently the CHIEF NO OFFICER, as they have to say NO in tight capital rationing situations. If the CFO does not exercise this power, we would have far too many calls for cash investment, usage and ROI will decrease or be sub-optimal.

Send bad news early

As CFO, consider the Need for Impairment early in your tenure.

The market and all stakeholders will be looking for a guide from the new incumbent CFO as to what they are finding and assessing and needing to action positively and negatively.

One major issue is whether the previous CFO incumbent had been honest and vigilant re depicting the real state of the financial position, recorded book value, financial solvency or sustainability of the business, and its respective lines of business or business units.

In particular, is there a **need for impairment** of any asset values on the books: are there any unsustainable asset values that need writing down – hence a charge to the P and L or retained equity, which will not necessarily be viewed with joy by the board or senior management and especially by the investors.

Our message is that you must **send any bad news early** in your First 100 Days in the Job or at least by end of the First 100 Days. Don't hold back. However, do it with judgement and seek professional advice and support: use independent experts to support your views and actions.

As the CFO, you know that senior management and the Board will be looking to you to clean up any financial mess that may exist and there is an expectation that you will quickly come to grips with any bad news and skeletons in the closet.

Bad news is often discovered in; assets on the books at inflated or not supportable values; unprofitable Business Units; contingent or non-recognised liabilities or provisions – where less than full and honest estimation or accounting has been taken prior.

They will be expecting decisive action in assessing any write downs or impairment adjustments that may be needed and that you will be alert to the need and be decisive: don't disappoint them and ensure that all bad news is delivered quickly and swiftly and without fear: you have one chance to get this right and you should not hold back.

Any changes to **accounting policies** should be assessed and highlighted with the Board early in your tenure, prior to preparation of the next set of formal accounts and prior to presentation to the Board and Shareholders. Discuss and agree the changes with your current auditors. Assess the impact of such changes on the Profit & Loss and Balance Sheet values and hence market valuations of the business.

Ensuring Corporate Compliance
As the CFO, you are responsible for ALL compliance across the organisation: the CFO has also been described as the CCO [Chief Compliance Officer] and as such, you must get your mind around and position yourself to be across this within the First 100 Days on the job.

Steps the CFO can take to adopt a pre-eminent role in **Corporate Compliance** include:

- Review the organisation's risk register, if one exists, or have this important register developed if none exists.
- Have Risk Compliance and Risk Management installed as a Standing agenda item for all board meeting agendas.
- Review the charter and then any minutes for any past FARM, Audit & Risk or Remuneration Committees. If no such Committees exist, have formal Charters developed and adopted by the board and establish board sub-committees of the board.

As the incoming CFO, you should immediately instigate a meeting with the Chair of the FARM, Audit & Risk and Remuneration Committees to understand the relevant issues and future focus which will affect your performance as CFO.

Focus on the following key areas of Risk and Compliance for your business:

- What debts does the business have?
- What bank covenants exist and are you compliant: past and present?
- What reporting arrangements are in place to forecast compliance in advance and then your organisation's compliance position in regards to covenants?
- Creation and management of internal financial controls.

Determine what sort of **Risk Reporting Matrix** is in place and whether it is suitable for your business, known as the Risk Likelihood and Risk Consequence Model discussed on page 210 of Risk Management and Risk Mitigation.

Organisational Structure and Tax and Legal Arrangements

One of the most common dilemmas for an incoming CFO is any existing complex organisational structure. Examples of common structures are: various legal entities; multiple subsidiaries; differing tax domiciles; transfer pricing arrangements; management reporting lines or business units which have grown topsy but have no logic in terms of the current legal, management or board reporting structure; and optimum tax compliance arrangements.

It may be costly to change structures [regulatory and legal fees, stamp duty, banking arrangements and covenants] but there may be good sense to do so. You need to **make this assessment** but based on good advice and understanding past logic and future directions of the business.

Don't be afraid to make an assessment by the end of your First 100 Days, to then make it a project for the Second 100 Days in the position, to bring down a new legal taxation domicile or management reporting framework or structure. Your board and/or CEO will be expecting this review, so avoid disappointing them.

Complex and legacy structures are expensive and do not help with the proper conduct of an appropriate and optimal Corporate or Group business structure. It also creates the ability for those seeking to hide the truth to be non-transparent.

Work with the CEO on a more appropriate legal and management structure, especially if there is a possibility of rationalisation of the business units within the group. **The benefit of this review may be tax optimisation and a better management reporting structure**.

As the CFO, you are the public officer and as such, by the end of the First 100 Days you must be able to say without any doubt that your organisation is TOTALLY COMPLIANT in respect of all taxation and government reporting obligations [all returns lodged and always on time and all provisions complied with, no funny business].

Conduct a **Tax and Legal Compliance Assessment** for the whole group and produce a report for the Board and Executive team highlighting:

- All compliances and good practices
- Any non-compliances or areas requiring rectification.

You may need to consider conducting an independent Tax Compliance Review by a group of independent tax experts to be able to assure Senior Management and the Board of your assurance that you are appropriately and optimally structured. To assist your review, we now discuss taxation compliance and management policies and practices.

Taxation Compliance and Taxation Management Policies and Practices

As the new CFO, tax compliance is a MUST and a big FOCUS for you in the new role: all tax filings and taxation payments must be made according to **regulatory deadlines**. You need this assurance and a certificate for tax compliance from whoever is responsible within the business, possibly your statutory accountant or tax agent.

Far too often we see a cavalier attitude to tax compliance and missing taxation payment deadlines. Failure to meet tax deadlines in some countries, especially in Australia can result in director's being held personally legally liable.

A further issue is that the organisation for which you are now the Chief Figurehead in Taxation [even though you may have a Taxation Manager reporting to you] must be adopting totally **ethical policies** in regard to revenue recognition and expense claiming and that there are no untoward treatments that could bring discredit on your organisation: for example any suspect transfer pricing policies or income shifting arrangements into international tax regimes or domiciles.

As the CFO, the Board of Directors will be looking directly to you to provide them with **assurance** that their business is totally tax compliant and that it is paying the correct amount of tax and that any and all taxation arrangements or schemes are entirely legal, ethical and transparent. Evidence to support your position such as the appropriate certificates and independent expert opinions may be required.

A good assurance for your position is to immediately appoint or instigate an independent and professional taxation audit – which is a qualified and confirms your organisation's compliance.

Ensure that your organisation has a **Tax Compliance Policy** [published] and a **Taxation Manual** – which brings together all taxation policies and procedures, checklists, standard forms etc

New Leadership in the Role:

BCG [Boston Consulting Group] Advice and Counsel

The Boston Consulting Group 'Perspectives Research Paper', *"Assuming Leadership – The First 100 Days"*[14] discussed the challenges and then recommendations for new Leadership assuming their role in any leadership positions.

They say "Many will be recruited or promoted to the top post in their companies. Their performance during the 'First 100 Days' in office will be crucial: friends and foes alike will be watching for signs of long-term success or failure."

BCG developed the concept of a "First 100 Day Scorecard" where successful candidates can reflect on **four areas of Focus or Determinants of Success in the new position:** these are:

1. What did they initially intend to do in/with the job– their goals and intentions
2. What they actually did or achieved
3. What they regretted doing
4. What they regretted NOT doing.

Create a Matrix / Box to segregate the 4 points above.

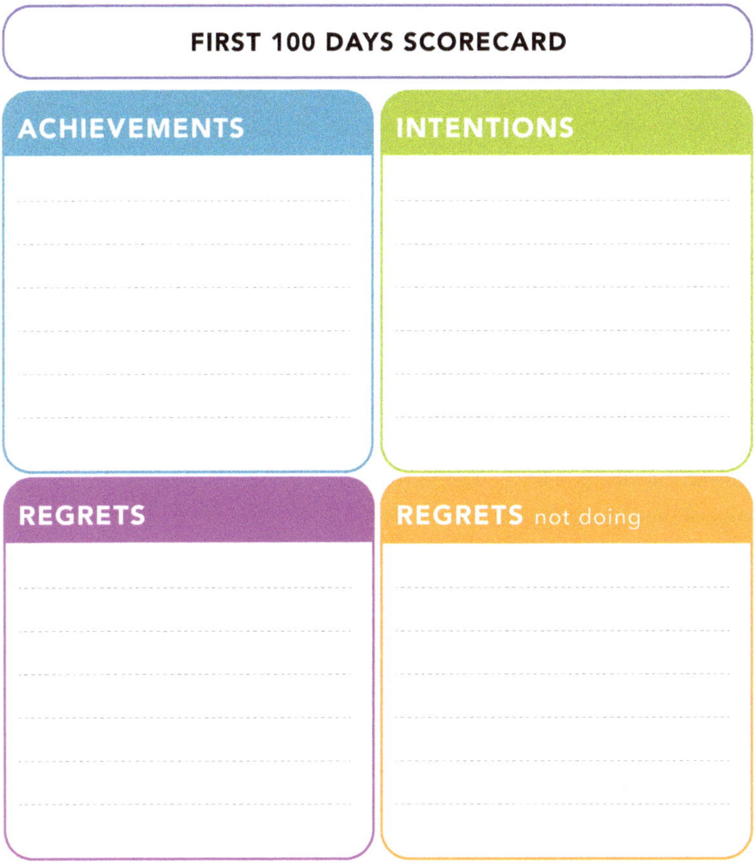

FIRST 100 DAYS SCORECARD

ACHIEVEMENTS

INTENTIONS

REGRETS

REGRETS not doing

Figure 16: My First 100 Days Scorecard

Complete your Scorecard Worksheet Section on p296

There are two ways to examine your determinants of success from the matrix.

The top row exhibits your winning **[Achievements]** and those that you had failed to do **[Intensions]**. The bottom row exhibits what you shouldn't have done **[Regrets]** and those **[Regrets of not doing]**, which are to recognise and learn by the mistakes whilst providing a watch and monitor alert to you.

The alternative way to view is the left hand side is historical and won or lost, against the right hand side that may still provide opportunity to engage and act.

This is an interesting general reflection of intent and then the achievements for and from the First 100 Days. Obviously if you progress past your probation and move into the Second 100 Days in the Job, then this is a worthwhile reflection point to take stock and move forward.

BCG's counsel for Managing the First 100 Days *from a personal perspective* were as follows:

- Diagnose first, decide second

- Follow your instincts, it is personal

- Take notes, then prioritise and act second

- Understand that as the leader, you have only three topics: people, strategy and values. Everything else is secondary

- Pick a kitchen cabinet of people you trust and use them for problem solving.

BCG's advice for the Ten [10] Actions during the First 100 Days **for any manager** are as follows:

1. **Assess** the company's management team [your direct reports] and complete the necessary initial round of changes within the first 30 days. But Do Not Discount old-timers who carry corporate memory and may be invaluable over time.

2. **Communicate** *your vision* for a better organisation and ensure employees understand how you will get there. Convey the basic values that serve as a framework for future decision making. Convey your clear management style of how you will treat others and how others should treat or deal with you. Be very clear *on your style* but not prescriptive too early in decisions.

3. **Meet and discuss** with ten of your salespeople *on the frontline* and ask them what the organisation should be doing: you will hear all the customer complaints, especially quality problems and be able to predict future trends in sales even before your finance people can. They will simply love to talk to you and chew your ear; and you will find out how you can support them.

4. Following on from point 3, then meet with *ten top customers* for an outside-in view of the business. Listen carefully, receive feedback graciously and then **act on the valuable ideas**. Consider then bringing your senior staff (well briefed and respectful, not argumentative) together with your customer's senior personnel to resolve your way forward.

5. Pay attention to your personal habits, as they are a reflection of you and **your projected image**. Consider what time you arrive at work, how you relate to people in the hallway, how you allocate your time, how thoroughly you prepare for meetings and your style in meetings – do you take notes or rely on your memory? If you wish to be seen as an action person, pick two aspects or outcomes that you wish to change very quickly and decisively.

6. In a turnaround situation or when you have limited time to be seen as effective and decisive, or there are significant concerns over available cash flow, halt all discretionary spending until you have **determined your business priorities**. Cash is KING and reflect this in your focus. Create a shortlist of priorities and ensure they are well funded and well tracked.

7. **Understand** *the businesses key profit drivers and critical success factors;* the leverage points and develop a simple reporting mechanism so you are regularly appraised of these. What is your profit engine and how do you drive that for growth and retention?

8. Assess and understand the *problems that reside on the* **Balance Sheet** and communicate that you understand them and will be addressing them early in your tenure: this is a nice way of saying get a handle on debt and gearing ratios, obsolete inventory or non-recoverable receivables, excessive goodwill which can't be supported or unresolved customer complaints and further festering litigation.

   Also get a handle on any OFF-BALANCE SHEET commitments. A good starting point as a new broom is to clear the decks and get a clean start: consider and deal with any impairment or necessary write downs of assets or urgent sale of caustic operations. Better to sell off the problem child for $1 than have an open pit draining cash.

9. Develop the ability to **detect** *HIDDEN THREATS* and *OPPORTUNITIES* and get them out there for consideration and action. Keep a running list of quick successes such as new product promotional programs or new contracts with suppliers or customers or new board reporting presentations. You would want to fix everything all at once but you will have a list of what needs addressing over the next 12 months once you get past your First 100 Days in the Job.

10. **Manage UPwards**: manage the *expectations of your Board of Directors* with communications upwards and support from your leadership team below. Speak with one tongue and voice. Set expectations and exceed them.

At the end of your FIRST 100 DAYS, you will have moulded and met expectations. A strong Performance Report Card during your First 100 Days in the Job will set you on your path and with a tone for the next 1,000 days.

CFO: Shared Services Review
The NEXT wave of Corporate Efficiency

Shared services were all the go in the late 90's and into first decade of the 21th century, but do they still deliver the benefits that were envisaged and suit your new organisations' management model?

You will need to assess if these Shared Services models, as adopted, still suit your business or you foster the discussion which is about the 'Next Wave of Shared Service Centres'.

KPMG in its "Being The Best: Inside the Intelligent Finance Function"[25] said: **The Next Wave of Shared Service Centres will cut deeper and deliver even bigger benefits for the organisation: the C-Suite Group must look for bigger and better shared solutions and applications**.

The recent 2020 Covid-19 experience has forced and informed businesses that working from home remotely can be achieved and results in potentially more efficient overhead cost management and less centralised HO floor space and operations.

As CFO, you will need to *determine your position and direction on Shared Services* for your particular business and the way that customers and suppliers are engaged with your business. Certainly, cost pressures continue to be an important focus for the CFO and various techniques like Overhead Valuation Analysts and Expense Reduction Analysts will provide benefits and savings that a new CFO can bring to the business.

Any such **Benefits Realisation Models** are worth considering as it is a gain at no cost unless both the gain is realised and achieved and can be quantified.

The whole discussion of Shared Services functions, centralising corporate services, Off-shoring or In-shoring, etc. will all be part of your focus for your First 100 Days in the Job and will have been tested out at the initial and secondary interviews. You need to be able to describe your position on Shared Services as an option and your past experiences in successfully implementing such a model.

You will need to look, listen and understand your future organisations current attitude to Shared Services centres, what competitors are doing, any history within your business, what the risks are in security of information and control processes, and then help coach a way forward for your organisation.

Risk Management and Risk Mitigation

What are your Top 20 risks and how would the Audit and Risk Committee rate their Likelihood and Consequence?

KPMG framework for Enterprise Risk Management [ERM] [26], links the organisation's business strategy to the Risk strategy. This figure below is a brilliant way to build shareholder value for risk mitigation and management. This example has been included in CIMA's Gateway Series No.49 [11] for ERM.

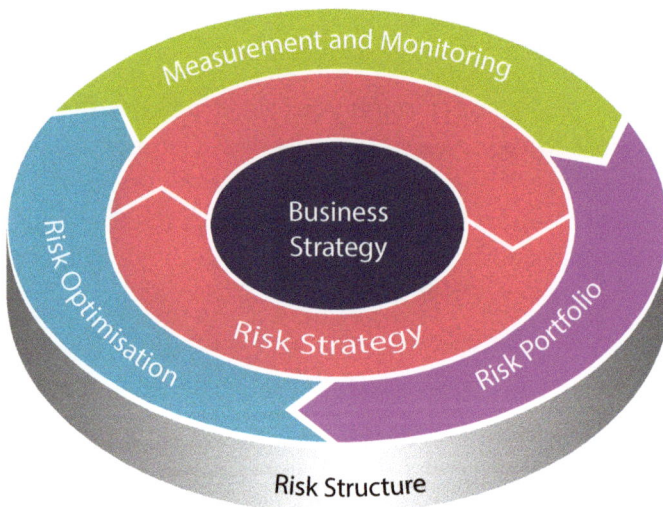

Figure 17: Enterprise Risk Management

Source: Enterprise Risk Management: an emerging model for building shareholder value, A KPMG White Paper, KPMG, November 2001.

Once you have determined your Top 20 risks, they can be placed on the Likelihood-Consequence Matrix. You can raise the discussion on risk and then mitigation with the senior management team and then the board.

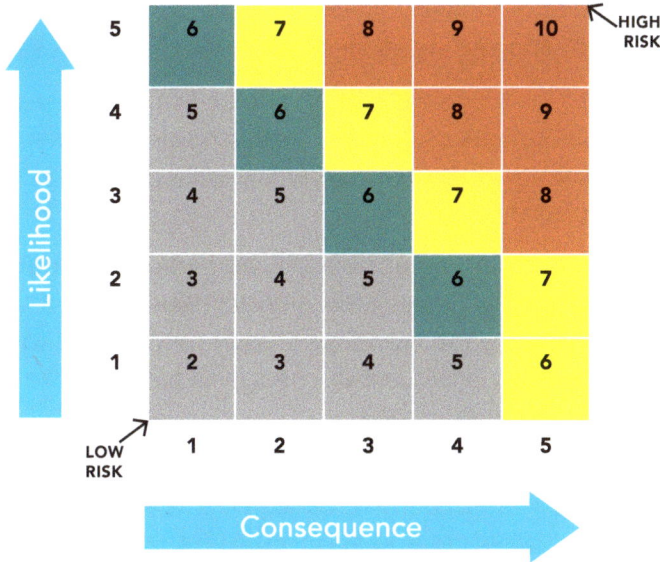

Re-examine the risk exposure after mitigation:

Finally you need to have a formal meeting with your external auditor to understand their issues and areas of concern from a formal audit perspective. Further we suggest an informal questioning of 'how are we going' and 'what are the unwritten situations or concerns that have not yet made it to the Audit Management letter'.

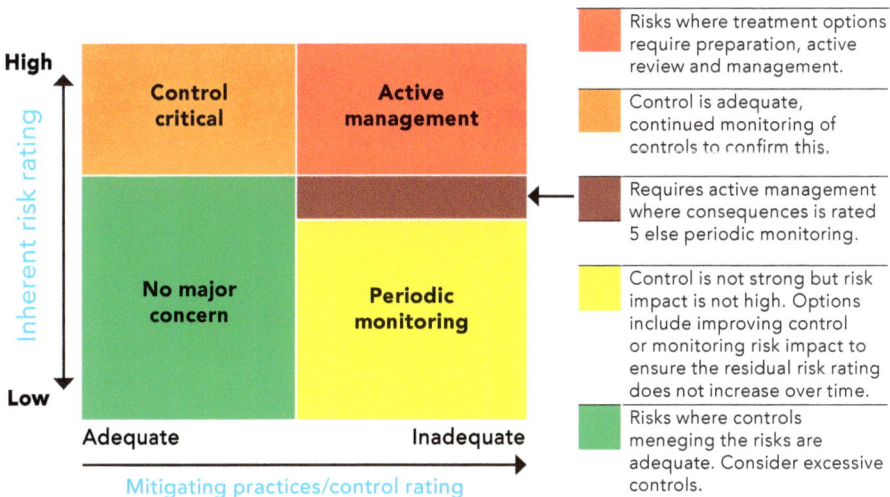

Risks where treatment options require preparation, active review and management.

Control is adequate, continued monitoring of controls to confirm this.

Requires active management where consequences is rated 5 else periodic monitoring.

Control is not strong but risk impact is not high. Options include improving control or monitoring risk impact to ensure the residual risk rating does not increase over time.

Risks where controls meneging the risks are adequate. Consider excessive controls.

CFO Positioning
Case Study: McKinsey's[10] 'Starting Up as CFO – First 100 Days'

An important International study concluded that the learnings for a CFO in their First 100 Days in the Job included:

- The CFO position involved an increasingly complex strategic role focused on driving the creation of value for the business.

- CFO's need to understand the key drivers of the business: and that the critical drivers of success best considered are sources of growth, operational improvements, and changes to the business model of the business.

- Insightful CFO's on being appointed, immediately conducted a Strategy Audit and a Value Audit – understanding how capital markets would value the business's fundamentals and focus on getting the strategy right: cut or change to focus on the big ticket Value creating activities.

- Big emphasis was placed on meeting & liaising downwards with business unit chiefs: these Executives need support and confirmation of progress and support from the chief exec and chief financial person.

- Major theme was the CFO aligning with the CEO and the Board, avoiding any appearance of conflict or disharmony with the top team: a logical step to the CFO becoming an executive director on the board of directors.

- At the end of FIRST 100 Days, the CFO MUST initiate fundamental changes to their finance functions' core activities – they must pick 3 or 4 big issues or approaches   and move ahead to implement change over the second 100 days in the position. These will involve reengineering the finance team in the following aspects or areas of focus:

- Fast Monthly Close and Reporting
- Rolling Quarterly Forecast [RQF]
- Customer Profitability Analysis
- Board Dashboards and Measures That Matter [MTM] models.

Summarising McKinseys' findings, the BIG FOUR areas of focus or attention for the CFO were:

1. Conducting a strategic and value audit

2. Building strong relationships with business unit managers

3. Building trust and relationships with the CEO and Board

4. Working out the big three or four projects to transform the finance team to make it operationally efficient and at best practice.

CFO: Finance Walking a Mile in My Shoes

Walking a Mile in their shoes is a concept we discussed at the end of Chapter 3 that a CFO must do, but for your position we have an additional extended version for you.

The Finance function is one which must practice the 'Walk a Mile in My Shoes' approach: Finance is a central service to provide operational management with critical information on the performance of their business unit and function. To do that, finance must be out and about helping operational management to understand their results and key drives and how to better their performance with pricing and cost management.

If Finance is to be the team that will manage and oversee performance reporting, then understanding finance from the recipients' or providers' perspective is important.

As such, the CFO specifically must:

- Understand the resource and time pressures of providing control information upstream to corporate management.
- Identify the cost to properly provide operational and cost information to operational management including customer profitability and cost control information

- Assess whether the current reporting requirements and deadlines are too onerous and could be reduced without impacting the control reporting you wish to have in place for your corporate requirements.
- Focus Performance Reporting on the 'Measures That Matter' [MTM].

The message that you as CFO have an OPEN DOOR POLICY is crucial – the CFO is here to hear – tell me what is on your mind and how or whether the figures we give you tell you the real story or success or progress of your respective business unit or the group as a whole; what must we tell you on a weekly or monthly basis.

Beware too much open door though, leave it open but with a booking system whereby each day there is a block of time for any staff to book a meeting. Enabling two hours for this sees you are not interrupted during planning or your other external meetings and yet you are still available.

Highly successful CFOs have almost inevitably conducted training programmes focused on Finance for Non-Finance Executives or Commercial Skills Training Programs for Senior Non-Finance Executives: to help guide and educate them on what finance professionals know and take for granted and how management can understand the basis and meanings of those reports; help management to decide what action they need to take based on these reports.

In this way, the Finance team is seen as helpful, supportive and wanting other non-finance executives and managers to understand the terms, methods, nuances of finance so all are on the same page when it comes to assessing and reporting progress up and down the organisation and the decisions they must take.

What makes the CFO stand out and gain Respect - Day 1?

The following personal traits and demonstrated abilities will help you at interview in the selection process and then ensure your authority is stamped when selected for the CFO position and established within the First 100 Days in the Job.

You must demonstrate the following ten traits or qualities:

1. Uncompromising **integrity** and **ethical** standards

2. **Strategic vision** and ability to influence, express and implement business plans

3. **Communications** skills in not just financial terms but ability. to describe and relate to non-financial drivers and concerns or initiatives: communicating being both up to Board and senior management and down to operational Business Unit Managers

4. Sound financial accounting, cash management and business management reporting principles to ensure best of breed **financial management and solvency**

5. **Problem solving abilities:** able to suggest alternative solutions when current traffic seems blocked or snarled

6. **Strong work ethic** as the second in command and the one capable to step in or up for the boss who may be preoccupied with other more pressing 'presidential' matters or conducting other representational roles

7. Ability to be the **trusted advisor** and/or confidante of the CEO and Chairperson of the Board

8. **Self-confidence** and hence ability to represent and present at the Board and to Executive management meetings

9. **Results-oriented focus** on the corporate plan and having the actions and outcomes tangibly determined, measured and reported against.

10. A **team builder** such that you are not a one person band but build a reliable and promotable team of finance professionals.

These competencies for a CFO form the basis for our 'CFO AbilityMap' as discussed shortly.

Training for CFOs for the FIRST 100 Days

For greater scope and in-depth training the **CFO of the Future** workshop is the leading CFO course for CFO's founded by Mr. John Petty, facilitated and further enhanced through Coachability Pty Ltd. The course can be undertaken as intensive over 2 days or over a 6 month duration. This leading course is the first of its kind that is updated regularly for your latest techniques and fundamental measures as CFO. No course has ever compared, worldwide, and this is why IFAC awarded articles of merit for some of these tools.

The Australian Group100, [the Group of 100 CFOs] conducts a professional development program for emerging CFOs covering the First 100 Days in the Job.

The chapter/program modules cover the following 13 topics/aspects:

1. Stakeholder communications
   [focus on Stakeholder management and accountability]
2. Developing your Strategic Plan for your organisation
   [focus on strategic planning in the organisation]
3. Mergers and acquisitions
   [Growth, expansion and how to buy well]
4. Capital and funding strategies [Banking & sources of finance]
5. Driving value through integration
   [Efficient core service management]
6. Financial reporting [Statutory accounting]
7. Tax management [Tax planning and compliance]
8. Role of CFO and finance function
   [CFO skills, relationships and team building]
9. Fraud, bribery and corruption prevention, detection and response
10. Risk management and Risk Reporting
11. People, culture and change management
12. Productivity
13. Program management [Businesses run by dividing into programs that are managed and achieved].

How many of these 13 topics/aspects would you say you excel in?

This is an excellent checklist of the areas that they believe an emerging and developing CFO should be familiar with and able to prove evidence of experience and competency. You should develop an answer of how you have an example of excellence in each of these core responsibilities.

When it comes to training Finance and CFO teams, you should look no further than the **Finance Business Partnering** workshop developed by Coachability and working with CFOs to develop for their teams.

To help you at your interview, we have included interview questions generously shared by Chandler Petty CFO Search and Advisory recruitment and then move into a suggested first 100 days, by the day account as compiled from a survey of leading CFO's.

CFO Position Interview Questions

Chandler Petty
CFO SEARCH & ADVISORY

Chandler Petty CFO Search & Advisory – Interview Questions for the CFO Position:

The authors do many CFO Interviews and Appointments in addition to their CFO Recruitment Agency. We see many CVs and Covering Letters that will either make or break a candidate's ability to proceed to the interview [refer section 1 for your preparation]. We know how to successfully recruit High Performing CFOs and as such can prepare and advise on potential CFO recruits.

Generously we are sharing the biggest insight to your interview to prepare for. Our series of selected but pointed questions directed at a CFO's knowledge, skills and approach, relationships with the Board, CEO, other senior management members and management of their CFO team;

1. Give an example of where you have participated in or made a significant contribution in the Strategic Planning processes/ outcomes of a business. What do you believe is the role of the CFO in strategic planning?

2. What do you understand by the Blue Ocean Strategy [BOS] framework? Have you participated in any BOS workshops and what was achieved?

3. Please give an example where you reassessed the Business Model adopted by your organisation and with what outcomes? What do you understand the concept of a Corporate Business Model entails?

4. Block Chain – what is it and how or where have you implemented it in a previous role as CFO?

5. Please give us any examples where you have had to make hard and unpalatable decisions where the organisations future had to be put in front of personal positions and how you handled those situations?

6. Please tell us of a situation where you brought about radical and improved reporting to the board and executive management team: how did you do it, what were the obstacles and how did you overcome any obstacles?

7. Do you think that Board and management reporting are different and how have you handled these differences?

8. Have you adopted or introduced a Corporate or Balanced Scorecard Reporting pack, with what success, what do you think of Finance reporting Non-Financial metrics?

9. Have you developed a Report On A Page [ROAP] reporting model and how did you gain Board and Management support for this model, if applicable?

10. What do you understand by the concept of RQF {Rolling Quarterly Forecast} – have you adopted it in any past roles? What is your position on the use of detailed monthly budgeting for control and management reporting?

11. Have you ever had a situation where you have disagreed significantly/violently with your Board/Chairperson or CEO and how did you resolve this conflict or disagreement.

12. Can you give us an example where you have used external authorities / auditors etc. to bring about change in your financial management systems or board reporting model.

13. Describe how you have assessed and introduced a Customer Profitability Analysis [CPA] program in a business. What did you learn and what were the critical success factors? Have you developed a Customer Caused Cost model in any business? Do you know how to develop a Cost 2 Serve customer cost analysis model?

14. Please describe your involvement as the CFO in the Risk Management policies and positioning of your business.

15. Describe your understanding of Sustainability and Corporate Social Responsibility [CSR] and your involvement as CFO.

16. Please give examples of CSR that was adopted:
    - By your organisation where you were involved
    - By you personally in the community.

17. What have you learnt most from your experiences as CFO in a public listed organisation?

18. Who is on your CFO team: what roles? How would you describe your management / leadership style with the staff members on your CFO team?

19. What do you understand to be the Strategic Scorecard and please explain where you have introduced it in a past situation?

20. What is your view of the relationship between CEO and CFO? How do you intend to support the CEO? See if they answer as a back seat driver, awaiting the 'please turn here' sign, or are pro-active in suggesting strategic plans to facilitate the CEO's vision, in line with the overall Organisation's Plan.

21. The role of the CFO has been describe in terms of Systems, Process, People, Profits [Cash] and Probity. Please comment on your views in respect to these factors:
SYSTEMS, PROCESSES, PEOPLE, PROFITS, PROBITY.

22. The following diagram on page 221 is the IFAC [International Federation of Accountants] [21] CFO Domain Model: please comment on your competency in respect of these areas of focus and competency: where do you excel and where do you need further attention/skills development?

Future Focus of CFO's

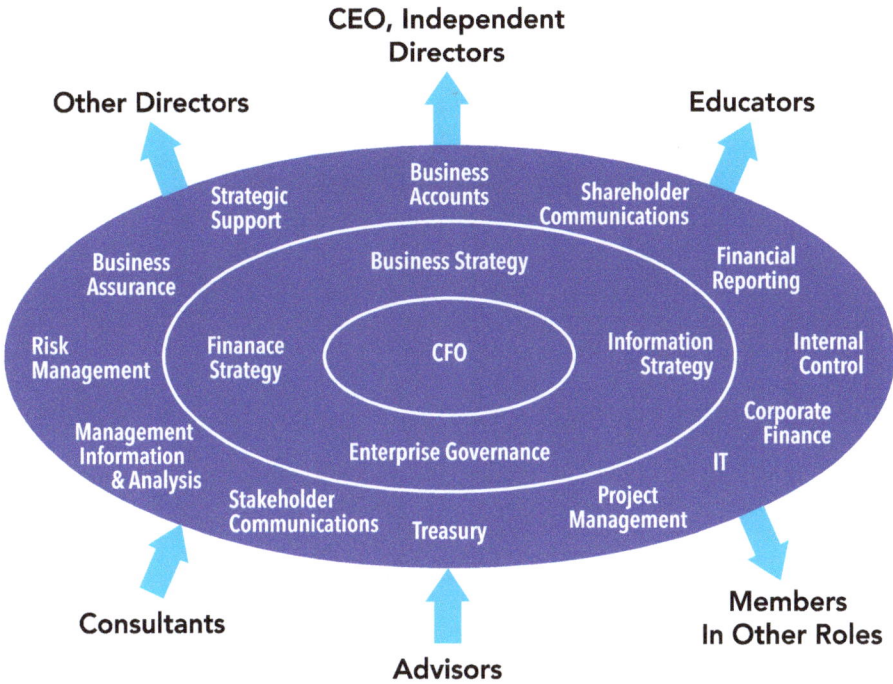

23. What attracts you to this position at our organisation?
24. What will be your goals for the First 100 Days in the job as CFO of this organisation? What will be your style of leadership of finance and interaction with other senior executives of the organisation?

Work Template for CFO First 100 Days

Provided below is an actual work template for working through a 100 Day Plan in the Job for a CFO Position. We surveyed many CFO's as to their first 100 days and reviewed their diaries. Our findings led us to this particular case study of a successful CFO candidate who WON the recruitment contest, did the TRANSITION in organisation and twelve (12) months later was offered a board position as the Executive Finance Director. We combined his win with that of another highly SUCCESSFUL female who also won the recruitment, and now successfully holds the same position on a number of boards:

My 90 day plan

This approach focuses on the following important drivers and areas of role:

I. People

II. Processes

III. Systems

IV. Cash (including balance sheet)

V. Business model (how the organisation makes money)

-30 to 0 Days

Pre engagement is all about the **research and insights** you can gain on the organisation through:

- **Publicly available information:**
  - History
  - Structure (legal entity, trading entities and people from Board to the shop floor)
  - Business model analysis (annual company reports, stock exchange data for info) – what stage are they achieving goals, aligned, diversified from the model?
  - Business model – is it a transformative business model, B2B, B2C, B2G, C2C
  - Grants won – blogs, news and LinkedIn brags exhibit most
  - Financial performance
  - Products or Services – current offerings, by type,
  - Brands
  - Market information and trends of the industry, demands, supplies

- Media releases
- Future forecast of demand for products
- Future forecast of ability to meet supply
- Tech trends that may impact both positive and negative

- **Organisational information if permitted:**
  - Board reports for past 2 years
  - Management reports past year
  - Current financial statements

- **Stakeholder Engagement**
  - Familiarise with the Organisational structure
  - Research Board and CEO profiles
  - Organise calendar to meet with stakeholders
  - Meet with CEO for expectations alignment
  - Research and if reasonable, contact the predecessor CFO to gain insights as to hurdles and expectations
  - Discuss organisational culture and work culture

Day 1 - 10

The big **introductory period** where egos remain in check, no bragging, just listening and observing, with the ability to confirm your prior research as to financial health, business models etc. Meet with key internal stakeholders including board members, executive leadership team members, management and finance team members. Obtain as much background information with respect to the company's:

- Strategy (short, medium and long term)
- Business model and organisational goal per board minutes
- Operating entities and relationships
- Financial performance and health check
- Key Customer and Supply Relationships
- Key priorities for Executive team
- Risks and risk mitigation
- Business acquisition opportunities.

Review corporate documents relating to the above as well as prior external and potential internal audit/diligence reports and tax return memorandums.

Organise my calendar, which will include:

- Establishing weekly 1:1 meetings with finance team members, CEO, COO and CPO.
- Establishing monthly 'ADEPS' with direct reports, CEO and COO.
- Establishing monthly finance team meeting.
- Establishing regular meetings with operating entity management and work with them to determine most appropriate time frame for ongoing meetings.

End of week two - CFO

You will have **compared the financial accounts**: [Balance Sheet: what the organisation owns and owes: the Profit and Loss or Income Statement – where the revenue comes from and where it is spent: with the reality of the cash management of the business; and now have a better view of what is working financially and what now needs to be evaluated and possibly changed].

You will have **spoken to all key players** and formed a view of who you can trust, who you can work with and what needs more detailed analysis: you should have formed a view importantly on the Balance Sheet factors for the business and the revenue, cost and profit drivers. Remember CASH is KING and your rein will be judged by your cash management performance: cash user and abuser or cash generator and accelerator.

You will have **reviewed the in place strategic plan** of your new organisation, and started to assess whether it is relevant and to be supported or in need of a massive makeover, which will take some time to mobilise. You won't change performance and outcomes in a week but will form a view on whether you can and will support the in place strategic plan longer term and what and how to reassess its relevance going forward.

Day 11 - 16

Focus is balanced between **understanding of management and executive support:**

- Meetings with operational management.
- Understanding key drivers of the business model.
- Assess the adequacy/appropriateness of decision support to key management.
- Understand current executive and downstream reporting timetables and assess suitability for action taking.

Day 16 - 20

Increased **Finance focus** during this week 3 whereby you review cash balances and related forecasting processes and systems. This could include creation, improvement and review of:

- Weekly cash flow forecasting
- Bank reconciliations
- Purchase to pay process
- Order to receipt process
- Capital expenditure approvals and operational expenditure controls
- Banking relationship and facility review / covenants monitoring
- Working capital and terms of trade management; review all working capital management performance and scope for improvement

Day 21-40

Weeks 4-6 offer key observations and insights as to **intra-month and end of month reporting** to allow you to assess credibility of the numbers.

Review all financial and management reporting including copies of previous external reports, board reports, management reports, reporting processes, balance sheet reporting, and key reporting and performance metrics used and indicators:

- Review, agree and establish key metrics to better understand performance and highlight any risks and concerns
- Notate and analyse differences between reporting to executive, board, management and statutory

- Initial assessment of the finance and inventory system regarding applicability and scalability
- Review the sales reports – pipeline and commitments
- Create a flash report if one doesn't already exist
- Review divisional reporting
- Understand the yearly finance calendar and related key processes (e.g. budget and reforecasts)
- Assess budget and forecast accuracy and budget methodology
- Determine WIP reporting and metrics used against accounting standards and analyse for recommended management improvements
- Effectiveness and efficiency review of Procurement management
- Recommend revisions to reports (internal and external) and improvements to processes where necessary
- Balance sheet review: gearing and residual NTA – economic worth
- Assess gearing and liquidity ratios against industry standards.

Day 41-50

You are now passed the settled in phase and observed intra and month end and your team are settling into your leadership style. It is time to **conduct a review into your finance team**.

- Review CVs and employment contracts
- Review and improve clarity around individual role and responsibilities with 6 to 12 month objectives for each team member
- Establish finance team project plan outlining key projects for completion
- Establish training schedules
- Delegate tasks
- Redefine optimal finance team structure highlighting and any vacancies or 'wrong fit' issues
- Establish a 'plan on a page' for the finance team.
- The intent is to head a Top Performing Finance Team that is Best of Breed.

Day 51-55

Review **key contracts** and potential **contingent liabilities** to ensure no surprises and work with legal adviser(s) to understand any key risks.

Determine viability of **stock** levels and obsolescent stock.

Review **leases** and major contracts to establish your registers and any potential internal and external factors that may be cause for concern.

Day 56-60

Meet with board and key external stakeholders including auditors, investment community, lenders, and key shareholders/trustees.

Day 61 -80

Conduct a deep dive review into the **control and system environment** including:

- Review of the core accounting and ERP system
- Understand current system capabilities
- Establish requirements [demands and wishes] of the system
- Review of finance policies including intra-group and inter-group related party transactions
- Review all insurance policies and insurance management
- Identify control weaknesses
- Review annual compliance certificates signed off by management and implement such a scheme if none exist.

Day 81-90

Resolve any outstanding urgent and important issues stemming from the activities discussed to date and **prepare** a report to be delivered to the board and executive leadership team including key material findings and recommendations.

This involves **summarising** your findings from your First 100 Days in the Job and your summation/positioning and way forward for your 2nd 100 Days in the Job.

Day 90-100

Reflect on your First 90 Days and **Plan** for the Second 100 Days and then your First 1000 Days in the organisation.

At the end of your First 100 Days in the job, you are ready to facilitate an Executive and Board Retreat, using the Blue Ocean Strategy approach to develop the organisations' SWOT 3x3 Matrix Action Plan. You should suggest and initiate this retreat as you have just taken control of strategic development and the strategic planning for your organisation.

You will also help to develop the **Measures of Success [MOS]** for the Innovation and Business Growth Quadrant of your Scorecard measuring such outcomes as:

- Number of new patents applied for
- Revenue from new products or services launched to market in the prior two years
- Number of suggestions from staff: suggested and them implemented
- Number of Technology or New Product Awards
- Number of Co-Operative Research Projects with Industry or Academic Research organisations
- Number of Industry Grants won
- Number of Industry accreditations or product/service awards.

Strategic Tools for your First 100 Days

Being Strategic and deeply involved in the Strategy Development and Implementation of the Strategic Plan is what a CFO thrives in and is demanded upon them. To develop strategic plans, assess and recommend changes within your first 100 days, and to truly add value requires a few very valuable strategic tools.

We have included these strategic tools in Appendix for your focus and technique:

    I.   Was/Is/Will Be

    II. SWOT

    III. CIMA Strategic Scorecard

    IV. Business Model

    V. DIFOTis

    VI. BCG Growth Share Matrix.

The First 100 Days in the C-Suite will be head down, many meetings and assessments and bringing to the fore your expertise in strategy, finance, customer focus and business management. You will want to make a difference and stamp your mould on your organisations team or at the board and the executive level.

As we get to the end of the First 100 Days in the Job, you need to demonstrate your calibre as a STRATEGIST and how you have the skills and techniques to help position the organisation not only in the Present but also for the Future. You must be strategic and be seen to be the strategic partner.

Key to this will be the areas of focus or techniques in the rear Appendix that you can use as models to facilitate strategic planning in your new business.

78. COO [Chief Operating Officer]

A very important, but much misunderstood and much maligned role as described by HBR article titled: Second in Command: The Misunderstood Role of the Chief Operating Officer by Nathan Bennett[6] and Stephen A. Miles, is one we want to unravel and help you in your first 100 days.

The COO role is so important that regardless of services or products that your firm may offer, regardless of being a not-for-profit or a public or privately listed organisation, the need for operational leadership delivers results.

The role of the COO is, well, different. Our research since then has put a finer point on the difference. Through in-depth conversations with dozens of executives who have held the position and with CEOs who have worked with COOs including ourselves, we've gained insight into a subject that has been largely neglected by organisational scholars.

In this chapter we expand upon and share the success and failure factors we've identified, as well as our analysis of such related questions as: Are there circumstances in which a number two role is particularly useful? Are there situations when it will inevitably produce tension and discord?

Understanding what makes for a successful chief operating officer is vital because **the effectiveness of COOs is critical to the fortunes of many companies and could be to many more**. As we will suggest, the high-ranking executive that is on par with the CFO or reporting to, is a role that by rights should become increasingly prevalent. It is prevented from doing so, perhaps, because it is so misunderstood and therefore also poorly recruited.

Role of the COO

The accreditation to a COO is through the rank, having proven experience as a CPO [Chief Procurement Officer] or CSM [Chief Supply Manager], a CLO [Chief Logistics Officer], an Engineering Manager, or a **Chief Production Manager [CPM]**, being the main ladders to this senior executive role. Having worked alongside many CPM's we can confidently advise that this is the **predominant promotion to COO**, as they are already performing management duties of a COO, but without the governance, the risks and other elements that a COO is now responsible for.

The role of the COO includes:

- Production management
- Risk prevention management and strategy
- Operational governance management
- Logistics management
- Warehouse management
- Research and Development
- Procurement management
  [CPO or CSM are direct reports to you]
- Customer service and sales management
- Establishing KPIs for all managers reporting directly to you and your team
- Forecast and budget accountability for your departments
- Capital expenditure requests.

The controversy of sales reporting to operations is one we need to quash. Customer service and sales are on the front line reliant upon production and thus they both impact one another. To discuss issues in supply and demand requires both departments to WORK COHESIVELY and as such, this provides good basis for why a CSO and CPO should report to the COO.

Another way to view this is from supply and demand that both the CPO and CSO represent. To output at **equilibrium** is to have these two both work cohesively. Let's look at the first 100 days in the job of a COO.

The First 30 Days

The **first week** is your week to meet directors, C-Suite executives and unit managers. Due to your large subordinate hierarchy you will need to plan this well so as to **prioritise meetings with key stakeholders** internally.

Weeks two to three will be one of **observation** of the processes conducted by each department whilst exploring the products and services offered. Refrain from suggestions of improvements you may see as you perform your exploration, it is too early to suggest and without a well-researched strategy, it is immature.

Week four is a good time to observe the **month end procedures** each department are currently performing, notating time spent to prepare month end if any. **Review the last stock take** performed as to the volumes of stock write-off due to lost or obsolescent stock; both of these provide indicators a good starting point as to efficiencies.

The Next 60-100 Days

Leadership to so many units that do come together to produce the product or service for the organisation requires the **best strategic thinking** experienced manager to deliver the organisation's goals. The board and C-Suite will be judging and scrutinising your strategic plans that you share within your first 100 days on the job. Time flies but so to does the pressure to prove your worth.

Now is a good time to use process flowcharts to assist your **design and presentation of operational strategies**. Further tools of DIFOTis explained under the CPO header will measure utilisation of equipment, capital, floor space and manhours. This tool is a COO's best friend. Measuring DIFOTis on a regular quarterly basis will reduce downtime, increase outputs and really capture how you are using the capital invested. It may unearth the need for updated capital, shift changes, staff changes, etc.

Warehousing may be centralised or if many sites will be regionally centralised, requiring you to review the organisations business plans to align the storage facilities to suit with emphasis on inventory days and **risk mitigation** to pre-empt natural disasters. Further review of operating system integration, tracking and barcoding will also need analysis.

Alignment of warehousing management with logistics management and the style of procurement ordering [just-in-time, consignment, import, etc.] begin to paint the picture of the direction your strategic plans will take. Procurement management must be cash efficient whilst considering min/max levels with lag delivery factors. We suggest you refer to the CPO and CSM chapters to oversee the depth of these roles during your tenure.

Determining new service or product launches, peaks and troughs in demand will formulate your operational schedule triggers to better balance utilisation of labour and capital whilst again providing clearer advanced forecasting for procurement, warehousing and logistics.

Organisations that wish to stay ahead of competition will continually seek to improve or introduce new services or products as soon as the most recent launch of a service or product, through research and development. You will need to **observe and assess the R&D**, it's demand on labour, equipment, floor area and finance to take this into your overall strategic plan.

Any good leader delivers best practice ethics and corporate governance regardless of the type of organisation. Ensuring your team, managers and employees understand more than just their responsibilities, as it is their **accountability, ethics and patriotism** to the organisation. This includes leaks of new launches, issues within the business or sharing of information. Governance takes many forms including reporting and compliance whereby standards are not be short-cut or covered up.

Deliver your strategic operational plan before the 100th day. It will be a high level plan for senior executives, to then be expanded further into detail for each unit manager during the course of the next few months. It will deliver performance growth and other kpi measures whilst improving efficiencies, decreasing risks and streamlining processes.

Business Partnership with the CFO and CEO should involve regular weekly meetings to keep them informed, to support and assist you. The role is big, employees many, contractors many, external stakeholders many, but it is a rewarding role that is the heartbeat of the organisation.

79. CHRO [Chief Human Relations Officer]

Human Capital is of great importance and often under-valued as those trying to make work to keep themselves employed. This could not be further from the truth and it is up to the CHRO executive to share their strategic plans to prove as such.

Managing and leading all aspects of human resource management, industrial relations, training, practices and procedures, employee contracts and dispute handling is a vital role. You will be reporting either directly to the CEO or alternatively may be to the CFO.

Technology has changed the size of HR departments from large to thinly scaled. Many a question is raised as to where does payroll sit, under a CFO or CHRO? The truth is both. The payroll operation itself is definitely reportable to the CFO and as such most report to this department. However, the HR contracts of employment, although they are payroll related, are only provided to payroll upon being completed and checked off by the HR department, this makes sense as it is this department that hired the employee.

Government compliance has increased the importance of the HR department. The ability to **scope talent** is one refined to a HR dept or alternatively an agency. When a HR department exists, there must be good substantiation for use of an agency and the cost involved. Agencies are experts in talent scouting through the thousands of applications utilising their ATS to reduce the number of eligible candidates.

Role of the CHRO
The role of the CHRO includes:
- Delivering employment reporting and analysis
- Manage Employee Succession planning
- Develop an Annual Talent Strategy plan
- Talent acquisition and Termination management

- Drive employee training and development
- Balance CSR initiatives to talent recruitment
- Leading employment complaints, disciplines and negotiations
- Driving Enterprise Bargaining Agreements [EBA's]
- Strategic structure of employment to meet the organisation's goals
- Forecast and budget reporting for employees
- Increasing employee wellness satisfaction
- Foster Culture awareness management
- Responsible for Compliance to regulatory and ethical workplaces
- Updating equal opportunity practices and procedures
- Execution of all employee contracts and forms
- Advising the CFO, CEO and the Board of workplace accident claims, legal employment issues, union impacts, serious injuries and near misses.
- Developing initiatives for increased employee engagement
- Building employee promotional programs
- Enabling disability friendly workplaces
- Advising unit managers of employee patterns of sick leave
- Arranging executive strategic planning days and training off site
- Training management in WFM [Workforce management]
- Employee engagement surveys
- Performance and Remuneration reviews
- Remuneration sub-committee member
- Accountable for employee accessories; keys, passes, lockers
- Induction/Onboarding Training Programs for all departments
- Create awareness of scouting for intrapreneurs and where feasible, implement a supportive procedure for these exceptional employees
- Lead employee risk management programs
- Liaise with government departments on OH&S issues.

The list above is extensive and the reason why your team that you inherit must be up to the task to assist and support you. As an executive you will not be required to report regularly at board meetings, however your data analysis will be required regularly by the CFO.

The First 30 Days

Your **first week** on the job is quite different to that of other executives in the style that you meet where you are not **focused on** product or service but on **humans, real people, their welfare, training, culture and promotional opportunities**. Your week will be packed full of introductory meetings of Directors and Executives.

During these meetings you will be judged on your **warmth and compassion**, whilst also displaying your **strong ethical leadership and corporate culture skills**. Whilst meeting directors it is important to utilise this time to ask them what they feel could be improved, needs to be and is working well. Three simple questions, that will provide good insight.

Your **second week** will continue on the **exploratory observation** and **listening** to the positive and negative undertones of staff. It is important you retain a positive approach at this time to avoid being bogged down in petty disputes as you find your feet, knowing disputes will be waiting but requiring a full culture check assessment prior.

The **next two weeks** will be spent **examining** the current employment contracts, EBA's, policies and procedures including complaints, harassment, drug and alcohol, privacy, etc., and the organisation's business model and strategic plan. Learning of the **level of training programs already in place** and the calendar of prior committed workshops will assist your understanding in the commitment to human capital investment that the organisation has been undertaking.

Complete a week during this period to **observe the month end process** your employees may be involved with, any reporting provided, and any talent acquisition that may be occurring.

The Next 60-100 Days

It is time for you to begin developing your **strategic talent management plan** that will include training, succession planning and promotional level categories. Further to this will be the need to present your **analysis of each business unit** to the unit managers of leave patterns that may indicate culture issues within the unit requiring you to **implement training and measures**.

The strategic plan you develop will **align to the organisations goals** whilst addressing current major issues that may be present in the workplace. These may be the SIFR [serious injury frequency rate] that should always be low or ultimately zero, or the near misses that are otherwise preventable.

Human safety should be at the forefront of best business practice, from painting lines, installing a barrier to ensuring two people are always in the same department working in case of a fall, and that there is safety in terms of sexual harassment risk aversion.

This period will see you judged like any other employee, having spent 100 days in the job, as your eager peers, managers and staff are enthusiastic to learn of how you will change the workplace and their careers. **Your strategic plan will reduce employee turnover, increase employee engagement that will drive employee performance and productivity**.

80. CIO [Chief Information Officer]
CTO [Chief Technology Officer]

Like many C-Suite titles, it is the incumbent who understands the confusion between two similar titles and not necessarily the employer. For those who are unaware, a **CIO looks inwards** whereas a **CTO looks outward**. Many in the roles find there is not a CIO and CTO and hence the ability to perform both roles is often placed on the new incumbent.

To better understand the differences between the CIO and CTO we have split their duties as follows:

CIO duties:
- ERP [Enterprise Resource Planning]
- iOt [internet of things]
- Internal access controls
- Internal Technology Architecture: hardware and devices required by staff
- Software upgrades
- Research into softwares that can improve the organisation's performance

- Internet supply provider [ISP] management to maximise speed and performance
- Boardroom and training equipment
- Cyber security management
- Process improvement management
- Manage IT staff and outsourced contractors
- Streamline business processes
- Manage staff and business unit requests
- Responsible for budget of internal technology, internet, hardwares, softwares and security.

CTO duties:

- Technology strategic plan
- Manage all technology infrastructure
- Customer-centric focus for a highly satisfied buyer experience
- Responsibility for external technology; website; online sales tech
- Manage outsourced contractors of engineers and web developers
- Review and assess external technological progress for potential deployment
- Accountable for all external technology budget expenditure
- Enable big data analytics, AI capability and cloud collection
- Monitor and manage social media platforms.

Comparing the two distinct differences in duties provides us with a better appreciation for the need for both roles, subject to the size of your organisation and financial capability. Both roles report to the CFO or if no CFO, it will be reporting to the CEO. Questions have been asked as to why not direct to the CEO, and it is simply due to the strong business partnership between a CFO and CIO or CTO that provides for more immediate urgent response when changes are needed in real time, or is of a capital nature.

To assist you in determining which is needed ask if it is internal digitisation of the organisation you need or is it improving and service customer technology requirements, remembering one is internal focussed and the other is external focussed.

For those with an app based business you would consider hiring a CTO and then a CIO as you grow. However, if you are a hospital or university it is both that you must have at the onset.

With the danger of increased hacking and cyber attacks, you may need the services of a **CSO**, a **Chief Security Officer** whose task is to place the greatest levels of *barriers to prevent cyber invasive penetration*. The CSO will also test your system but as this is the person who is an employee, we ask is it an inherent risk due to the lack of independence to test from an external perspective whilst being an internal employee, aware of the architecture of the system. For this reason, it is suggested that an external contractor is hired to test your website and barriers who is independent. Recent demand has created this niche market of experts such as CSO Security in Australia.

The First 30 Days

Your **first week** is per the outline at the start of this section, **involving meeting** all key stakeholders and your team, and asking questions to ensure you have a really good grasp on the organisation's goals.

The **second to third weeks** are spent **interviewing** each unit manager and a staff member from each unit to understand grievances, ongoing issues, and what works well. This will take a while as you document the systems used, the **systems that are integrating and barriers occurring**. Both the CIO and CTO will undergo these interview assessment meetings.

The **fourth week** involves meetings with all **external providers** to understand what the current contracts are and your assigned reps that you will need for your future renewals and amendments.

The Next 60-100 Days – as CIO

Armed with findings from interviews and meetings, your **strategic plan** will be prepared during this period ready for preparation toward the end of your 100 days. This period is where we remind you that you are being judged, observed and on display to prove your worth that you sold to your employer.

Due to the expansive role a CIO undertakes, the need for segmentation of the strategic plan into two to three plans may be best practice, these could be:

- Internal security [cyber protection, internal controls]
- Technology architecture [hardware and software used by staff]
- Performance providers [speed of internet, data capability and storage]
- Team hotline and maintenance [urgent requests, registered requests, upgrades]

Viewing the first item, a sound **review** and **update of internal controls** is a necessity at this early stage, especially as a security requirement. A thorough **audit of access** to systems to ensure past employees do not have access, your payroll access is restricted and each team member only has access to that which they are to have access to per their authorisations. Secondary to this is the all to forgotten need for a director to be provided access to the organisation's full password list for best risk management procedures.

The Next 60-100 Days – as CTO

Similar to the CIO you have conducted meetings to formulate your **strategic plan** that your executive peers will be eager to learn. With an outward focus your role is also quite challenging and to map your plan into one strategic plan may be difficult, whereby it would be easier to have a strategic plan for:

- Trade and Website Management [online sales, website, customer experience]
- External security [big data collection, cyber protection, AI]
- Social media platform management [Instagram, facebook, linkedin, twitter, etc].

To present your strategic plan/s it is best as an executive to have a full presentation from overall high summary, to then break down into each segment. As a senior executive you will be presenting to the C-Suite and in some instances, the Board may wish to see a short summation of your strategy. Like many roles that are not directly creating sales, your worth is only as good as the information you share of the planning, progress and success that you and your team have achieved.

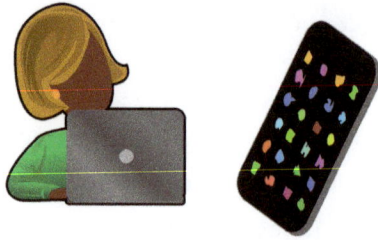

I.T. is a niche area, just as you do not specialise in tax or law, so it is up to you to keep your CEO, C-Suite colleagues, staff and if required, the Board informed of milestones and best practice preventions.

81. CMO [Chief Marketing Officer]

A Chief Marketing Officer [CMO] is an executive responsible for all marketing activities and the development and implementation of the **strategic marketing plan**, that includes all forms of management and monitoring of communication, marketing, advertising and branding.

Typically, a CMO reports to the CEO or alternatively the CFO. Your primary focus is to **increase growth and brand recognition** through your strategic marketing plan, that will support the value proposition statement to drive sales growth and strengthen competitive advantage to position the organisation in the marketplace.

Other duties that harness the CMOs experience stem to market research, competitive and technological advancements, demographic geographic and sociographic marketing campaigns and counsel on consumer pricing expectations.

Duties of a CMO will include:
- Drive brand awareness growth and sales performance growth
- Strategic marketing plan development, implementation to execution
- Design to execution of effective marketing campaigns that provide ROA
- Outsourced marketing services management
- Marketing forecasts – financial and non-financial
- Evidence based Market research

- Trend analysis
- Competitor substitutes and advancements to your offering
- Customer surveys for market research including Net Promoter Score [NPS]
- Industry Conferences, trade shows and events representation
- Manage KPIs for marketing department that align to the organisational goal
- Responsibility for marketing budget
- Management and accountability for CRM, SEO and SEM
- Marketing reports and analysis including presentations
- Business partnering with the CFO, CTO, CSO, COO and CEO
- Social Media marketing
- Design of annual reports
- Responsibility for external advertising pamphlets and brochures
- Appreciation and understanding of price discount and increase strategies.

The First 30 Days

Your **first week** is per the outline at the start of this section, involving meeting all key stakeholders and your team, and asking questions to ensure you have a really good grasp on the organisation's goals.

The **second week** is spent mostly **observing** the products and services your organisation is selling. No matter the industry sector and whether a NFP, educator, government, public or private business, there is a product and/or service being sold that requires **your placement of the organisation in the marketplace**.

The **third week** sees your talents begin to flourish. Having observed the products and services, you need to determine what the overall HERO product or service is of the organisation. Once your hero is determined, identify from each product line the hero of each line. Dialogue with the CFO is critical at this point to understand the most profitable product that may or may not currently be the highest volume sold. The result of your discussion needs to be discussed with the COO as to feasibility of production capability.

Investing in a campaign is one thing, supporting the rollout and ability to meet demand is another. **Feasibility studies** to ensure you achieve equilibrium for demand and supply is of paramount importance prior to investment in a campaign. Refer to your Chief Economist or alternatively seek direction from the CFO before investing the time and cost into your next rollout. Use of a SWOT analysis will be helpful in assessing products and services as to their performance, so too will be the BCG Growth Share Matrix, refer Appendix A8.

The Next 60-100 Days

A month spent already in your new role has provided you with a large insight into the organisation, its **products and services**, but do you know what campaigns worked and failed prior and for which products? It is time to meet with your peers, staff and executives to ask some hard questions about why they felt from an organisational view and from their own perspective, campaigns excelled and others failed.

Taking this information will help you to learn some other not so marketing related issues that may have evolved. Feedback may have exposed internal politics, budget restraints or poor marketing from your predecessor. Relationship management for a CMO is very important to receive cohesion within the organisation and support for your work.

What about the **external services** you are so heavily reliant upon? Were these used effectively, methodologically, to reach the target buyer that the product was sold to? Questions need to be asked during this period and hard questions of those whom provided the services. Ask for the contractor's perception on whether the campaign could have been run better using various or other means. Examine the statistics of the campaigns reach and success, the demographics, etc. Was it a push or pull product that was marketed in the opposite/wrong way or not reach the target buyer?

A good CMO will campaign, a great CMO will change the buyers life.

There will always be a limit on expenditure and it is up to you to work within this or if you see the budget provided is not adequate for the new campaign, you need to work with the CFO to re-examine this using best practice methodology, understanding their will always be a limit.

When we discuss your methodology a proven simple one that many CFOs do not understand is **ROA [return on advertising]**. Often we see the majority of expenditure upfront in a campaign that has a lag factor in returns. It is up to you to provide a flowchart of the campaign expenditure and when returns are expected. Include in this your ratios of local campaign to that of brand awareness.

Please remember that not everyone is creative as you when it comes to envisioning what is not in their daily role, or capacity to do. Further breaking your ratios into the types of media, the researched proven traffic flow exposed to that media and the basis for modelling of sales from the types of advertisement will not only substantiate your worth, but provide you much respect and ability to increase your budget when required.

Whilst sitting in your role for now a few months, you have had time to **examine the website** and see that its last update and its simplicity of use combined with functionality may or may not be working. Customers like to see even slight changes to websites that they visit, it shows progress and care about what they experience. Engage with your website designer and CIT to create a draft for update, upgrade or improvement of the website and social media pages.

By the end of your First 100 days in the job, your fellow executives and senior directors will want to see a sound **marketing campaign** draft and your review of the outsourced services that will reduce cost and reinvest that cost into better and more far reaching campaigns. You are the enthusiastic CMO that will push their product or service to a greater market share, they need your progress monthly to keep that excitement a buzz. Provide your marketing strategy to the CEO that aligns with your organisation's goals.

As you progress and have your feet firmly on the ground, put your hand up to assist in the Annual Report booklet. Advertising pamphlets were expected to receive your touch but the Annual Reports and Sustainability reports are often overlooked and yet it is these that the shareholder peruse, who ultimately keeps you employed.

82. CSO [Chief Sales Officer]

A sales executive is often confused with the CMO, however as you know but others reading this may not, your role is to **lead and manage sales**, **to meet the sales growth and revenue** targets, that is quite different to marketing products, services and brand awareness. Your leadership is to those on the frontline who seek to successfully *convert* the lead into a fully executed sale.

Often this position is created due to the size of the organisation, being large, across expansive countryside and selling globally. Dependant on the type of organisation, digital sales have lowered cost to sell significantly, whilst there is always a need for an enquiry to reach a human to respond. To not enable responses by humans after asking a chatbot or searching FAQs results in negative experiences for the consumer.

Reporting to the CEO or CFO, the **Duties of a CSO** will include:
- Sales strategy development, implementation to execution
- Reporting of sales per CFO directive
- Training and education of the sales team
- Implementing language barrier reduction for customer service
- Customer service management and training
- After sales customer service management
- Customer complaints management
- Development and enhancement of sales techniques performed
- Customer-centric behaviour training of sales team
- Manage KPIs for sales department that align to the organisational goal and revenue targets.

The First 30 Days
Your **first week** is per the outline at the start of this section, involving meeting all **key stakeholders** and **your team**, and asking questions to ensure you have a really good grasp on the organisation's goals.

The **second week** will be your understanding of the products and services you are selling through an **observation exploration**. Observation of your team's practices is also of importance. The business model is one for you to study as you must understand who the target audience is and how the marketing channels are reaching them.

The remainder of this month will be to **review** the current sales strategy and **develop** a more **robust strategy to drive performance growth**. Analysis of conversion rates and sales metrics will assist your consideration as to the improvement required. Use of a SWOT analysis will be helpful in assessing products and services as to their performance, so too will be the BCG Growth Share Matrix [refer to Appendix].

The Next 60-100 Days

Firmly across all products and services being offered, and your staff techniques, you can start to build your sales strategy. Examine the Net Promoter Score [NPS] to develop a training program to **improve and strengthen customer service**.

Diagnose issues that **customer's experience** as they journey from an interest to a converted sale and post sale service. Often the bad experience may evolve from a team member or it may be from difficulty in finalisation of online sale, payment types offered online, or even how they search online for a product. What of those organisations not selling a tangible visual product?

The ability to sell a service or membership is even harder for your team, reliant upon best practice salesmanship to **convert the sale** reliant on receiving the benefit/s as outlined by your team. Training your team is of upmost importance, not once, but continuing training. How to handle negotiations and win a deal are two key training programs that should be considered.

Observing and assessing your team's capabilities you will have inherited a team that may need training, may not be fit for the role or may be disgruntled having applied for your role and missed out. Handling this situation delicately is a must, so to as encouraging those remaining in the team that you will lead, train and support them to achieving the new KPIs that you set.

C-Suite executives want to see you making changes, they want to learn of your strategic sales plan. The entire organisation works hard as a team, but it is only your team that the public interact with, being the face of the organisation. Marketing has provided the initial broadcast to create the interest in your product or service, it is now up to your team to convert the sale.

Your **strategic plan** should include your strategy, resources, technology, people, processes and tactics that will enable targets to not only be met, but to be exceeded.

---

83. CRO   [Chief Revenue Officer]

CDGO [Chief Development Growth Officer]

CGO   [Chief Growth Officer]

Predominately in the USA, the CRO has become a more frequent role driven by Silicon Valley especially in the Technology sector. In other countries such as Australia, this role is referred to as a CDGO or CGO.

The role is an executive role seated within the C-Suite, reporting to the CEO or alternatively the CFO or COO. Where this role is in place, it replaces the role of CMO and CSO due its incorporation of the roles. Multi-national FMCG's such as Mars and Kimberley-Clarke have recently taken on CGO's to replace CMO's, whilst Coca-Cola employed a CGO who successfully met his KPI's to ultimately retire and not be replaced indicating that this role is still to be proven as long term or short term, which is not within our scope to determine.

Harvard Business Review published a study, authored by Behnam Tabrizi, [33] June 23 2015, claiming 75% of cross-functional teams are dysfunctional. They said, *"This is just one example of the dysfunction that exists in cross-functional teams. In a detailed study of 95 teams in 25 leading corporations, chosen by an independent panel of academics and experts, I found that nearly 75% of cross-functional teams are dysfunctional. They fail on at least three of five criteria: 1.) meeting a planned budget; 2.) staying on schedule; 3.) adhering to specifications; 4.) meeting customer expectations; and/or 5.) maintaining alignment with the company's corporate goals.*

Cross-functional teams often fail because the organization lacks a systemic approach. Teams are hurt by unclear governance, by a lack of accountability, by goals that lack specificity, and by organizations' failure to prioritize the success of cross-functional projects."

The need to reduce individuals who place their needs above of the overall organisation's goals is already being met head on by aligned KPI's, however these are only as good as those who agree, monitor and govern them for the C-Suite. Should the need for a CRO not be welcomed by the board, the individual CSO, CMO and other C-Suite executives can create a **Portfolio Governance Team [PGT]** whereby they must work together on the project to achieve the same goal and be held accountable through the PGT.

Role

Brilliant sales, marketers and CRM geniuses, the CRO or CDGO will **drive revenue / sales growth**. Responsible for all three areas as a CRO or CDGO, your role is to align the three pillars of sales, marketing and CRM to collegiately develop the best customer experience through a strategic customer journey plan.

McKinsey [15] conducted a six year study as to the consumer journey to conclude that those who optimised this consumer journey increased their revenue growth by up to 10%. Subordinates of the CRO will primarily be the Sales Manager, Marketing Manager and CRM Manager.

The ability to harness big data to drive strategies and adapt real time is a skill that this role thrives in. The technological change to big data over the years has pushed the CRO to be tech savvy and to fully understand how those technologies work, and to appreciate and stay up to date with the fast evolving AI [artificial intelligence].

Responsibilities

In addition to managing the overall cohesive performance of sales, marketing and CRM to drive revenue growth, a few major responsibilities are:

- Annual and 3 Year Strategic revenue growth plan
- Increasing and exploring the Omni-channel customer experience
- Major customer, CRM and marketing supplier relationships management
- Developing the value proposition statement
- Managing business products and services
- Increasing revenue growth
- Retaining existing customer relationships whilst increasing market share

- Negotiating with major stakeholders
- Reporting information to management and executives
- Briefing the CEO is evolving industry trends, considering threats and opportunities
- Managing customer research projects into demands and needs.

The First 100 Days in the job will be subject to the current urgent projects at hand, however your first week will be an introductory, listening and learning week amongst your peers, the CEO and if requested or available, the Board.

The following days during this period can be referred to as an alignment of the responsibilities of the roles included in these chapters as a guide, being CMO [Chief Marketing Officer], CSO [Chief Sales Officer] and the role of CRM that we have not expanded into.

84. CPO	**[Chief Procurement Officer]**	
CSM	**[Chief Supply Manager]**	

The titles are often confused by many, however there are two subtle differences. A **Chief Procurement Officer [CPO]** is an **executive role** whereas the **Chief Supply Manager** is a level down and more of a **tactical and operational focussed role** responsible for the daily operational sourcing of procurement.

The CPO will attend board meetings when requested, be responsible for the management, administration and major supply contracts and negotiations, whereas the CSM will in addition to attending to the daily procurement operations, will be responsible for stock replenishment levels, processes and procedures.

All organisations that produce an end tangible product, will have a person in charge of procurement, being the CSM. The larger organisations will have a CPO. These two roles are critical to efficiency of production and costs. The trick to understanding the difference is whether they are a manager or an officer.

Having conducted extensive research and business partnered with both roles, we will examine each of their roles in relation to their first 100 days on the job.

Chief Supply Manager [CSM]

The CSM may report to the CPO, but will work closely under the watchful eye of the CFO. A good CFO will make a lot of cost saving measures through the CSM, with no cause for disruption to production and in fact will influence production through improved reporting metrics. It is vital that these three C's work collaboratively.

The First Week

By the end of week one you will have conducted a **Discovery Week**:

- Meetings with all unit managers [incl. admin and marketing as it may be a simple unresolved need for paper orders to marketing materials] to understand and ask about their needs.
- Ask what is working and ask what is not.
- Meet with employees on the production line or construction build, etc to ask what are the failures by procurement and what works well.
- Ask if there are regular lag factors in delivery from particular suppliers.
- Ask what the substitute products are for major goods.
- Meet with all major suppliers
- Meet with all C-Suite executives to understand their needs
- Meet with the CFO to learn of immediate issues, projects and needs
- Meet with the logistics and warehouse managers to understand their needs.

The Second Week

This is your Systems week. Your focus needs to be a good understanding of how the **procurement system** works:

- Understand and observe how the software determines stock needs, stock levels, to then order the stock, to delivery
- Review the controls of limits on quantities and costs per staff member with access and authorisations
- Attend a toolbox meeting to learn of current issues
- Meet with the Financial Controller to learn of recent stop supplies

- Meet with the Financial Controller to learn the procedures for establishing new credit terms, standards the organisation will accept for trading term durations and procedures to finalise invoices
- Spend a day observing the procurement team ordering, processing, following up and note concerns to be discussed at a later time.

The End of the First Month

You should well and truly have your feet on the ground, understanding processes and met with key suppliers, management, executives and employees who are on the shop floor so to speak.

It is vital that you allowed the procurement system to run its daily course during this period right up through to the end of month process to grasp the true **current health status of the procurement efficiencies and their flow on impact**.

Refraining during this period is very important so you are not perceived to be the new kid on the block wielding a club around at everything that may include some very good processes. Patience also paints you in a warm approachable manner of a professional who will listen to others, observe, notate and prepare a very good strategic review of the overall efficiency and effectiveness of the procurement function.

The next 60 – 100 days

This period allows you to begin strategically planning how procurement can be improved with direction from your CPO if you have one, or alternatively this will be up to you to create the vision.

There are a number of really good tools that you can use in this role and again if you have a CPO and/or a CFO, they may instead perform this role. We have reduced these to effectively month 2-3 due to allow for your month 1 meet and observe period. These are expanded in detail in the CPO section:

- DIFOTis
- Inventory Days
- % of Orders by Cost placed per Day
- Major supplier trading terms
- Min/Max Levels and Lag Factors

- Bulk Pricing Volume Discounts
- Obsolescent Stock
- Substitute Suppliers.

The list will require engagement of the CFO for **quantitative and qualitative aspects** that you may require assistance with. Each week you should be attending to one of these items to create a results report that you can share with your team and other unit managers to create **strategic improvements** that will drive performance growth, risk management and free storage space in the case of obsolescent stock.

Outsourced and Centralised Services

Where there is import procurement for supplies, especially in a global market where tariffs and free-trade agreements can provide greater access to a better supply, there will be a review in addition to that of your procurement team as to centralisation and outsourced services are the best fit.

Subject to your organisation's need, if most procurement is imported, and in large volumes, it may be feasible to conduct a review of the cost to use an outsourced service or to use your inhouse staff. In the study you must include the time exhausted on such logistics, the prices for customs, ports and broker fees, delivery to/from ports be they by sea, rail, air, etc.

A review of using a centralised service may be required if you currently have a de-centralised team for procurement. This will also include the capability and full utilisation of software and its integration using your ERP.

The next 4 – 6 months

Your role is one of most importance and as such there are many areas you thought you would attend to in the first 90-100 days on the job. Time to observe, plan and action is one that must occur with the best research and outcomes, therefore it is in the next few months that you can undertake a few other actionable measures that require more in depth time allocated:

- Price negotiations
- Purchasing Power of Supplies
- Consignment Stock for continuously used smaller items
- Trading term renegotiations and procedures including removal of directors' guarantees

- Use of Bill of Materials where able for standard 3+ stock items used to create one sellable item
- Manage the update of inventory listing in software
- Review classification of inventory parts.

Our experience has shown that organisations will hire more CSMs than CPOs simply due to cost and need. Blockchain has provided for fully automated inventory systems to be embraced, reducing the role of the CSM to a more high level project style role for specialty stock ordering. This does not mean the CSM is obsolete or the CPO, it means you need to **refine your skills** and **hone** the **negotiation skills** that are required and **expand** your use from an operational level **to a tactical and strategic level**.

Chief Procurement Officer [CPO]

Leading the procurement team is the CPO delivering the most experienced **best practice procurement aligned to the organisation's strategic goals**. In addition to the introduction we provided, the executive is responsible for the management, administration and supervision of the **acquisition program**. This includes trade procurement and other procurement of assets that are not within the scope of the CSM. **High level negotiation** is a key attribute the CPO possesses.

The first week is per the outline provided at the start of this section. The second week sees a move into the role to observe the procurement operation whilst it is thereafter that the role truly begins to flourish.

Weeks 3 – 6

Examining the business model for your organisation will ensure your **procurement strategy** will align to and formulate the solid foundation you need to **deliver efficiencies.**

Building on your foundation, you need to *understand the organisation's goals* as it is critical to your planning. Goals will involve change management, new, reduced and eliminated products and services, that must be accommodated in your future plans. Ask about lease duration, changes in location, acquisitions and improvements to property that will impact your supply volumes and management, and the special project negotiations you will be managing the acquisitions for. This is your **planning period** where you will develop your roadmap ahead, your strategic plan at a high level.

The next 60 – 100 days

Successful implantation of your strategic plan requires a well thought out approach to implementation. Who will assist you, who will supervise as you drive each pillar of the plan? This is the time where you involve your business unit managers and CSM to collaborate a full team focussed approach.

The key elements for your role to focus on are:
- Deliver Cost reductions
- Improve processes and procedures
- Capital negotiation sales and acquistions [tangible assets]
- Increase compliance standards
- Risk management through:
  - substitutable supply arrangements
  - stock controls; reorder, min/max levels, lag factors
  - regulatory change effects
- Govern control of procurement authorisation
- Maintenance and review of procurement tenders and contracts
- Centralised procurement management
- Outsourced contract management
- Maximise purchasing power
- Drive sustainably responsible procurement
- Communicate and advise procurement status
- Report to the COO or alternatively if no COO, the CFO
- Business Partner to the CFO
- Optimisation of Inventory Days
- Simplification of Categorisation, UOM, BOM
- WIP management of orders
- WCM of maximisation of cashflow for supply management
- Reporting for monthly Management and monthly or quarterly Executive.

Some of the above tasks may seem duplicative of that of a CSM, however the differentiation is the levels at which management occurs and that of micro to macro involvement.

For example the CPO will be involved and lead the major outsourced contract negotiation, whereas the CSM will act as secondary in the negotiation to remain vigilant of the agreed terms, to then manage the maintenance and approval of jobs, persons, approval of invoices, etc on an operational basis.

Further tasks you will perform during this period are:

- **Collaboration** with Logistics Manager to adapt a full inventory storage system to track, trace and accommodate continuous stock supplies compared to that of lessor used stock, including **risk mitigation** of perishables to non-perishables stored on shelves
- **Classifications** and itemisation of uniformity of stock items
- Process for manual stock order requests
- Stop Supply and Interference to Supply procedures.

Tools
DIFOTis

The most successful game changing tool for measurement of customer satisfaction and supply chain success is DIFOTis. This is one of **the best tools** you can use in finance that drives utilisation and improves performance and yet … it is *non-financial*. You may wonder why this impacts you. Performing this on your suppliers will provide you with the full review of just how well you are being serviced by your suppliers. This is also used in the reverse as a measure for sales of product and service from your organisation.

The concept when broken down is simple but powerful.

DIFOTis **D**ELIVERY **I**N **F**ULL **O**N **T**IME **I**N **S**PEC

Delivery in full on time - Did we deliver the order in full by the date required?

Expand this one step further – was the order what the customer purchased? Was the specifications of the order correct? Was it in Spec?

In the role of procurement, the delivery you placed should be received in full per your order and delivery time slots, but the due date, and in good order. You would know from returned goods and credit note requests that cost the organisation in time, in production and costs. The result to aim for of DIFOTis is 90-95%, with 100% being exceptional but also may be an indication that the calculation is incorrect.

Please refer to Appendix A7 for expansion.

Inventory Days

Inventory procurement has developed over the years to provide improved ordering systems. Your CFO will be able to assist with this useful ratio that measures efficiency of inventory ordering through average days of inventory held in stock prior to use or resale. The goal is to maintain low inventory days, maximising working capital.

% of Orders by Cost placed per Day

A big oversight by procurement which may be due to a lack of understanding and/or communication from the finance manager, is how to place orders to maximise monetary retainment.

The aim is to have the bulk of the cost of orders placed in week one of the month with a standard 30 day net EOM trading applied, resulting in usage of the invoiced delivered goods [assuming delivery within week one] for 50 days on average until payment is due. This is a best practice working capital model use of procurement cashflow.

Perform this calculation against each day to obtain the current ratio of when orders are placed and by the cost involved. Once you have obtained this, aim to increase week one ordering [assuming your terms are 30 days net eom] whilst decreasing weeks two - four.

85. CLO [Chief Logistics Officer]

In an era of digital buying, world trade magnification and pressure on being able to transfer goods or services in dynamic time, the role of CLO has finally received the appraisal so well deserved.

Facilitation of smooth logistics operations that are efficient, productive and maximise utilisation of equipment and storage are a primary role in addition to strategic logistics leadership and management. Reporting to the COO or directly to the CEO, **your role is determined on whether your role is leading the logistics for a services organisation or division, or whether you are leading a products organisation or division**.

Organisations that are service providers may require a CLO to manage the logistics for large organisations. An example is an airline. The CLO will manage the inflight entertainment, the catering transport, other goods required at the ports or onboard, but not the catering content itself as this is the CPO's lead.

The main roles for a CLO remain within goods providers or transporters of goods. Despite technology at the forefront of growth, it is freight that has explosive market growth in the past two years.

In 2020, during a global pandemic, those who lost jobs transferred to employment in the industry to try to meet consumer demand from citizens being locked inside their homes for days and in some overly ineffective instances, for over half a year by their government. Pressure on logistics became huge, transitioning factories, warehouses and the way consumers could collect goods. The CLO was pivoted to importance in the C-Suite.

Fast efficient and effective management of transfers in and out of the organisation will be yours to lead.

The many duties of a CLO are:
- Strategic inventory logistics planning
- Manage logistics methods: air, sea, rail, road
- Manage training of staff
- Manage warehouse staff
- Responsible for all inwards and outwards goods
- Responsible for capacity/volume quotas
- Manage utilisation of equipment
- Risk management of materials and handling
- Risk management of third party services for logistics
- Warehouse storage management
- Risk management of warehouses
- Storage strategy
- Technological improvement planning and implementation [eg. semi or fully automated warehousing; tracing; gps live tracking; blockchain; ERP integration of logistics]
- Sourcing and procurement of logistics providers and contracts
- Capital and facilities requests for logistics operations

- Forecasting and budgeting of logistics
- Tracking and control of inventory
- Responsible for failure to deliver
- Regulatory and legal compliance including registers
- Logistics and 3rd party contract logistics welfare and team culture
- Policies and procedures
- Logistics audits
- Compliance reviews
- Logistics program efficiency and effectiveness review incl. DIFOTis
- Contract and tender negotiations
- Stocktake procedure, process and management under the guidance of the Financial Controller, Finance Manager or CFO
- Logistics reporting as and when required
- Support and partnership to the CPO
- Operational process mapping.

The First 30 Days

The first week is per the outline provided at the start of this section. The **second week** sees a move into the role to **observe** the logistics operations whilst it is thereafter that the role truly begins to flourish.

Having met with stakeholders, listened and observed it is time to move into the bigger areas of **key supply arrangements to logistics**. These may be your freight forwarders and handlers, your domestic transport, distribution network and the process map that is in place.

On a macro view, assess and notate the process map and how your strategic planning could improve time efficiencies, cost and reduce risk. Hold onto your ideas, ready to wrap into your overall strategy as you see from your duties there are many aspects yet to consider.

During **week three** extend time to meet with the CFO to understand the **cost drivers of your department and claims** that may be ongoing or repetitive in nature, including **high risk incidents** that may have occurred.

Also meet with the CPO who will provide you with their insights as to what did work, what has failed to work, and what they would like to see improved in order to fulfil the procurement orders in a more effective and efficient way. It is not always the CLO who causes the cost increase, it may stem from the CPO [Chief Procurement Officer] so be careful to evaluate the requests to that which would see your department unnecessarily inflate costs.

Week three is a discovery week with your peers as you obtain insights into how logistics has been engaging with other departments and what their needs are. The CSO [Chief Sales Officer] will have the information of successful deliveries in both partial and full orders, meeting deadlines and warranty claims or credit returns that relate directly to delivery.

The alliance you create during this week understanding and allocating time to hear of grievances whilst reassuring you are there to develop a logistics strategy that will support the organisation with improved efficiencies, will develop greater business partnership amongst senior executives.

During **week four** review the contracts and create your own contract register summary that provides any list of duration, contacts, any overlap of services and the notice required to cease the contracts. This period has been a **review of outsourced services** provided whilst creating partnerships within your team.

The Next 60-100 Days

Assessing your department's process will require you to observe day to day operations and month end procedures if any are in place including reporting and how orders are closed.

During this period it is suggested that your warehouse/s are assessed in term of:
- Mobile Equipment [no. of, ageing, type of, suitability of].
- Utilisation of organisation owned transport in a 360 degree utilisation capacity [deliver goods and return with a full load of procurement orders collected]

- Roles of staff members, numbers of, shifts worked.
- OH&S management within warehouses and delivery channels.
- Shelving and storage [types, styles, suitability, ageing, accessibility].
- Natural disaster risk to storage [perishables stored per height, elevation of warehouse/s in topographic risk, generators, etc].
- Pallet and container suitability, ageing, style and use of.
- Inventory categorisation method and its subsequential classification assigned to each SKU or product.
- Utilisation of storage space with attention to peaks and troughs demanded throughout the year and ability to support those peaks.
- Obsolescent stock [age, storage space, plans to sell at cost or remove]
- Traceability of inventory through the entire picking to destination process
- Authorisation controls and procedures
- Reporting procedures and quality of reporting captured to relevance of what you would like to have measured in order to improve processes.

The list is plenty but your days are those spent that formulate your strategic plan. A primary measure for you to use if **DIFOTis**, **Delivery In Full On Time In Spec**. You will find DIFOTis located under the CPO and CSM and may have noted the term DIFOTis mentioned throughout the book.

The DIFOTis metric measures how especially for your department your logistics is working. Primarily it is understood for departing goods and services, however it can also be used for the reverse by procurement as the receiver/customer and you in turn can use it to assess how well you are receiving stock in from time of order to store and how well you are delivering stock.

The term in Full refers to did you fullfil the order or was the order fulfilled that you received. If not, why not? This simple metric delivers performance growth and is a vital measure performed by leading CFO's.

You have a full bag of information gained, observed, assessed and are now ready to deliver your strategic plan within 100 days, probably just prior to this ending, to allow time to have fully understood the organisation. The CEO, C-Suite executives and the board want to learn of your **Strategic Logistics Plan that will drive performance growth, deliver cost savings and reduce risk**.

86. CSO [Chief Sustainability Officer]

The role of the CSO is a newly created 21st Century role to address, action and hold the organisation to a responsible level of sustainability.

The term sustainability many first think of as green, as this is where the role first emerged from, but it has expanded to include more than the environment, too uphold accountability to the community, stakeholders and the public.

The title of CSO has emerged by some as a Chief Responsibility Officer amongst other titles. The word and title of 'responsibility' is one that can be subject to manipulation, is grey and hierarchal debates and as such we do not recognise this title at this time.

Competitive advantages are evidenced of those organisations who do undertake a sustainability strategy, reporting and employ a CSO or a Sustainability Manager. The transparency shared to stakeholders and the public, commits the organisation's social stewardship, economic objectives and environmental commitment initiatives, that are becoming more frequently demanded by citizens and consumers.

CSO Role

A CSO will **develop, define and manage the organisation's corporate economic, social and sustainable responsibility strategies**. The focus of climate change enforcing organisation's to be accountable, responsible and rethink the impact and long lasting effects they have on the environment and the local community support, have created a need for reporting that is referred to as Quadruple Bottom Line Reporting [QBL], reporting non-financial measures, to later become a report of its own as a Sustainability Report.

It is a **self-governing role** for many organisations and can also act as an accountability role for those complying with government legislature. Despite external legislation, it is the complexity to align the organisation's goals and core values to that which the CSO envisions and strategically plans as the first undertaking, to then ensure that considered vision complies with legislation and/or seeks to meet the Global Reporting Initiative [GRI] Standards guidelines.

Leading and driving change is key, in fact across many areas that include full scrutiny of shareholders and directors, up to third party suppliers who you require to uphold your same primary values.

Ability to **project manage** is required to champion the sustainability plan and thus projects contained therein. In addition the need to be creative, innovative and investigative is also required.

A few good examples of a best of breed CSO are:

1. **Sustainability with economic and environmental focus:** Examine the current packaging that is recyclable, to investigate changing it to a better recycled product, whilst not exceeding cost limits. The change in the particular packaging materials resulted in a decrease of the timeline of natural breakdown [halving the disintegration/breakdown time] of a type 1 international category material to remain as a type 1.

2. **Sustainability with economic and environmental focus:** To reduce the travel taken by the organisation through adopting digital technology and an adjusted travel policy. The change resulted in reduced costs, downtime of travel, and in turn reducing the carbon footprint which in turn has enabled greater sustainability for the organisation.

3. **Social responsibility – People:** To create a community employment inclusion program whereby those who were residing within the immediate and close surrounding community would be considered above other applicants, subject to the qualifications and experience required. This went a step further to consider a gender balance equality and age balance.

CSO's are influential persons who have good relationship management skills to lead and unite organisation's to achieve sustainable operations.

The First 100 Days

The First 100 days in this role will be initially meeting with the C-Suite and where possible, the Board to gain an understanding of the organisation.

The **second week** would be to understand and examine any current projects and their alignment to the organisation's goals. Further to this we suggest you read the board minutes to learn of the journey that the organisation is undertaking and targets they are headed toward. It also allows you to gain insight into the way they think, consider and vote on subjects.

By the end of **week four**, your learnings should provide you with enough insights to commence an annual and three year **strategic sustainability plan**. The aspects included in this must include your **core pillars of economic, environmental and social initiatives**. The next 60 days will be invested in your new strategic plans in addition to managing the current projects that are in place.

The multidisciplinary subjects that can consume a plan are too great to list, however the aim to at least proceed toward a considered GRI membership, meeting the GRI guidelines, does provide for measures that can be undertaken to improve particular transactions.

Prior to the end of your 100 days we recommend your presentation of your *strategic sustainability plan* to the CEO with the intent of receiving approval, feedback and ultimately presenting this to the board.

The **next 200 days** will be spent implanting your strategic plan, whilst commencing strengthening *Sustainability related policies and procedures and inclusion of sustainability related objectives* such as in the recruitment protocols.

87. BxD [Boards]

The over-arching governing body of a company is a board of directors, whereas a Board of Advisors are informal members of the board. To understand these positions briefly will assist you to understand what it is that they may be needing or requesting from you. This is a quick high level intro to the positions held by directors at board level.

Those wishing to pursue the role of CEO should spend considerable time to understand the workings of the board and those whom they will sit alongside or report to dependant on whether a directorship position is offered.

In addition to the CEO, the CFO will be called upon to provide regular reports and as such, it would be advantageous for those pursuing this role to also study it in depth.

88. Director [Director of the Board]

There are two types of Directors, those having an interest in the entity being an Executive Director and those having no interest remaining independent being a Non-Executive Director [NED].

Directors will be provided with the tenure terms prior to application with the standard being three years with an application to nomination required thereafter if they seek to remain.

Roles may be paid or unpaid. Unpaid roles are primarily for NFP's [not-for-profit]. Remuneration of outgoing expenses are paid per the organisation's policies.

Directors are sought for their governance, their skillset, and proven experience to [as the name suggests], **Direct** the executive team to lead and manage the day to day operations of the organisation, whilst **holding the organisation accountable** through best practice **governance reporting** to the shareholder/s.

The number of directors will always be an *odd number* to allow for successful voting rather than stalemates.

Each Director should be unique in the value they will provide to the board. This begins with their qualifications and experience to then their expertise, recognising that by the median age of a director being 63: *per Harvard law school, How Board Skills Vary by Director age groups, Tomas Pereira, Equilar, Inc April 4 2018 study of 500 equilar companies*, they have a few or many disciplines to offer. The findings proved that it is not the age of the director that effects performance but the tenure that must be limited to provide **constantly refreshed boards.**

Examples of board arrangements by director skillsets are:
- A medium size private entity delivering an App product:
  - Finance and Strategy
  - Governance and Risk
  - Legal Commercial Contract Law and/or Intellectual Property Law
  - Technology Architect and AI
  - Marketing.

- A publicly listed FMCG in confectionary foods:
  - Finance and Strategy
  - Governance and Risk
  - Legal Commercial Contract Law
  - Sales or Marketing
  - Packaging or Logistics
  - Procurement or Operational Management
  - Food Scientist or Research.

The examples above are not set in stone, they are merely a guide to show you how **a board is diversified in skillset to be unified in the organisation's goals.**

Dependent on the size of the organisation, the regularity of board meetings and the commensurate remuneration will vary but as a standard practice, directors will be expected to work approximately 12 hours per month ordinarily with allowance for exceptional circumstances such as mergers and acquisitions, disasters, new product or service launches.

89. CHAIR [Chairperson of the Board]

Seated at the top of the hierarchy is the ***Chair holding the most power and authority on the board of directors***.

The chair's primary role is of **governance and leadership to direct and guide officers** of the organisation and executives, whilst ensuring the constitution and other codes applied are upheld throughout the organisation.

The chair is the **liaison to shareholders** and also the gatekeeper between shareholders and the board, ensuring that shareholders are informed of major changes and/or risks, informed of the health of the organisation and ultimately providing the news of dividend returns.

Unlike employees, directors are voted in with the chair being the first voted, to then uphold the conduct of the vote to fill the remaining vacant positions.

It is discouraged to have a CEO with dual positions on the board, and moreso as Chair. We warned of this in the CEO section, and will repeat it here for the role of Chair.

CEO with a Dual role as Director

There is some confusion for the CEO as to the requirement to be a Director in addition to their role. There is no actual regulation in Australia and New Zealand for a CEO to be a director, however it is recommended for efficiency of board meetings that the CEO is provided such a seat at the table to enable ease of briefing of the organisation's performance and operations each meeting. The interchangeable title of a CEO holding a board role is MD [Managing Director].

It is discouraged to have a CEO holding a dual role as Chairperson of the Board. Good risk management would see such a person not hold so much power as it provides for inability and difficulty to manage the CEO especially when removal of the CEO is required.

The Difference between CEO and Chairman of the Board

While the CEO directs the operational aspects of a company, the board oversees the company as a whole, and the leader of the board is called the Chair of the Board. The Board appoints the CEO and the Board is the ultimate authority and is said to be responsible for the Corporate Governance of the organisation. The board has the power to overrule the CEO's decisions, and the Board, through its Chairperson sets the terms and conditions, authority and powers of the CEO.

Board meetings are chaired by the Chairperson. The CEO normally reports to the Board in a formal and structured Board Report to the Board. In some cases, the Board will meet without the CEO [called a Private Session] where aspects of the organisations progress or the CEO's performance are discussed in the absence of the CEO. This private session shows the power and presence of the Board and the Chair, relative to the CEO as the Chief Executive Officer.

The Role of the Chair

We mentioned above the **governance** in the role which includes upholding and abiding by the constitution, compliance whether regulatory or guidelines adopted by the organisation such as ISO standards or membership codes.

Pledging to uphold an **efficient** and **effective board**, the chair must ensure this occurs using specific techniques to measure and effect within the board. **Achieving organisational goals** through direction and execution of strategy such as approving business plans, the business model and budget for example are a few of the primary roles expected of a chair to lead the board to discuss and decide upon, that they must perform well.

Once could say *the chair is the conductor of the board* whilst chairing general meetings, board meetings and annual general meetings. To ensure the running order of the board meeting is timely, with clear information is important, yet it is the encouragement of involvement of all board directors that the chair will seek. The chair will seek to direct discussions in a manner whereby every director will understand what has been discussed and if a vote, has been agreed upon.

Extraordinary board meetings occur when quick decisive decision making is required that cannot wait until the next board meeting, which the chair will control and manage the format required. Often an extraordinary meeting starts with an email brief, to a follow up teleconference or digital conference whereby any discussions can be held with the view to a quick vote.

As a best practice leader, the Chair must ensure the **shareholders** of whom they are the representative to, are **communicated to** when and is necessary, including in times of disaster.

Finally, the *Chair will oversee the board positions being filled*, being held by the relevant skillsets, within tenures that provide for a healthy board being rejuvenated with a ceiling cap on the tenure a member can serve, be gender balanced, age balanced, number of positions with assurity of odd numbers, experience and cohesion of members.

Should the chair be independent?

It is accepted good corporate governance practice in Australia (like in many other countries of the world) that the chair should be an independent director, although there are differing schools of thought on this topic, for example, in USA where the concept of a combined chair/CEO continues to have reasonable appeal.

Ultimately where the chair is free from potentially conflicting relationships with the organisation creates unbiased decision making. For example, being an executive or professional adviser to the organisation within the last few years, being a substantial shareholder or supplier, and having no material contractual relationships with the organisation.

Australian good corporate governance practice also recommends that, where the chair is not an independent director, it may be beneficial to consider the appointment of a lead independent director. This person can act as a conduit for any material issues that independent directors on the board may wish to raise with the CEO or executive management team.

For more information, see the ASX Corporate Governance Council's Corporate Governance Principles and Recommendations 3e (2014)[4], Recommendation 2.5: *"Australian good corporate governance practice also recommends that, where the chair is not an independent director, it may be beneficial to consider the appointment of a lead independent director."*

What are important personal traits for a chair?

A balance of desirable personal traits for a chair include:

- Leadership by example
- Tact, diplomacy and sensitivity
- Strength and clarity of purpose
- Encouraging
- Influencer and negotiator
- Able to leave the ego at the door
- Manage and remove non-performing and under-performing executives
- Delegation through example.

This completes your specialist executive learning area.

Thank you for engaging your learning in the first 200 days of your EXECUTIVE CAREER TRANSITION.

GOOD LUCK WINNING THROUGH to your next career position.

Winning Through

Executive Career Transitioning

Appendix

My Strategic Career Journey - Was / Is / Will Be

Conduct a Strategic Planning session focusing on your career journey:

Conduct a **WAS IS WILL BE** review of you.

This is the blank canvas or template which you can use as a starting point. Ask your mentor or coach to work through this with you. If you do not use a mentor, you may wish to rethink this, however in the interim, try it yourself.

Begin with **Was** and **Is**. Then once you have read this book, return to complete **Will Be**. If you did elect a mentor or coach, work through this exercise with them, then discuss their conclusions as to what it tells them about your new strategic journey.

WAS/IS/WILL BE			
	Your Past journey **WAS**	You Currently are **IS**	You Aspire to **WILL BE**
Role / Title			
Organisation Size [S/M/L]			
Organisation ext. : T/O, EBITDA			
Sector			
Industry			
2 Major Achievements			
Accolades			
Prof. Skills Training, Degrees & Certificates			
Personal CSR: charity, donations, volunteering			

Once you have completed this, review and update it each time you are contemplating your next position.

Complete your Strategic Career Journey worksheet on p297

A2. Continuous Days

We talk of the first 100 days pre your new position, we talk about the next 100 days in the job, but what about post this? Your job doesn't stop so why should your planning?

Suggested below is a simplistic form to allow you as you head toward reaching each milestone, to plan for the next 100 days thereafter right up to 1000 days where you will have been in the position three years, preparing to move on.

Milestone or Result or Flag on the Hill	Achieved Y/N
First 100 Days in the Job *What is my goal? Observe, Inquire, Understand, 1 Yr Strategic Plan*	
Milestones to reach the goal: BCG SWOT Was/Is/Will Be	
Second 100 Days in the Job *What is my goal? Establish Strategic Plans that align with my 1 yr plan, by department*	
Milestones to reach the goal:	
First Year in the Job *Introduce or utilise the Rolling Quarterly Forecast, provide meaningful reporting*	
Milestones to reach the goal: RQF Dashboard Reports Reporting Survey to Board, Execs, and Management	
First 1000 Days *What is my goal... my FLAG ON THE HILL? CEO*	
Milestones to reach the goal: MBA Directorship nominee Mentor	

Complete your First 100 days milestones worksheet on p298

Appendix

Being Strategic and deeply involved in the Strategy Development and Implementation of the Strategic Plan

Conduct a Strategic Planning session focusing on the organisation's strategic journey:

Conduct a **WAS IS WILL BE** review of the business.

This sample of a **WAS IS WILL BE** journey was conducted with a sporting club that was growing, but as you can see, wanted to diversify not just to purely provide sport, but to become a cultural friendly club offering many services.

Note the change in focus over time from where the organisation has come from, to where the organisation is now positioning and have the capability and how big a stretch your organisation plans or wishes to take in the future to achieve its goals and future.

This exercise and the outcome clearly maps the journey of where the business has come from: its successes and achievements, what has worked, where it is now – its strengths and weaknesses and where it aspires to be over the next three years.

The Sporting Club Business Planning Journey

CA

Where the Greek Club has been: **WAS**	Where the Greek Club is now: **IS**	What we want the Greek Club to be and to achieve: **WILL BE**
SMALL Club founded by part of Greek Community **HIGH PROFITS**	**BIG / LARGE** Largest single club in Canberra with largest member base largest Greek Club in South Hemisphere **LOW PROFITS**	**BULLET PROOF** Have a large property / building portfolio with high sustainable profits/cashflow **SUSTAINABLE PROFITS**
OFFERING	Premium catering venue, best bistro/Asian and Italian / Mediterranean restaurant	Maintain position & original charter of Hellenic Club: social venue for Greeks
WHY THEY COME	Leader in Governance & in CSR Well branded – across Australia	Promote Greek culture in Canberra Community
AWARDS	Club of the Year Great Sports Bar	More focus on SPORTS eg Sports ground procurement
	HIGH LEGISLATION	HIGHER LEGISLATION
RESOURCES	2 SITE CLUBHOUSE + others	2 CLUBS + 2/3 CAFÉ + 3 / 4 Properties
ROI	Significant & continuing profits, strong cash flow and high tax losses: no tax payable for 7 yrs Good gaming venue + good gambling GAMBLING IS TOUGH!!	Good gaming venue with good gambling policies & systems in place Las Vegas types shows and service GAMBLING will be TOUGH
	First IPP Property secured	Daycare & child care centres. Maybe 3 if 1st a success
A Small Business Operation	A Corporate Operation	Social Community Corporate Operation

The Was – Is – Will Be technique is a great and reflective tool to present the journey of the business you have joined, that ultimately becomes a good reference for the organisation's 3-5 year long term plans.

This blank canvas or template is located in the Worksheet Section for you to use as a starting point. Have your Group and Business Unit Managers attempt to complete this template and then, discuss their conclusions as to what it tells them about your new organisations' strategic journey – from where to where, and what in the future.

Where the firm has been **WAS**	Where it is now **IS**	What we want it to achieve **WILL BE**

Complete your Strategic Journey Organisations worksheet on p299.

The **WAS   IS   WILL BE** methodology is a great way to assess and assemble the journey of your business and more importantly the critical focus to make your business what you want it to be.

Where has the business **come from:** what lessons; mistakes; learnings; and achievements, etc?

Where is the business **now placed:** successes; resources; capabilities; customers; brands, etc?

Where is the business intending and capable of **progressing to** in the future?

Introduce and conduct a SWOT ANALYSIS [2x2 model] review of the business and then develop a SWOT [3x3] ACTION PLAN

The CFO and the CEO will find a SWOT Analysis useful to focus on what to improve, reposition and refocus and action as you analyse the business and its positioning. However, if you are a C-Suite executive you may find this useful to apply within the scope of your responsibility, such as a CSO, right through to the CTO.

You need a method, an approach at this point to guide you and hold your own actions accountable to develop and reposition your role. Being asked 'What is your assessment so far of the organisation, what are its' issues and future directions?' requires you to be prepared. Using a SWOT for this request that is included in your professional presentation as a simplistic starting diagram, will have you well positioned and respected.

You can use the traditional SWOT tool to help strategically direct the business, to then action using a change management tool that your fellow management may not previously have seen or used.

We start with the 2x2 SWOT STRATEGIC POSITIONING template.

Once you have the foundation you can move to the revolutionary 3x3 SWOT ACTION PLAN technique: POSITION and ACTION.

Firstly the 2x2 SWOT Strategic Positioning Tool:

The top two boxes focus on your organisation's INTERNAL current positioning and resources within the business, what the business is good at and are recognised for [capacity, brand, resources, technology, supply chain and distribution networks] and what you cannot do or deliver [incapacity, poor brand and inability to perform, inadequate marketing resources, poor locations, distribution limitations etc.]

The bottom boxes look to the future and focus on EXTERNAL factors to the business where you can create a glorious future but also must recognise the threats coming at your business from external and uncertain areas or pressures or competitive threats.

This 2x2 SWOT analysis will tell you what you have to work with and on [your Strengths and Weaknesses] and where to address your external environment [your Opportunities and Threats] – a great positioning tool and presentation.

Complete your 2x2 SWOT Strategic Positioning Tool worksheet on p300.

You should prepare this table before you start in the job. Sounds strange but it will test the external view, to then confirm it in the First 100 Days. This 2x2 table will have you well placed to ACTION and perform well in the new position – with a strategic focus.

SWOT is a well-known but not so well used tool to strategically assess your organisations' position and potential directions for the future and for you to use personally in a new management position.

We do not stop with a 2x2 for the SWOT as it sits in a *static reported format* that is not analysing how it can be actioned.

Let's turn the SWOT on it's side to become a matrix, an actionable matrix.

REPORTING IS GOOD, BUT ACTIONING DRIVES RESULTS.

Secondly develop a SWOT 3x3 Action Plan:

	OPPORTUNITIES	THREATS
S W **O T** ACTION PLAN MATRIX 3 X 3		
STRENGTHS	ACTION NOW BOX 1 **S** **O**	CONTINGENCY ACTION BOX 2 **S** **T**
WEAKNESSES	ACTION WITH CAUTION BOX 3 **W** **O**	CRITICAL ACTION OR ELSE BOX 4 **W** **T**

Complete your SWOT 3x3 Action Plan worksheet on p301.

Actions developed can be shown under box headings:

= Using STRENGTHS to take advantage of OPPORTUNITIES
  [Box 1]

= WEAKNESSES to be addressed before OPPORTUNITIES possible
  [Box 2]

= Using STRENGTHS in the face of THREATS
  [Box 3]

= WEAKNESSES and THREATS together means decision time.
  [Box 4].

Expanding upon these:

Box 1 – do it now and it is a no brainer. It will provide the organisation focus on the big game changers: play to strengths [how sensible] to take the opportunities to advance that must be pursued and funded.

Box 2 – fix or supplement resources/weaknesses to move forward with presently available opportunities.

Box 3 – strategically use your positioning to align or reposition to head off threats – called the Strategic Alliance box.

Box 4 – Oh no! this is the must do something box as if it is left unmanaged, it could wipe the business out – called the Action Now box or critical box. It tends to be a rear guard action but it is very important to action to avoid disaster.

Introducing the 2x2 SWOT Strategic Positioning and 3x3 SWOT Action Plan will have you well placed in the management team to lead the organisations' future plans.

We as professional mentors, strongly suggest the full SWOT 2x2 to 3x3 is conducted every two to three years. The market changes and so must our ability to continually reassess our goals and ability to succeed.

Appendix

Develop and regularly produce for the Board and Senior Management a Strategic Scorecard

This internationally acknowledged presentation tool is probably not known to your business and executive team.

The CIMA Strategic Scorecard [12] *was a governance changing development* that emerged from key findings formed by a project led by the International Federation of Accountants [IFAC]. IT is all about strategy and evaluation.

It is a simple yet brilliant matrix that depicts where your business is positioned strategically, whether there are other strategic options available which you have not pursued and whether your current strategic direction is being implemented effectively.

These are very valid questions that must be considered on a regular basis [six monthly to annually] that you bring to the consideration of the board and management team by presenting this technique, that you will action upon the board's deliberation.

CIMA Strategic Scorecard

STRATEGIC POSITION

This section lists the areas of importance for the organisation. **No more than ten issues** and listed in order of importance e.g.

- Regulatory developments
- Technological developments
- Competitors

STRATEGIC OPTIONS

This section lists the major **'strategic bets'** and should contain no more than five.

- Merger in related business
- Outsorcing major process
- Major divestment and refocus of business

STRATEGIC IMPLEMENTATION

This section lists the major strategic projects that are in progress. Should be **different** from items listed under **Strategic Options**.

- Development of major new delivery channel
- Major relocation
- Expansion into Eastern Europe

STRATEGIC RISKS

This section lists the key strategic issues, in terms of appetite, process and actual risk

Risk appetite:
Process issues
- Risk review process

Strategic risks:
- Employee retention
- Reputation

Complete your CIMA Strategic Scorecard worksheet on p302.

Add into the matrix –

Strategic Position box: -Production and Supply Chain model, [where are you strategically positioned?]

Strategic Options box: [what can, what should we do strategically?]

Strategic risks box: add next to reputation / brand.

By the end of your First 100 Days in the Job, we recommend that you have drafted your new organisations' Strategic Scorecard and have it discussed and reviewed with the Executive team and at the Board

It is our experience that the author or architect of the Strategic Scorecard will be well positioned to guide and direct the strategic focus of the organisation.

A6. Business Model

Review and Revitalise the Organisations' Business Model

One of the most significant and defining aspects of refocusing a business going forward is to **assess and review the relevance, the appropriateness and validity of its current business model** – how the business operates its business.

McKinsey's in their 'CFO – First 100 Days' Research said one of the critical roles of the CFO was to assess the organisations' existing business model, to determine if it was still appropriate and engender discussion on an alternative business model which may serve the business better and differently for the future.

McKinseys suggested that it is good practice to conduct a 'Strategy Audit' and a 'Value Audit' to ensure the business understands whether the existing strategy was working or if there is a better alternative strategy and whether the organisation Added Value in the way it thought it did by conducting a Value Audit.

The Value Audit is an honest assessment from the customers perspective of how the organisation adds value [or contributes] to the customer and hence to its business model being effective.

You will determine through the value audit whether Your Organisation's Business Model provides help and support to your

Customers Business Model: if not, you may not continue to have access to that customer.

Certainly in the First 100 Days, the new recruit must assess:
- how the business deals with customers
- how it provides its services and products
- how it engages with employees and other suppliers
- where it makes money and profits
- where it loses money and profits
- what is its competitive advantage – a strategic review of who, what we are and do, and the value to the respective players/ partners to the organisation.

The IBM 2013 Global C-Suite [20] study said that one of the two major foci for the C-Suite was, ***"To reassess whether the existing Business Model was working and help to create new business models to set the business apart from its competitors."***

As the new CEO or CFO, you will make your mark with the Board and in the Executive by engendering this discussion on whether the organisation is following or adopting the most optimum Business Model to achieve its Goals and Objectives and create a sustainable financial business model.

A7. DIFOT

Operational management be it in sales or procurement is gifted with one of the best practice tools that provides insightful off-book, non-financial insights to drive performance growth.

DIFOT **D**elivery **I**n **F**ull **O**n **T**ime **I**n **S**pec

For Inwards Goods, Procurement and Logistics it asks "Did we deliver? Was it to the full order? Was it delivered on time as advised on the order? And finally was it to the Specifications?

For Outwards Goods, Sales and Logistics it asks "Did we receive the delivery? Was it to the full order? Was it received on time as advised on the order? And finally was it to the Specifications?

At this stage, it tells us a lot but not enough. For procurement we seek to determine our handling and correctness of the order placed, how efficient the order placement was including additional costs to receive it into store, and how efficiently our warehouse transacted the receipt and was it in good order.

At this point of DIFOTis we can extend the measure for the analysis of the customer experience, that is as a CSO, CLO and CFO you will find analysing this measure will certainly drive performance more, however the CPO will stop at this point.

From a sales perspective for our customer, we want to know how **Efficiently** our team performed, extending our measure to DIFOTisE. To factor this into your findings, ask if Standard Labour hours were used to perform the service or produce the goods or was it subject to overtime to complete? Did a standard delivery occur or were there excess fees for fast delivery. Were the goods or services delivered in perfect order or were there damages. Were the goods or services delivered as per the specification.

You are seeing here how asking a question and reviewing a specific product, service or project, that you can unravel the unknown and make it known, and to tell management if there were extra costs involved. This is a good thing. It is how we correct one-off or continuous errors and inefficiencies that sometimes stem from the sales rep placing unachievable timelines on your organisation, or a sneaky overtime rort occurring.

Appendix

If you have reported DIFOTisE then you have already helped your organisation rectify and improve efficiencies and performance. Let's not stop there and measure how well the sale went: Did we **Add value**? Did we upsell? Do you want fries with that? Did we sell a will and upsize as an executor of the estate and update property titles? Did we book a holiday and sell a tour, a cruise? We are now at DIFOTisEAV

To finally ask was it in **compliance**? Did we deliver our service or product within regulations? If it were a hospital surgery did we provide best medical services within regulations without any mishaps? Did we produce a product within our emissions targets?

This is **DIFOTisEAVIC**. A brilliant tool designed and developed by Sandra Calvert that you can use now that you have extra hours available from your fast closing. Use it to review the manhour or machine utilisation, logistics, sales and operational performances to cut costs, increase effiencies and drive compliant performance growth.

Calculations:

We suggest calculating **DIFOTisEAVIC** as follows:

Calculate each measure individually as a percentage. Aim for two combined measures: D I F O T is as the first measure; DIFOTisEAVIC which is your second added value, efficiency and compliance measure, the 'cream on the top' performance growth and operational cost reduction measures.

eg. DIFOTis

1. **DIF:** No. of deliveries made in full incl. UOM / Total no. deliveries x 100 = %

2. **DIFOT:** No. of deliveries made in full incl. UOM that were made on or before the requested delivery date / Total no. deliveries x 100 = %

3. **DIFOTis:** No. of deliveries made in full incl. UOM that were made on or before the requested delivery date and met full specifications / Total no. deliveries x 100 = %

Continue adding measures to achieve DIFOTisEAVIC. Report the individual steps to the relevant managers to improve each stage and set KPIs.

Boston Consulting Group created the Growth Share Matrix as an analysis tool of the role between business units to highlight how your future profit margin looks. The grid requires you to place your business units subject to their market share and market growth rate in the matrix. Once input, you can analyse the relationship between the two.

Examine the baseline of the Market Share. How much of the market does each business unit represent? Is it low or high?

Examine the left hand side of the Market Growth. How much growth does each business unit represent now??

Each quadrant represents an action you need to take with your business units, be it to continue, invest or terminate:

CASH COW: This very RELIABLE product or service business unit continues on unhindered requiring little investment. It generates cash used to invest in other business units. It is stable and commonly has a large market share but in a slow growing industry.

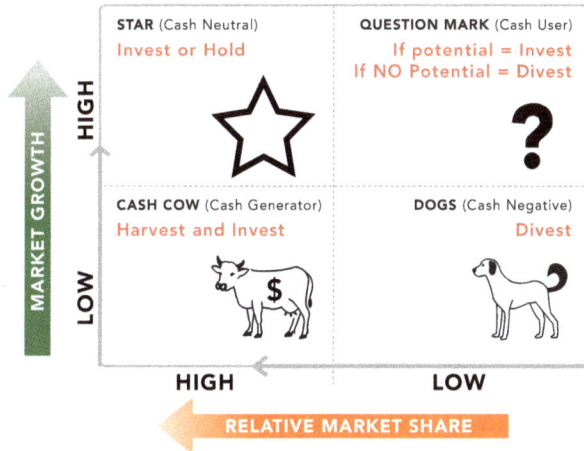

STAR (Cash Neutral) — Invest or Hold

QUESTION MARK (Cash User) — If potential = Invest / If NO Potential = Divest

CASH COW (Cash Generator) — Harvest and Invest

DOGS (Cash Negative) — Divest

MARKET GROWTH — HIGH / LOW

RELATIVE MARKET SHARE — HIGH / LOW

Source: BCG Growth Share Matrix, 1968 Bruce Henderson, Boston Consulting Group

THE STAR: A true performer generating cash but in a rapidly growing market it does require investment to continue and maintain it's status. Once a star matures, if it remains SUCCESSFUL it will become a cash cow.

QUESTION MARK: Questions hang over business unit that has not grown in market share. The QUESTION remains as to whether you keep investing resources into this or terminate it. It may have potential or may not.

THE DOG: It requires substantial cash but TIES UP RESOURCES, our capital that could be deployed elsewhere. Unless the dog has a strategic purpose for remaining it should be liquidated, or moved on and out.

Appendix

Index

Index

Bibliography

[1] AbilityMap. Proprietary property of AbilityMap Pty Ltd, Sydney, Australia, 2020. 68

[2] Aruti, Sam. What to Do in the First 100 Days of Your New Job, CIO, Jan 14 2006, https://www.cio.com/article/2447752/what-to-do-in-the-first-100-days-of-your-new-job.html. 171

[3] Ashton, Kevin. How To Fly A Horse: The Secret History of Creation, Invention, and Discovery. United Kingdom: Random House, 2015. 4

[4] ASX Corporate Governance Council. Corporate Governance Principles and Recommendations, Edn.3, 2014. Australian Securities Exchange. https://www.asx.com.au/documents/asx-compliance/cgc-principles-and-recommendations-3rd-edn.pdf. 267

[5] Bahar Hewertson, Roxi. Lead Like it Matters...Because it Does: Practical Leadership Tools to Inspire and Engage Your People and Create Great Results. United States: McGraw-Hill Education, 2014. 140

[6] Bennett, Nathan and Miles, Stephen A. Second in Command: The Misunderstood Role of the Chief Operating Officer. Harvard Business Review. May 2006. 229

[7] Bolles, Richard N. What Color Is Your Parachute? 2020: A Practical Manual for Job-Hunters and Career-Changers. United States: Potter/Ten Speed/Harmony/Rodale, 2019. 53

[8] Brandon, John. 10 Unusual Interview Questions to Ask Every New Job Candidate, Inc.com, October 23, 2015, https://www.inc.com/john-brandon/10-unusual-interview-questions-to-ask-every-new-job-candidate.html.' 110

[9] Chapman, Jack. Negotiating Your Salary: How to Make $1000 a Minute. United States: Ten Speed Press, 2008. 121, 123

[10] Chappuis Bertil E., Kim, Aimee and Roche, Paul J. Starting up as CFO. McKinsey & Company, Mar 1, 2008, https://www.mckinsey.com/business-functions/strategy-and-corporate-finance/our-insights/starting-up-as-cfo. 212

[11] CIMA. Enterprise Risk Management, Topic Gateway Series No.49, Jul 2008, https://www.cimaglobal.com/Documents/ImportedDocuments/cid_tg_enterprise_risk_management_jul08.pdf. 210

[12] CIMA. Strategic Scorecard, Mar 2005 https://issuu.com/cimaglobal/docs/tech_execsum_strategic_scorecard_boards_engaging_i/1?e=1740886/5033179 278

[13] Coyne, Kevin P. and Rao, Bobby S.Y. A guide for the CEO-elect, Aug 1, 2005. McKinsey Quarterly, https://www.mckinsey.com/featured-insights/leadership/a-guide-for-the-ceo-elect#. 180

[14] Ducasse, P and Lutz, T of The Boston Consulting Group. Perspectives Assuming Leadership: The First 100 Days, Edn. 1/03 #401, Feb 2003. 204

[15] Edleman, David and Singer, Marc of McKinsey and Company. The new consumer decision journey, Oct 1, 2015. Full article available on Harvard business review, Competing on customer journeys, Nov 2015, https://hbr.org/2015/11/competing-on-customer-journeys. 247

[16] EnhanceCV.com. Marissa Mayer's Yahoo CEO Resume Example (2020), https://enhancv.com/resume-examples/famous/marissa-mayer/#famous-resume. 39

[17] Formerly First100.com. Leadership Consultancy FIRST 100 144

[18] Haden, Jeff. The Motivation Myth: How High Achievers Really Set Themselves Up to Win. United States: Penguin Publishing Group, 2018. 105

[19] Hargrove, Robert. Your First 100 Days in a New Executive Job. Createspace Independent Publishing Platform, Book Depository, United Kingdom, 2011. 159

[20] IBM. The Customer-activated Enterprise: Insights from the Global C-Suite Study. United Kingdom: The IBM Institute for Business Value, 2013. XX, 198, 280

[21] IFAC PAIB Committee [International Federation of Accountants]. The Roles and Domain of Professional Accountants in Business, Oct 31, 2005. 220

[22] Jessica Thiefels. "4 Great Personal Statement Examples for Your CV - & Why They Work" cites Chris Mumford MD of Aethos Consulting Group, January 30, 2019, https://www.glassdoor.co.uk/blog/cv-personal-statement-examples/. 28

[23] Kelly, K. Top Jobs: How They are Different and what You Need to Succeed. United States: FT Press, 2009. XII

[24] Korn/Ferry. New CFOs: the First 100 Days. CFO Magazine, Sep 8, 2004, https://www.cfo.com/human-capital-careers/2004/09/new-cfos-the-first-100-days/. 190

[25] KPMG. Being the best: Inside the intelligent finance function, October 2013. 209

[26] KPMG. Enterprise Risk Management: an emerging model for building shareholder value, Nov 2001. 210

[27] LEGO® SERIOUS PLAY® methodology, 1996. LEGO Group. 157

[28] Oakley, S. and Petty, J. CFO: the True Meaning Behind the Title. Sanvon Investments Pty Limited, 2018. 190

[29] Pressler, Paul. CEO Gap. Cited by Chiefexecutive.net/depts/routetotop2003/186.htm. Route to the Top: White-Collar Climb, by Freedman, Catherine, Vol.186, Mar 2003. https://studylib.net/doc/8269752/route-to-the-top-white. 159

[30] Rivkin, Steve., Trout, Jack. Differentiate Or Die: Survival in Our Era of Killer Competition. Germany: Wiley, 2010. 158

[31] Saddleback College, Student Resume Critique/Review Survey (2020), https://www.saddleback.edu/jobs/resume-critique-survey. 41, 42

[32] Smith, Jacquelyn. Why half of all new executives fail can be narrowed down to 4 reasons, March 3, 2015, Business Insider, https://www.businessinsider.com.au/reasons-executives-fail-2015-3. 138

[33] Tabrizi, Behman. 75% of Cross-Functional Teams are Dysfunctional. Harvard Business Review. Jun 23, 2015. 246

[34] Watkins, Michael. The First 90 Days, Updated and Expanded: Proven Strategies for Getting Up to Speed Faster and Smarter. United States: Harvard Business Review Press, 2013. 137

Worksheets: Personal Career Skills Review

Current Personal and Career Skills:

Current Role and Position using these skills:

Current Skills not presently being used:

Where do you want to be in 10 years and how will you get there: What is your ultimate Flag on the Hill Role? eg. CEO

Which positions/roles do you need to undertake to reach your Flag on the Hill? eg. CEO via CFO

Skills Required to Reach your Flag:

Skill Deficiencies to Overcome:

Skill Development Program to reach next milestone and thereafter:

1.

2.

Worksheets: Mindmap Landscape

Name:

My skills:

I am appreciated for:

I like doing:

I am an expert in:

What is IMPORTANT to me?

Current & Past Roles Attributes:

I dislike or am NOT GOOD at:

My dream job:

My second [plan b] option:

Worksheets: One Page Career MudMap

SWOT:	Actions / Directions / Possibilities
Strengths:	
Weaknesses:	
Opportunities:	
Threats:	

Worksheets: Self-Evaluation and Diagnostic

What are your Personal, Technical and Business Skills and Competencies that you have and should play to?

What do you offer the new employer? What is your brand and reputation? What are your distinctive experiences and proven abilities?

What will hold you back in this position? What are your lesser skills or deficiencies that will become obvious and you will need to address re remedial actions, training and development programs?

How do you rate as a Candidate for this Position? What makes you Stand Out?

In essence, you need to conduct your own personal SWOT POSITIONING ANALYSIS on yourself as explained below. Your PERSONAL SWOT is a Self-Assessment of Your Career and the Skills positioning in that Career Positioning Analysis.

What are your personal:

STRENGTHS – for the position:

WEAKNESSES – for the position:

OPPORTUNITIES – to fulfil the position:

THREATS – to fail in the position:

Worksheets: SWOT: Personal Positioning

STRENGTHS

WEAKNESSES

S W
O T

OPPORTUNITIES

THREATS

Worksheets: Review Self-Evaluation & Diagnostic Checklist

Personal & Professional Feature	Your Assessment / Evaluation
What are you GOOD at? (your proficiencies)	
What are you known for or recognised for?	
What is unique about you?	
What are your greatest achievements?	
What are you POOR at? (your deficiencies)	
What personal developments do you need to enable you to be the person you want to be?	

Worksheets: Convocation Map

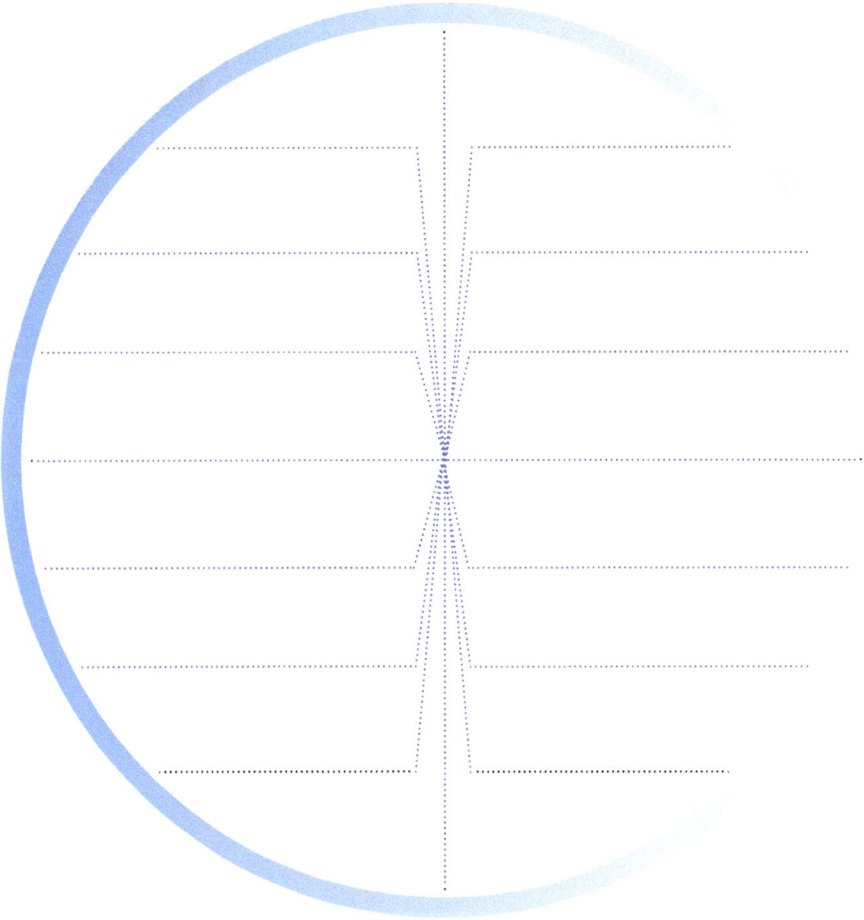

Create your own convocation map: Fill out the boxes below and populate the map above the numbers represent display from top left to bottom and return to top right to bottom.

1.	2.	3.	4.
5.	6.	7.	8.
9.	10.	11.	12.
13.	14.	15.	16.

Worksheets: First 100 Days Scorecard

FIRST 100 DAYS SCORECARD

ACHIEVEMENTS

INTENTIONS

REGRETS

REGRETS not doing

Worksheets: My Strategic Career Journey - Was / Is / Will Be

	WAS IS WILL BE		
	Your Past journey **WAS**	You Currently are **IS**	You Aspire to **WILL BE**
Role / Title			
Organisation Size [S/M/L]			
Organisation ext. : T/O, EBITDA			
Sector			
Industry			
2 Major Achievements			
Accolades			
Prof. Skills Training, Degrees & Certificates			
Personal CSR: charity, donations, volunteering			

Worksheets: First 100 days milestones

Milestone or Result or Flag on the Hill	Achieved Y/N
First 100 Days in the Job *What is my goal? Observe, Inquire, Understand, 1 Yr Strategic Plan*	
Milestones to reach the goal: BCG, SWOT, Was/Is/Will Be	
Second 100 Days in the Job *What is my goal? Establish Strategic Plans that align with my 1 yr plan, by department*	
Milestones to reach the goal:	
First Year in the Job *Introduce or utilise the Rolling Quarterly Forecast, provide meaningful reporting*	
Milestones to reach the goal: RQF, Dashboard Reports, Reporting Survey to Board, Execs, and Management	
First 1000 Days *What is my goal... my FLAG ON THE HILL? CEO*	
Milestones to reach the goal: MBA, Directorship nominee Mentor	

Worksheets: Strategic Journey Organisations. Was / Is / Will Be

Where the firm has been WAS	Where it is now IS	What we want it to achieve WILL BE

Worksheets: SWOT 2x2 Strategic Positioning Tool

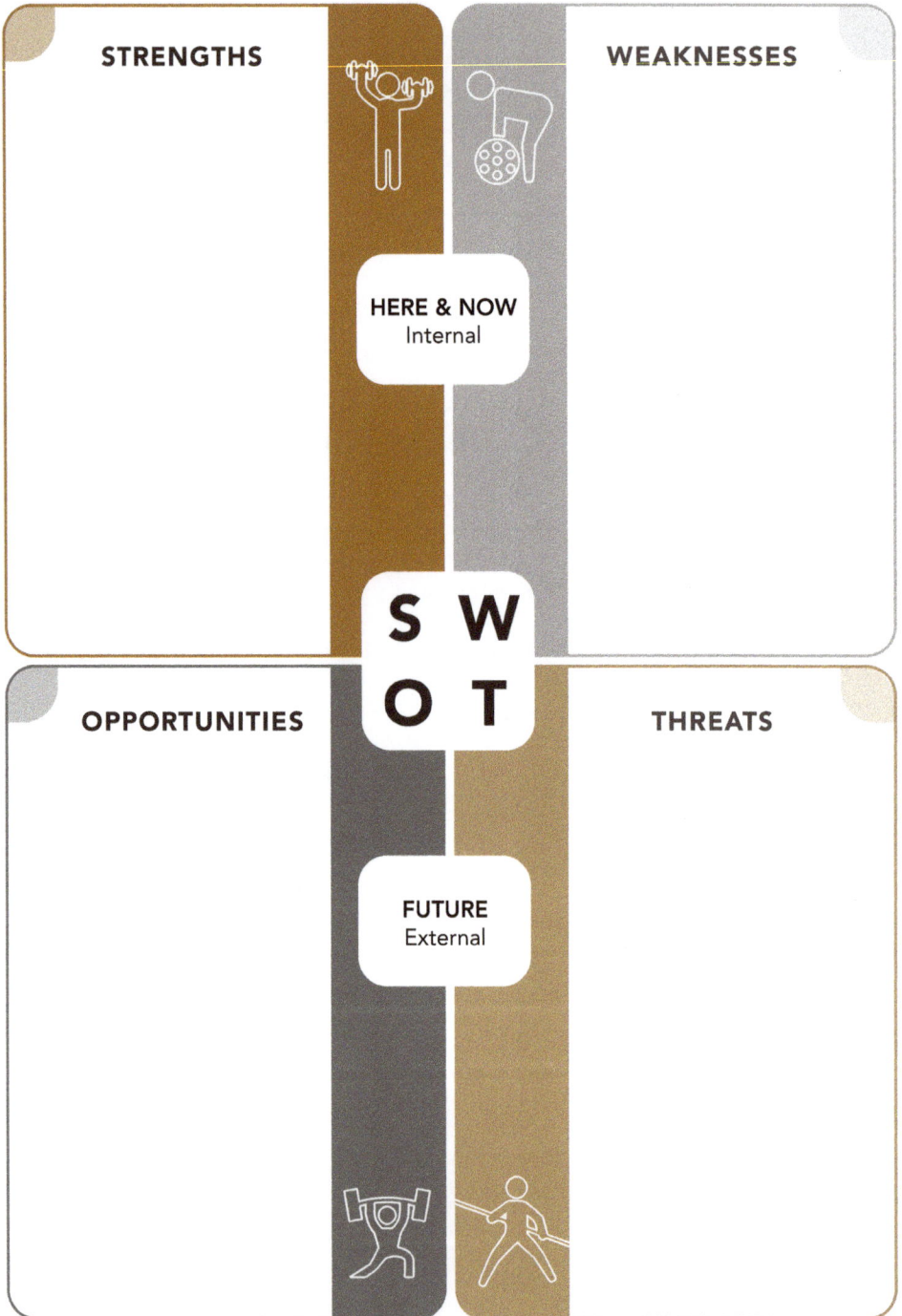

STRENGTHS	WEAKNESSES

HERE & NOW
Internal

S W
O T

OPPORTUNITIES	THREATS

FUTURE
External

Worksheets: SWOT 3x3 ACTION PLAN

THREATS

OPPORTUNITIES

SWOT
ACTION PLAN MATRIX 3 X 3

S	W
O	T

CONTINGENCY ACTION

BOX 2

S
T

ACTION NOW

BOX 1

S
O

STRENGTHS

CRITICAL ACTION OR ELSE

BOX 4

W
T

ACTION WITH CAUTION

BOX 3

W
O

WEAKNESSES

Worksheets: CIMA Strategic Scorecard

STRATEGIC OPTIONS

STRATEGIC RISKS

STRATEGIC POSITION

STRATEGIC IMPLEMENTATION